D0243649

THE ESSENCE OF
Abnormal Psychology

THE ESSENCE OF PSYCHOLOGY SERIES

Forthcoming titles
The Essence of Cognitive Psychology
The Essence of Biological Psychology
The Essence of Health Psychology
The Essence of Organisational Psychology

THE ESSENCE OF
Abnormal Psychology

David A. Holmes
the Manchester Metropolitan University

PEARSON
Prentice
Hall

Harlow, England • London • New York • Boston • San Francisco • Toronto
Sydney • Tokyo • Singapore • Hong Kong • Seoul • Taipei • New Delhi
Cape Town • Madrid • Mexico City • Amsterdam • Munich • Paris • Milan

Pearson Education Limited
Edinburgh Gate
Harlow
Essex CM20 2JE
England

and Associated Companies throughout the world

Visit us on the World Wide Web at:
http://www.pearsoned.co.uk

First published 1998 by
Prentice Hall Europe

© Prentice Hall Europe 1998

All rights reserved. No part of this publication may be reproduced,
stored in a retrieval system, or transmitted, in any form, or by any
means, electronic, mechanical, photocopying, recording or otherwise,
without prior permission, in writing, from the publisher or a license
permitting restricted copying in the United Kingdom issued by the
Copyright Licensing Agency Ltd., 90 Tottenham Court Road,
London W1T 4LP.

Typeset in 10¼/12pt Plantin
by Dorwyn Ltd, Rowlands Castle, Hants

Printed and bound by CPI Antony Rowe, Eastbourne

Library of Congress Cataloging-in-Publication Data

Available from the publisher

British Library Cataloguing in Publication Data

A catalogue record for this book is available from
The British Library

ISBN: 0-13-748633-2

Transferred to digital print on demand, 2006

Contents

Preface

When I was asked to write a compact Abnormal Psychology text, I saw a golden opportunity to create the book I had been searching for during my many years of teaching the subject. Such a book was to be inexpensive and small enough to be carried around when revising for exams. However, it also needed to cover a wide range of material, in depth and to a high academic standard, but still be understood by people who were not students of the area. I felt ready for this challenge.

I hope this book represents a remarkable achievement in that it meets the conflicting demands of comprehensive coverage and compactness, the main feature of the Essence series of texts. Within this slim volume, there are all the elements normally associated with much larger and more expensive texts. *Abnormal Psychology* provides a thorough introduction to the approaches in abnormal psychology, suitable for the lay reader as well as the advanced student. The book roughly divides into two parts: an introduction to the area, followed by the main categories of abnormal behaviour as they are currently classified. Thus the definition, history, treatment, diagnosis and context of abnormal behaviour are clarified before coverage of the individual disorders. These major areas of mental disorder are then described, evaluated and illustrated by case studies. In order to maintain the anonymity of individuals, the case studies are constructed from the features of a number of real cases combined to present a realistic illustration of the disorder in question. Each topic has its critical issues and recent research explained and discussed. For the lay reader, there is a glossary of the technical terms used and suggested further reading for each chapter. For the student, a comprehensive reference section has been included at the end of the book, together with chapter summaries and self-test questions at the end of each chapter. In addition to this, other aspects of abnormal psychology such as community health, legal and forensic issues are explained, along with descriptions of the work of the many professionals involved.

Abnormal Psychology is a European text, but as such it also *translates* the subject for those students familiar with existing abnormal psychology texts, the majority of which tend to be very much based on the American experience of abnormal behaviour. Thus the reader will easily recognize the names of disorders, while being introduced to the different approaches and examples that are more characteristic of the UK and the rest of Europe.

Although the book is intended for students of psychology, medicine, nursing, social work and law, it is just as appropriate for police, politicians and any member of the public who wishes to be *fully informed* about a subject which is a constant focus for media attention and a source of much controversy and misguided opinion.

I would like to thank the editorial staff at Prentice Hall and Rupert Knight, who originally coerced me into the task. Books tend to be written in isolation, but this does not mean that others do not suffer. Could I therefore show my gratitude to Dee for remarkable stoicism and superior reading abilities. Thanks to my family, friends and colleagues for their extreme tolerance, to Sara and Don for persistent encouragement, and John Stirling for cheerfully answering random questions.

David A. Holmes
the **Manchester Metropolitan University**

CHAPTER 1

Abnormal psychology: past and present

In this chapter

What is normal? defining abnormality

Throughout evolution, abnormal or deviant individuals have been driven from various groups of humans and other creatures. Such ostracism would clearly isolate such individuals, prevent them from breeding within the group and may even have resulted in physical attack or death. Thus, this crude defence is a double-edged process. On the one hand, it partly excludes overtly abnormal genetic and environmental influences from the group, and on the other, it rejects the affected individual themselves. Humanity is not alone in having limits to its accepted 'normality', but it is alone in trying to define and justify it. Offer and Sabshin (1991) present a detailed examination of **normatology**, the study of normality, and have outlined some of the difficulties of defining normality and abnormality.

Various approaches to such a definition have been proposed and all have their limitations, as the following examples show:

► **The statistical model** assumes the average to be normal and
deviations from the average to be progressively more abnormal.
Although this makes sense logically, it is not practical in terms of
abnormal psychology. Being schizophrenic may be a statistically
infrequent occurrence, but so is being able to run a mile in 4 minutes.
Clearly, the exceptional is not average, but such athleticism does not
fit our concept of abnormality.

▶ **The psychometric approach** is related to the above, in that the psychological measurements taken are said to be abnormal when they deviate sufficiently from the average. An example would be a measure of a client's **intelligence quotient** (IQ), where this single score is compared with the average for various age groups to determine his or her '**mental age**'. This mental age may be *abnormally* low according to a predetermined criterion (e.g. an IQ of less than 70 would be in the abnormal range). Such rating instruments (often questionnaires) are used to measure individuals along dimensions such as 'neuroticism' or 'impulsivity', but these traits have to be determined in advance and, as with the statistical model, can work both ways. Thus an IQ score of 150 may be outside the normal range, but is it abnormal? Many students have produced 'abnormal' scores on 'neuroticism' and continue to function well and are (or seem) clinically normal.

▶ **The Utopia model** identifies a minority of individuals who are in perfect mental health as being normal. In this, the rest of us mere mortals fall short of the ideal and could thus be seen as abnormal. Rogers (1951) assumes this in his therapeutic approach, encouraging clients towards '**self-actualization**' to realize their full (utopian?) potential.

▶ **The absence of pathology, deviant or bizarre behaviour approaches** rely on clearly differentiated behaviour or symptoms to identify the abnormal individual. It is obvious that what is deviant varies between social groups, so-called **cultural relativism**. For example, levels of drug-taking and provocative dress in the youth culture would cause alarm among more rigidly 'respectable' social groups. Unfortunately, this approach does not distinguish clearly eccentricity from pathology, leaving nonconformists such as 'new age travellers' open to the label 'deviant'. In other words, there would be a large grey area of individuals who are not easily eliminated from the abnormal group by this approach.

▶ **The systems model** sees normal functioning as a set of systems which interact in harmony and adapt well. This approach recognizes the interplay between such independent but interacting systems such as biological, occupational and emotional adaptive functioning. Although this model accounts for maladaptive functioning, it is less useful in determining what is normal or abnormal.

The definition of abnormality is also hampered by its subject matter being mostly in the mental, rather than the physical plane. I once referred to **the mind** as a hypothetical construct squashed between biology and the environment, which is how many of the critics of the medical approach to abnormal psychology (psychiatry) would like it to stay. Szasz (1960) has played devil's advocate in this debate to great effect, reminding us that the 'mind' is not an organ of the body and therefore cannot be diseased as such. However, modern technology is beginning to overtake this position when it distinguishes between the problems of computer hardware and software. When we observe sophisticated computer software programs break down due to computer 'viruses', we may recognize a crude analogy for the diseased mind. Although these viruses are usually small, destructive programs deliberately written to replicate and infiltrate software, some occur 'naturally' in defective programs. To take the analogy even closer to abnormal psychology, such breakdowns can result from a fault in either the computer software ('mind') or the hardware ('brain'), and sometimes both.

A further complication in defining abnormality is the variation over **time** and **space** in what is thought to be abnormal. As mentioned above, cultural relativism refers to how behaviour that may be considered normal in one culture or social grouping may seem quite alien or abnormal to another. These differences may be socially generated (e.g. religious beliefs) or simply a result of geography. An example of the latter would be the old Inuit tradition in which a 'party' was held for an elderly, infirm relative. At the height of this occasion, a favoured younger relative would place the first hand on the rope used to hang the unfortunate elder there and then. This would seem barbaric in another country, but the Inuit environment was brutal and unforgiving for the old and infirm.

What has been considered abnormal has also varied over time. A recent example is homosexuality, which has in the past been considered abnormal and illegal, but is now considered in the West part of normal sexual variation. Throughout history, many of the acts celebrated during wartime were subsequently condemned during times of peace as abnormal behaviour. However, some abnormal behaviours seem to be **transcultural**: they are considered abnormal regardless of culture or era. Depression and schizophrenia are examples of these.

Producing an acceptable theoretical definition of abnormality would seem to be an imprecise endeavour built on the shifting sands of time and place. However, a more practical definition used in abnormal psychology holds that abnormal behaviour has the following features:

▶ It causes significant discomfort and distress to the individual concerned, or to their relatives and acquaintances.
▶ It causes significant impairment of their occupational or social functioning.
▶ It demands the attention of medical, legal or community authorities.

These criteria are the main reasons for individuals seeking or receiving therapy and are useful when applied in most cases. However, they have been abused in the past in order to remove individuals from society for *dubious reasons*. In a number of countries, individuals have been designated insane as a result of holding particular political views, or sometimes as an alternative to prison, providing permanent rather than temporary incarceration. In England during the early part of the twentieth century, young, unmarried, pregnant women were pressured into asylums by relatives, thus relieving them of this 'moral embarrassment'.

Despite such abuses, this working definition of abnormality provides for some flexibility in making clinical judgements.

Important concepts in abnormal psychology

Some terms used in abnormal psychology have survived both time and deliberate attempts to end their use. This is because the concepts they represent are valuable to both students and clinicians, though the terms themselves may be dated. Some examples are described next:

▶ **The organic-functional** distinction refers to whether the potential causes of a disorder are organic, i.e. biological in origin, or functional, meaning a product of function, generally speaking psychological in origin. This division is similar to the nature/nurture debate in developmental psychology in producing rather polarized views. The **medical model** in abnormal psychology assumes that mental disorders are similar to physical disorders in having a biological basis. From this viewpoint, Hunter (1973) believed that all functional disorders are actually organic disorders for which the physical basis is yet to be discovered. History would tend to support this view. For example, although schizophrenia was once listed as a functional disorder, its current aetiological status is far more biological in explanation (e.g. Cutting, 1985). However, current thinking has also emphasized the importance of psychological factors in precipitating episodes of schizophrenia. Thus, although there have been moves towards organic explanations as biological science advances, the organic-functional division still provides much debate in abnormal psychology.

▶ **The diathesis-stress** approach to the cause, or aetiology, of a disorder is a compromise to the above organic-functional debate. In this explanation, there is a predisposition to the disorder, which is usually assumed to be genetic, i.e. organic, and the disorder is then precipitated by environmental stress. The diathesis-stress approach is currently a viable explanation for schizophrenia.

▶ **The reactive-endogenous** distinction is a dated concept which was applied to depressive disorders. It was thought that some forms of the disorder emerged from within the body due to physical or biochemical change in the brain (i.e. endogenous type), and other forms were a reaction to external events (i.e. reactive type). However, this distinction was unworkable in practice as there is no clear cut-off point between these influences. The terms are still used to refer to internal and external sources of influence and can still be found in older texts on depression.

▶ **The neurotic-psychotic** division is one of the earliest used in abnormal psychology. From its original use, the term neurotic (referring to 'weak nerves') was reserved for less severe psychological disorders such as those discussed in **Freud's** case studies, which would now be classed as **anxiety, somatoform** and **dissociative disorders** (see Chapter 11). The term psychotic was reserved for severe disorders such as schizophrenia. A glib way of illustrating this distinction was to refer to neurotic clients building castles in the air, while psychotic individuals try to live in them. Later, the division was reinforced by the fact that neurotic patients mostly attended as out-patients at psychological medicine units, whereas psychotic patients were admitted to psychiatric hospitals. Such a simple division has not been maintained, especially as many disorders such as autism began to carry the term 'psychosis' in their description, which added to the confusion in the classification of disorders at the time. One current classificatory system, **DSM-IV** (see Chapter 3), has eliminated the term neurotic entirely. However, many professionals still use these terms, but with more specific meanings. Describing someone as neurotic does indicate that that individual is not severely disturbed, but also indicates a general susceptibility to anxiety, somatoform and dissociative disorders. The label psychotic is now reserved for individuals who display **hallucinations, delusions** and severe thought disturbance, i.e. psychotic symptoms.

▶ **The personality trait-episode** distinction is a very old concept in psychology, but one which creates many problems for abnormal psychology. It is often very difficult to distinguish enduring, life-long ways of behaving and reacting, or personality traits, from non-permanent episodes of behaviour disturbance. This is further complicated by the possibility of finding *both* influences on behaviour in the same individual at one time. This difficulty is acknowledged by the DSM-IV system of disorder classification, which requires the user to rate clients separately on different **axes** (dimensions of diagnosis) for current disorders *and* long-standing personality disorders, which may also be present.

A history of abnormal psychology: from ancient civilization to nineteenth-century medicine

Abnormal behaviour seems to have existed as far back as our means to detect it can determine. As with the rest of science, the further we go back in history, the greater the dependence on *beliefs* rather than *knowledge* in explaining abnormal behaviour. Skeletal remains from the **Palaeolithic period** show signs of what has come to be termed '**trephination**'. Circular holes about 5 cm in diameter had been bored into the skulls of some individuals with a primitive instrument, a 'trephine'. Bone growth around the holes indicates that at least half the recipients of 'trephination' survived their 'operation'. There are two competing explanations for this procedure. The first supposes that the hole was cut to relieve pressure following **head injury** and attributes these early 'surgeons' with rather advanced neural knowledge. The second seems more realistic in proposing that the recipients were disturbed and the hole was cut to release the **evil demon** that was causing their disturbed behaviour. Hence, the earliest known explanation for abnormal behaviour was **demonic possession**.

Similar beliefs and practices continued throughout the ancient world. Evidence has been found among the remains of cultures as diverse as the Incas, Chinese, Greeks and Egyptians, often with the introduction of a religious element, i.e. possession as a 'punishment from God'. Although still spiritually based, some of the approaches to the insane in **ancient China** were more humane. These included caring for them in institutions, more than 2,000 years before such care was available in other parts of the world!

The rise of the **Greek and Roman civilizations** was as important for the treatment of the mentally disordered as it was for the sciences. **Hippocrates** (460–377 BC), 'the father of modern medicine', rejected demonic explanations of abnormal behaviour. He believed in natural causes and the importance of physiological processes. He was also the first to separate psychological causes (**psychogenesis**) from physiological causes (**somatogenesis**). However, medical knowledge at this time was limited, perhaps due to religious proscriptions against dissection of the human body. For example, **hysteria** was the concept of the 'wandering uterus', where the organ was thought to wander within the female body (usually of virgins or widows) causing ailments relative to the place to which it was newly attached, a belief that persisted for several hundred years. Thus, limitations were also evident in the ideas of Hippocrates, who held that differing mental states resulted from the imbalance of four **bodily humours** (fluids): blood, phlegm, and yellow and black bile. He described three abnormal states: **mania, melancholia** and **phrenitis** (brain fever), terms that persisted in the thinking of his successor **Galen** and through to fairly recent descriptions.

Alexander the Great (356–23 BC) founded a number of institutions, **sanatoriums**, with regimes of exercise and occupation, which were used for the recovery of the insane. This practice continued until the decline of the Greek and Roman empires, under pressure from barbarian invasion and the rise of Christianity.

The **Dark Ages** (AD 400–900) followed. During this time the scientific approach also declined and religious superstition grew. Christian monasticism provided some care for the sick, but the knowledge that remained from previous civilizations was left unread in the monasteries. Many of the insane were left to wander as vagabonds.

Religious superstition began to influence the treatment of the insane in monasteries, including the concept of driving out the 'evil' influencing the sufferer. Various rituals accompanied this view, such as purging and all-night vigils. It was a short step from this type of belief to the return of **demonology**. By 1300, fear of the devil and belief in **witchcraft** were widespread, and those suffering from mental disorders were easily perceived as witches. Symptoms such as being withdrawn, eccentric, hearing voices and holding strange beliefs could be seen to characterize a primitive view of possession by the devil. Such views were supported by religious leaders, and 'treatment', usually some form of **exorcism**, was also within the jurisdiction of the Church.

During the fifteenth and sixteenth centuries, scientific advances began to contradict the teachings of the Catholic Church. The Church reacted to this threat to its power with force, persecuting its critics and sanctioning the pursuit of witches. In 1484, **Pope Innocent VIII** issued a papal bull to pursue witches. Following his orders, two Dominican monks published **Malleus Maleficarum** (the witches' hammer). This became a widely accepted manual for dealing with unnatural phenomena, giving 'signs', 'tests' and 'treatments' for witches and ungodly activity.

- ▶ **Signs** of witchery included loss of reason, red spots on the skin and insensitive skin areas. These signs could also be present in individuals suffering from somatoform disorders (see Chapter 11), delusions or cognitive disorders.
- ▶ **Treatments** for witchery usually consisted of imprisonment if the victim confessed under torture, or burning at the stake or hanging if they did not confess or failed 'tests' (e.g. *not* drowning after immersion in water!).

Zilboorg and Henry (1941) have estimated that thousands of insane individuals were killed as witches during these times. As noted above, psychiatric symptoms closely parallel the descriptions of witches and their reactions to interrogation would do little to save them from this fate.

The general population were very superstitious and fearful at this time, suffering plagues and religious wars and being very ready to find **scapegoats** for their troubles. However, some took advantage of the **Zeitgeist** (spirit of the times) to accuse others, even relatives, falsely to gain property or simply to rid themselves of those they disliked. In such cases deception was often used to reveal 'signs' of witchery. Victims became confused as a result of torture ('loss of reason') and retractable needles were used to 'reveal' insensitivity to pain. Thus, many sane individuals were also killed, usually for profit.

Those who objected to the witch trials were condemned as collaborators. In 1563, **Johann Weyer** produced a book claiming that the witches were insane or disturbed, ordinary individuals. He was fortunate in only having his books burned; other 'collaborators' were burned at the stake. During the Renaissance period **humanitarianism** began to spread, with increasing numbers of people in power opposing the charge of witchcraft.

Not all disordered individuals were accused of witchcraft during this period. Most were left to wander as beggars, though a few were taken into early asylums. These institutions were converted from leprosariums when leprosy declined from around 1200. Not to be confused with the efforts to care for the mentally ill of earlier civilizations, these institutions provided very poor conditions. One of the first purpose-built hospitals, which came to be used exclusively for the mentally ill in 1377, was **the Priory of St Mary of Bethlehem** (founded in 1243). The conditions within such institutions fell far short of clinical. A fair description would have to include the fact that they became tourist attractions for the paying public, who gave one or two pence to look upon sorry individuals chained to the walls of cells strewn with their excrement. The very name of **Bedlam**, as the early institution came to be known, now means a place of chaos. Many 'patients' were self-funding and when their funds were at an end they were given an 'official' badge to beg outside for their keep.

Insane relatives of the wealthy were 'put away' in a slightly different manner. They were often locked in remote rooms of the household and referred to as 'eccentric', or not referred to at all. If this was not possible, the unfortunate relative could be placed in private accommodation, usually some distance away. The desire of relatives to distance themselves from mentally ill family members reflected the **shame** they felt this brought on the family, rather than the inconvenience of coping with the disordered. Elements of this feeling of shame can still be seen today, for example, in Chinese communities. In less well-off families where the disordered relative was kept at home, they were often restrained by being chained to a corner of the room. The coal-house was commonly used for this practice, a practice still prevalent in the mid-nineteenth century. The disordered relatives of the poor were usually left to beg or, if they were fortunate, enter an institution of the type described above.

Around 1800, the **humanitarian** movement, which had first developed during the Renaissance, produced reformers with an interest in the treatment of the mentally ill. Symbolic of this *Zeitgeist* was **Philippe Pinel**, who ordered the removal of chains from patients at La Bicêtre, the Paris asylum he took charge of in 1793. He aimed towards 'moral treatment', with improvements to diet and hygiene, finding that patients became more manageable as a consequence. In 1796, **William Tuke** established the **York Retreat** in England, again using 'moral treatment'. **Dorothea Dix** (1802–87) in the United States raised vast amounts of money to modernize mental hospitals by her tireless campaigning on behalf of the poorly treated patients.

Despite reforms, the management of psychiatrically disordered individuals remained a compromise between *humane* and *secure* treatment, and these issues are still of primary importance today. Ignorance over the **aetiology** (cause) and therefore the **treatment** of disorders meant that patients mostly endured physical forms of calming and restraint, such as purging, bleeding, spinning, immersion in water, and various forms of holding down, pressing and chaining. The initial use of physical methods was complemented by the advances in science made during the nineteenth century. Thus as religious superstition abated, the medical or scientific approach to mental disorders was adopted. Although an **empirical approach** (i.e. objective) to the causes of insanity had been called for by **Thomas Sydenham** in the seventeenth century, early scientific methods were no match for the complexity of the human brain. However, the gradual association of physical illness with disturbed mental states, as in the case of **general paresis** (see below), and the emerging status of psychiatry as a medical discipline led to an assumed biological basis to mental disorders. This was given further respectability by **Emile Kraepelin** (1856–1926) with the production of a coherent classificatory system (e.g. Kraeplin, 1899). He identified the concept of a **syndrome**, a group of symptoms which tend to co-occur, and showed that a number of disorders could be identified and differentiated even though exact causes had not been established. This approach will be further examined in Chapter 2 under its current heading, the **biological paradigm**.

Special topic: General paresis of the insane (neurosyphilis)

The history of 'general paresis' provides a good illustration of how progress in medical science has often changed the way in which mental disorders are conceptualized, and how links between disordered thinking and physical damage or disease are slowly forged.

In 1798, Haslam described symptoms such as progressive dementia, paralysis and delusions which occurred together and were distinct from other forms of mental imbalance. In 1825 this syndrome was given the name 'general paresis'. Although the symptoms seemed to emerge slowly with no prior illness, contemporary thinkers (e.g. Wilhelm Griesinger) searched for physical causes to all disorders. By 1857, it had been established that some of the sufferers had contracted syphilis years before the onset of their paresis symptoms. In the next thirty years, the work of Louis Pasteur was to reveal how tiny organisms could invade the body and remain to cause progressive damage: 'germ theory' had been established. Following this breakthrough, a crucial, if unpleasant, study was carried out. In 1897, Richard von Krafft-Ebing introduced matter from syphilitic eruptions into the bloodstream of the paresis patients. The patients did not develop the disease and thus must have all contracted it previously. This link between the physical disease and the mental disorder was made explicit in 1905 when the syphilitic organism responsible was identified. What we now term neurosyphilis (tertiary syphilis) is a rare disorder as a direct result of such pioneering research.

All too often, the **psychological paradigm** has been seen in opposition to the supposed greater objectivity of the biological paradigm, whereas they should complement and confirm one another. Examining their historical origins can, to a limited extent, shed light on this conflict.

Many would consider the Austrian physician **Franz Anton Mesmer** (1734–1815) a case of *Ortgeist*, or against the thinking prevailing at his time. He claimed that patients with hysteria suffered an imbalance in 'bodily magnetic fluid', which he claimed to correct using magnetic rods. He would often use these in a theatrical manner, reminiscent of a magician's wand. Perhaps more therapeutic was Mesmer's use of **mesmerism**, producing a sleep-like, suggestible state in his clients, clearly related to hypnotism. The resultant dramatic show and Mesmer's claims of success drew some criticism from his contemporaries, and he was eventually discredited as a fraud by a committee in 1784. However, there did seem to be some value in the trance Mesmer produced. In 1841, **James Braid** coined the term **neurohypnotism** in place of mesmerism and emphasized the place of suggestibility in this process.

Initially forgoing his interest in hypnotism, the French neurosurgeon **Jean-Martin Charcot** (1825–93) returned to its use when work at the **Nancy school** (after Nancy in France) began to establish its use in cases of hysteria. Two of the Nancy school, **Leibeault** and **Bernheim**, not only treated hysteria with hypnosis, they also used hypnosis to produce hysteria in suggestible individuals. They also thought that hysteria might be a form of **self-hypnosis**, a suggestion that still has some merit today. Such work led to the serious consideration of psychogenic causes to abnormal psychological states. The work of **Breuer** and **Freud** followed from this and formed the basis of the **psychoanalytic paradigm** described in Chapter 2.

In Chapter 2, the development of other approaches to psychological abnormality will be traced from these historical origins to their establishment as a current paradigm, or way of conceptualizing disorders, in abnormal psychology.

The place of abnormal psychology today

The approach of abnormal psychology

The study area of psychiatry tends to emphasize a medical view of disturbed individuals. This does not exclude psychological approaches, but just as a book on psychotherapy would not emphasize medical treatments, a psychiatric text will consider the physical well-being of patients important. Although abnormal psychology *is* a branch of psychology, students are encouraged to view the differing paradigms within it in an unbiased (but critical) way. Thus each of the differing approaches to abnormal behaviour is considered to the degree that it is of value in practical terms, i.e. to the patient, and to the development of theory. In order to maintain this balance, the scope of modern abnormal psychology has increased greatly, providing information for a very wide range of professionals and students.

The status of psychological approaches

The potential for psychological approaches to disorders is vast, with an increasing need for **clinical psychologists** which constantly outstrips supply. However, the credibility of psychology is currently under threat. Psychology has become popular as a kind of lay science, with aspects being featured in the media every week. Thus, the public feel they have some expertise in abnormal psychology, which they would never claim for in an area such as surgical medicine. Further threats to status come from the fact that other professionals, such as nurses or counsellors, have taken on some of the traditional work of psychologists. Further towards the 'fringe' of therapy, there are practitioners who operate in the manner of **religious cults**. They are often unqualified, prey on the most vulnerable and suggestible clients and, sadly, may inflict even more harm on such distressed individuals. A current focus of attention has been **false memory syndrome**, where the therapists concerned have been accused of inducing 'memories' of childhood abuse in suggestible individuals. Such an accusation is difficult, if not impossible, to verify in fact. Many professionals would claim that the practitioners of abnormal psychology now need to be 'marketed' in such a way as to improve public confidence in their work.

The influence of the United States on abnormal psychology

A source of confusion for students of abnormal psychology has stemmed from the fact that the United States (US) has dominated the area of clinical psychology and consequently almost all abnormal psychology texts are American. This is important as there are differences in clinical training, practice and health service structure in the US compared with many European countries, including Britain. For example, in the US, clinical psychologists have doctorates and mostly work in private practice, whereas in Britain they (usually) qualify at masters level and work within the National Health Service. The latter difference leads to greater private financing of costly therapies such as psychoanalysis in the US, whereas in Britain such therapies are relatively rare. Although clinical psychology is developing rapidly in Europe, much of the framework for the study of abnormal psychology is still handed down from the US. Over time, differences may diminish as European countries move closer to the dominant (American) system.

The current context of abnormal psychology

New challenges are arising for the mental health services. Coping with the reactions of sufferers and the general public to **acquired**

immunodeficiency syndrome (AIDS) has made demands on psychologists in many individual professions, as awareness of the disorder and the disease itself have spread across the globe. Awareness of the prevalence of **post-traumatic stress disorder (PTSD)** has also increased, with therapists now finding themselves coping with the adult effects of childhood sexual abuse. As featured in the popular press, there is also expanding demand from the emergency services and those involved in civil conflict, for the very time-consuming therapy for PTSD. Perhaps the most daunting prospect for future healthcare is the increasing number of people with **chronic** and **age-related disorders**. This situation is made more difficult as the proportion of older people in the population rises and economic prosperity is concentrated amongst fewer individuals, leaving larger numbers of dependent individuals with insufficient resources to meet their basic needs. This is particularly evident in coping with disorders such as chronic **schizophrenia** and dementia (including **Alzheimer's disease**), where care provision is inadequate in many cases.

The current working environment for clinical psychologists reflects this stretching of economic resources, as well as changes in the aims of mental health care provision. Such changes include the move from in- and out-patients being catered for at large mental hospitals to supporting patients and service delivery in the community. Although the theoretical aims of this are laudable, the practice in a cash-limited context is far from satisfactory. In addition, mental health care has had a bad press, encouraging a **NIMBY** (Not in My Back Yard) reaction to **community care** from the public. In Britain, healthcare is increasingly run along business lines, so placing an additional administrative burden on clinicians. The cumulative effect of these factors translates into greater workloads and stress on the clinician, in addition to less public respect. Politics aside, in order to deal with the practicalities of the current environment, increasing use is made of 'economic therapy'. This most frequently means that one-to-one therapy sessions are a luxury, often restricted to brief therapy, with greater use of **group therapy**, and pre-therapy screening.

The current context for abnormal psychology also includes an increased focus on **ethics** and **litigation**. The rights of patients and participants in clinical research to **informed choice** as to what happens to them has been a key issue in recent years. Should a patient have the right to treatment, refuse treatment, or even choose whether or not to be a patient? Such a choice could clearly confound a therapist's attempts to use what is in their view the best treatment. Where research depends on patients participating without full knowledge of what is to happen to them, should their rights be subservient to work which may benefit future patients? This can undermine the view of the clinician as **scientist-practitioner**, that is, someone bringing specialist knowledge from one aspect of their work to resolve practical problems in the other. The current *Zeitgeist* tends to confirm the rights of the patient over research needs. This has coincided with the increased tendency of aggrieved patients to take **legal action**. Such activity was once thought of as an American practice, but is fast becoming normal in the rest of the world. Clearly a balance needs to be struck to avoid a situation where most healthcare funding is to be paid out to lawyers. One aspect of this moral dilemma, that of compulsory treatment and hospitalization, is more clearly defined and in most countries it is backed by legislation (see Chapter 4).

The professionals involved

The study of abnormal psychology involves looking at the activities of the many professionals and other workers in this field of mental health. The brief descriptions below are intended to outline the main roles played in this field.

- ▶ **Clinical psychologist.** The work of the clinical psychologist is central to the study of abnormal psychology in that it applies psychology to the area of mental health. Clinical psychologists begin as psychology graduates, who then gain sufficient experience as nursing assistants or assistant psychologists to enter a clinical psychology masters course (2–3 years), or doctorate programme (as is the case in the US). The **British Psychological Society** also offer a Diploma in Clinical Psychology. The society can also confer Chartered Psychologist status on psychology professionals, including clinical psychologists, who have sufficient postgraduate experience, in an attempt to reinforce the public credibility of professional psychologists. The clinical psychologist's major activities are psychological assessment and therapy. Their clients are referred by GPs to psychiatric out-patient departments, or within community mental health teams, although they will also see in-patients referred to them by consultant psychiatrists. Clinical psychologists are not medically qualified and cannot prescribe medical treatments, though this is being questioned in the US.
- ▶ **Psychiatrist.** Psychiatrists begin as graduates of medicine and then specialize in psychiatry for about three years, usually gaining recognition of the body governing the profession for that country, in England for example, the **Royal College of Psychiatrists**. It is then expected that they will work towards a consultant psychiatrist post. Because they are medically qualified, psychiatrists are able to prescribe medical treatments, including drug therapy, but can also give psychotherapy. Psychiatrists (especially consultants) are given more responsibility for in-patients than other professionals. Although a patient may be seen by a variety of therapists, they remain the responsibility of a particular psychiatrist. Psychiatrists also carry out assessments, but in addition, they will formally **diagnose** a patient's disorder.

▶ **General practitioner (family doctor).** General practitioners (GPs) are fully qualified medical doctors who have specialized in general practice. They have the central role in **community health care teams** and are the main primary care service delivery agents. Although they are mostly concerned with general medical complaints, GPs are usually the first port of call for individuals suffering an episode of mental disorder. GPs receive some training to detect signs of such disorders and can then refer them on to an appropriate specialist. Goldberg and Huxley (1980) describe this as the 'filter model' of family doctor referrals, demonstrating the general practice vs specialist division of labour in the primary care setting.

▶ **Psychiatric nurses.** Nurses form the largest group of healthcare professionals and have the greatest level of contact with patients. They cater for the daily needs of mentally ill in-patients including safety, security and restraint, as well as diet, hygiene, behavioural schedules and medication. Their training used to begin in general nursing training, though now this can be specifically psychiatric nursing training. Further training can change the career path to that of **community psychiatric nurse**, with slightly different emphases on outreach work. Along with families, nurses bear the brunt of disturbed behaviour, and there is a need for psychological support for the stress inherent in the job.

▶ **Psychiatric social worker.** Graduates of many disciplines undergo two years' professional training, which can include specialization in psychiatric work. The psychiatric social worker focuses on the social support available to the patients on their case list. This usually involves contact with the patient, their family and welfare agencies, seeking improvements in how these relate to the patients' needs. Further training can give **approved social worker** status for work involving compulsory admissions.

▶ **Educational psychologist.** Beginning with their first degree in psychology, the educational psychologist will train for a year or so to be a **qualified teacher**. Following a minimum number of years working as a teacher, they then undergo specific training, usually to masters level, to qualify as an educational psychologist. Their work includes assessing and addressing the problems of school-age children, which are stretching the limits of the regular teacher's professional capacity, such as hyperactivity, truancy or educational under-achievement.

▶ **Counsellors.** Once regarded as **semi-professional** due to the briefer training required, counsellors are now in great demand and can undergo an extended period of training. The **British Association for Counselling** is a relatively new overseeing body and approves Certificate, Diploma and Masters courses in counselling. They have helped to found the **European Association for Counselling** and many specialist counselling sub-groups in recent years. Counsellors see less disturbed individuals on a one-to-one basis, talking through their problems and giving constructive advice based on psychotherapeutic methods.

▶ **Health educators.** These often have a background in psychology, and are selected both for their specialist knowledge and ability to communicate and generate public interest. Their campaigns are aimed at prevention of ill health, promotion of good mental health and raising public awareness of mental health issues.

▶ **Paramedics and ancillary workers.** These terms cover a range of workers such as **occupational therapists** and **physiotherapists**, and tend to deal with the rehabilitation and support of patients. Their training is highly specific to the task and contains more practical elements.

▶ **Therapists.** These vary widely, from highly trained psychologists or even psychiatrists who have dedicated themselves to a particular form of therapy, to individuals with minimal training in an obscure therapeutic approach. Studies have discovered well over 300 ostensibly different therapies, though many of these will be variations on a theme.

▶ **Paraprofessionals and self-help groups.** Some untrained individuals with past experience as patients help relatively new patients. Others have the same ongoing problem as the patients they help, thus forming self-help groups.

▶ **Researchers.** Individuals from various mental health disciplines are increasingly found in contact with patients in the course of their research. Although not always involved in therapy, patients often find the attention given therapeutic.

A comprehensive list of those involved in mental health would seem endless, for example the **police** are now frequently involved in patient contact. An important current issue concerns the co-ordination of the differing services and how professionals work together in teams. These factors are often found lacking when failures of care result in tragedy.

Chapter summary

Abnormal psychology is dependent on there being a reasonably well-defined area of behaviour that can be considered abnormal. The study of the abnormality/normality division is termed **normatology**. Many **models of normality** have been proposed, though these are flawed or limited in various ways due to the varieties of human behaviour considered normal. The working definition of abnormality adopted involves the suffering of the individual or their contacts, and the violation of cultural or legal rules. There are important concepts in the study of abnormal psychology, which mainly focus on the separation of **biological** and **psychological** influences on behaviour. These tend to be irresolvable debates in which an interactive compromise, as in the **diathesis-stress** concept, is the preferred outcome. The history of abnormal psychology reveals a battle between a very slowly developing empirical **science** and **superstition**, the latter being supported by corrupt religious power. The historical emergence of abnormal psychology reveals some of the reasons for public scepticism of it, for example **Mesmer's** theatrical displays of 'therapy'. The developments that have taken place over the last century appear to dwarf what had gone before, although this has not been efficiently translated into improved care for the modern patient. Current issues for the student of abnormal psychology include: its **eclectic** view of mental illness; the strong **US influence**; psychology's public credibility; the changing environment in terms of **community care**, the prominence of ethics, political aims and use of litigation. The **professions** in mental health care are varied and a contemporary issue is to examine the way they interact and perform as **teams**.

Self-test questions

▶ Why is abnormal behaviour difficult to define?
▶ What is meant by the diathesis-stress approach?
▶ Historically, what is the earliest proposed cause of abnormal behaviour?
▶ Why were the early Greek and Roman approaches to abnormal behaviour considered enlightened?
▶ Discuss the development of the mental institution.
▶ What challenges the credibility of psychological approaches to abnormal behaviour?
▶ How do the roles of a psychiatrist and a clinical psychologist differ?

Further reading

Jones, K. (1972) *A History of the Mental Health Services.* London: Routledge & Kegan Paul.

Manzillier, J. and Hall, J. (1991) *What is Clinical Psychology?.* Oxford: Oxford University Press.

Micale, M. and Porter, R. (1994) *Discovering the History of Psychiatry.* Oxford: Oxford University Press.

Offer, D. and Sabshin, M. (1991) *The Diversity of Normal Behaviour.* New York: HarperCollins.

Palmer, S., Dainlow, S. and Milner, P. (1996) *Counselling. The BAC counselling reader.* London: Sage.

Persaud, R. D. (1992) 'A comparison of symptoms recorded from the same patients by an asylum doctor and "a constant observer" in 1923: the implications for theories about psychiatric illness in history', *History of Psychiatry*, **3**, 79–94.

Pilgrim, D. and Rogers, A. (1993) *A Sociology of Mental Health and Illness.* Milton Keynes: The Open University Press.

Prins, H. (1987) 'Understanding insanity: some glimpses into historical fact and fiction', *British Journal of Social Work*, **17**, 91–8.

CHAPTER 2

The development of the paradigms in abnormal psychology and their respective treatment approaches

In this chapter

► The biological approach
► The behavioural approach
► The cognitive and cognitive-behavioural approaches
► The psychodynamic approach
► The humanistic, existential and Gestalt approaches
► Group, family and cultural approaches
► The problems of paradigms: diathesis-stress and eclectic approaches

Chapter 1 covered the historical development of approaches to psychological disorder based on particular conceptual frameworks, or **paradigms**. These different ways of viewing abnormal behaviour were seen to tread very individual paths and even compete with one another. They each lead to differing **therapies**, which vary in their aims and the way they evaluate the outcome for the client. One limitation of the single paradigm approach is that this process can be viewed as a self-fulfilling prophecy. For example, if a behavioural approach is taken, the problem is viewed as one of need for change in *behaviour* and the outcome is measured in terms of *behavioural* change. Clearly, if the outcome were measured in terms of the client's feelings or thought patterns, it would seem less successful. The student of abnormal psychology is thus warned to be critical of unidimensional approaches and consider the alternatives given at the end of this chapter. However, as the following sections demonstrate, staying within a paradigm can produce a remarkable level of specialist expertise. Although there are a number of paradigms in the area of abnormal psychology, the following are currently considered to be the major theoretical divisions.

The biological approach

In Chapter 1 the beginnings of the biological paradigm were traced from early Greeks such as **Hippocrates** and **Galen**, with their limited understanding of the relationship between brain, body and behaviour, to **Kraepelin's** view of brain pathology causing a range of different disorders. The realization that apparently unrelated physical illness can produce psychological abnormality, somatogenesis was established in tracing the cause of 'general paresis'. Awareness of the true complexity of the nervous system has been slow to develop, often relying on the relationship between damage to the brain and the subsequent effect on physical or mental functioning. Many professionals have been reluctant to accept this causal link, fearing that to do so is to portray humans as biological 'robots' programmed to act out the instructions of their nervous system. This fear is ill-founded – the sophistication and interactive nature of human **neurophysiology** (the function of the nervous system) far outstrips the decision-making activities experienced by human consciousness. If this seems hard to accept, it is worth considering the many millions of decisions made by the hardware of a computer in order to represent this single sentence on the screen of a word-processor. How many of the decisions made by your brain while reading it were you aware of? In the following sections, different sources of biological influence on behaviour will be briefly described, then considered in terms of abnormal behaviour and the associated biological therapies available. Four major sources can be considered.

1. Genetics and neurodevelopment
2. Neuroanatomy
3. Neurochemistry
4. Neuroendocrinology

The basis of **genetic-neurodevelopmental** influence is the **gene**, its **expression** (the activation of its potential) and the mediating influence of the environment as development progresses. Thus the **genotype**, or trait information carried by the gene, will often differ from the **phenotype**, or actual trait expressed in the developing organism. Genes are chemical structures linked together in groups called **chromosomes**.

The human foetus begins with 23 *pairs* of chromosomes, one of each pair from each parent. Genes carry 'survival blueprints' from previous generations about how to construct a fully-functioning human being. In the main, they accomplish this by two basic processes: self-replication (**mitosis**) and releasing the information for the construction of **proteins (translation)**, which are important for the structure and function of the living organism. It is essential for the success of these processes that the **environment** of the developing human bears a reasonable resemblance to that of previous generations. For example, if the world were suddenly plunged into darkness, structures of the eye, such as the retina, would fail to develop due to lack of light stimulation causing a failure in the expression of the genes for eye development. Thus abnormal interaction between genes and the environment can lead to various disorders. However, past environmental change has made gene expression a *robust* procedure, enabling humans to adapt to fairly poor environments.

Sources of abnormality also include problems in the formation and division of cells. For example, once in about 1,500 births, a fault of division can result in three chromosomes instead of the usual two at the 21st pair (**trisomy**). The expression of this chromosome abnormality is termed **Downs syndrome**, with its characteristic facial features, retarded mental development and often shortened life-span. Not all disorders are a result of failures of function; some are by design. Some genes in the human gene pool are destructive, either singly or in combination. Although they are not always expressed, they are still passed on by symptom-free individuals who could be considered **carriers**, as in the case of **haemophilia**, which is expressed in males only. In some cases, the genetic influence causes a disturbance in the development of the nervous system which is only partially expressed, or varies between individual cases and may be resisted by manipulating the environment to limit the expression of the disorder carrying gene(s). Thus deviant **neurodevelopment** may be minimized by a developmental environment which suppresses the expression of abnormal traits.

Treatments based on genetic approaches are limited due to the difficulty in altering genetic information during the lifetime, a science which is in its infancy. **Genetic counselling** is increasingly used if a known sufferer or carrier of a genetic disorder is contemplating having children and may pass on the disorder. Impartial factual advice is provided so the individual concerned can make an informed choice based on the probabilities of transmitting the gene(s). For example, **Huntington's disease** (also known as Huntington's Chorea) is caused by an **autosomal dominant gene** and families with known cases are counselled, but because of its late onset, some parents do not discover they have the gene until after they have children. As there is no cure for Huntington's disease, early testing with genetic probes produces a further ethical dilemma: does the individual really want to know their own future is bleak? In other cases, a 'carrier' may not be certain they have a destructive gene(s), as this may have been simply inferred from a parent having it. On some occasions there may be a genetic **marker** for the disorder. A marker is an easily detected genetic trait which is inherited along with the gene for the disorder. This is due to '**linkage**', or the tendency for genes located close to one another to be passed on together. Researchers are constantly trying to find markers for the genetic components of a number of disorders. Where the disorder is not inevitable, e.g. where the **diathesis-stress** approach is appropriate (see end of chapter), advance knowledge for the potential sufferer could aid prevention: for example, avoidance of severe stress should a definite marker for schizophrenia be found.

Research into the genetics of disorders utilizes existing markers to help detect other causal factors for that disorder. **Family**, or **pedigree studies** look at the frequency of occurrence of the disorder in the different relatives in families to show the overall degree of heritability of the disorder. Another technique used in a similar manner is that of comparing identical (**monozygotic**) with non-identical (**dizygotic**) twins. **Twin studies**, as they are known, are used to apportion the relative influences of the environment and genetics by comparing the two types of twin where one of each pair (the **proband**) has the disorder. Ideally, identical twins reared apart (same genetic endowment, different environment) are compared with non-identical twins (fraternal) reared together (differing genetic influence, same environment). Thus, the greater the **concordance** of the identical twins (i.e. both develop it) for the disorder, the greater the genetic influence, and the more frequent the concordance among non-identical twins the greater the effect of the environment. In early twin studies, ascertaining the type of twin (**zygocity**) was difficult, the environments of separated twins were often very *similar* and all twins share an *identical* environment for the first 9 months in the womb. Many of these difficulties are avoided in **adoption studies**, especially where the *father* is the known carrier, whose genetic influence can be examined in their adopted children in the absence of *any* environmental contact, including prenatal.

The concept of eradicating a disorder by preventing it being passed on may seem plausible for some clearly inherited disorders. However, some caveats apply. Simplistic thinking along these lines brought genetic research into disrepute during the Third Reich in Germany. At present, we do not know (but strongly suspect) that gene combinations producing disorders could also be responsible for *positive traits* when in a different combination, or in the presence of other genes. For example, it is often found that in **bipolar disorder** (see mood disorders), productivity and creativity occur amongst relatives, and sometimes in the same individual at different phases of their lives. Thus the genetic predisposition that can lead to a disabling mood disorder could, under different circumstances, produce controlled rapid thought. Eradicating one may also eradicate the other.

Neuroanatomy is the study of the structural 'hardware' of the nervous system. The main focus for abnormal psychology is the **central nervous system**, which includes the brain and spinal cord. The remainder is known as the **peripheral nervous system,** which includes the spinal nerves, cranial nerves and **autonomic nervous system,** and is mostly of interest for the latter component only.

The autonomic nervous system is divided into two opposing subsystems: the **sympathetic** division, which prepares the body for activity and expenditure of resources, and the **parasympathetic** division, which stimulates organs to relax and recuperate. Demands of the environment trigger the different divisions. For example, when faced with danger, the sympathetic division prepares the body for combat or escape (the so-called '**fight or flight**' response), increasing heart rate, decreasing digestion, etc., and when not in any danger, the parasympathetic system predominates, aiding recovery from the activity. In the modern world this primitive function is confounded and often triggered in the absence of anything to be confronted or escaped, eventually resulting in stress damage to the body. In **anxiety states**, the sympathetic division is strongly stimulated in inappropriate circumstances, sometimes with no detectable environmental trigger. The autonomic system may be over-sensitive due to genetic inheritance or physical damage, or may have been sensitized as a result of experience. Most biological treatments (e.g. drugs) for anxiety reduce the effects of the sympathetic division of the autonomic nervous system.

Within the **central nervous system**, the different structures or subsystems of the **brain** are important in abnormal psychology. Although they are interconnected, these different brain structures develop specialist functions and may themselves be usefully subdivided by function. For example, the **hypothalamus** controls the autonomic nervous system, whereas the **cerebral cortex** is subdivided into many areas governing functions as diverse as the planning of actions to the experience of sight. Like a flower, the brain has evolved from its stem outwards, so in general, 'higher' controlled intellectual functions are located in the outer structures such as the cortex, and more basic functions closer to the stem. One way of conceptualizing this division of labour is to consider the 'higher' functions as **selectively inhibiting** the instinctive demands of the 'lower' structures.

Abnormal behaviour can result from injury, insult, infection or abnormal development of the brain's components. **Injury** can be from a blow to the head, intrusion into the brain or such events as a stroke (ruptured blood vessel in the brain). **Insult** is a term used to represent damage from toxic substances such as drugs. There are many **infections** that can temporarily or permanently affect brain function. Where the damage to the brain prevents the passage of information, the point of damage is referred to as a **lesion**. Some injuries, infections and drugs can mimic the symptoms of disorders that normally result from other factors. It is thus important to eliminate such biological factors *before* definitely diagnosing a disorder.

Treatments which deal with brain areas are usually permanent alterations to structure and as such are only used as a last resort. The early use of brain surgery was a crude procedure, resulting in a great deal of peripheral (**collateral**) damage. Jacobson *et al.* (1935) discovered that the removal of the frontal lobes of the brain of a very excitable chimpanzee made the animal far more even-tempered, without apparent change in intellect or other behaviour. The neuropsychiatrist **Egas Moniz** received the Nobel Prize for transferring this principle to humans, overseeing around 100 **pre-frontal lobotomies**. This procedure did not involve the removal of the frontal lobes, but rather random lesions made by cutting into them. One method was alarmingly convenient and could be performed in the physician's office. A **transorbital leucotome** was inserted under the upper eye-lid and driven through the orbital bone with a mallet into the brain and then moved back and forth to cut the white matter of the frontal lobes. Perhaps because the procedure was so quick and simple (*and* economic), thousands of patients had anxiety and obsessions successfully treated in this way and when examined, still performed well on standard tests of intellectual ability. After a number of years, however, a more careful examination of the patients' post-operative symptoms revealed irresponsibility, childishness and an inability to carry out planned behaviour. These findings led to the discontinuation of the procedure.

Accounts of neurosurgery such as these tend to confirm the alarmist views of those opposed to medical treatments, that it is some form of punitive butchery. The over-liberal use of such procedures without careful monitoring of side-effects, indicates reckless overconfidence and perhaps illustrates the lack of appreciation of the sophistication of brain function at the time. However, what is often forgotten in these early developments is the *profound suffering* of the patient *prior* to the procedure, patients who often sought relief in suicide. Modern procedures are rarely carried out in the absence of physical brain damage and are reassuringly precise in the brain areas they target.

Computer-aided X-ray technology now allows a neurologist to examine detailed 'slices' through the brain at any point along its axis. These are called **CAT scans** (Computerized Axial Tomography) and require high levels of X-ray radiation. **NMR** (Nuclear Magnetic Resonance imaging) uses a magnetic field rather than X-rays, but is more expensive. **Stereotaxis** is a method utilizing the similarity of brain locations between individuals, in which the skull is held firmly and the brain location is calculated in three-dimensional space by reference to a stereotaxic atlas. In this way a **cannula** (a hollow probe) can be inserted safely to the required point and cutting, chemical or freezing procedures are then accurately applied. By freezing (using a **cryode**), the lesions created can be temporary, enabling the effects to be checked.

In neuroanatomy so far we have considered the brain at the '**macro**' level, i.e. larger structures. At the '**micro**' level we have the tiny building blocks of the nervous system or **neurons** (nerve cells; also spelt neurone) as they are known. The cell bodies of neurons may be small, but they have projections (white matter) which may reach great distances. Neurons and the cells which provide their nutrients, **glial cells**, form the matter of the nervous system. Neuron function is the essence of nervous communication and as such, is more the province of neurophysiology rather than neuroanatomy. To clarify, the operation of neurons will be included under neurochemistry, to emphasize the biochemical dependency of their function.

The neurochemistry of the nervous system is dependent on the functions of the many neurons in producing and using chemical transmitter substances, or **neurotransmitters**. Neurons selectively pass electrochemical signals through themselves and transmit them to other neurons chemically across tiny gaps called **synapses. Frequency coding** is used in this, so the faster the 'pulse' of a signal, the greater its effect. Neurons receive signals at their **postsynaptic membranes** (the receiving side of synapses) on their **dendrites**. If sufficient stimulation accumulates, an **action potential** (a newly generated signal) is started at the base of the neuron's **axon** and passes along it by electrochemical depolarization across the axon wall until it reaches the axon tip(s), or **terminal button(s)**. Here electrochemical stimulation will encourage the release of transmitter substance into the **synapse** from **vesicles** in which it is stored. The transmitter substance travelling across the synapse then attaches to molecules called **receptors** in the surface of the post-synaptic membrane of the receiving neuron at the other side of the synaptic cleft. This begins the transmission process over again in the second neuron. Synaptic connections and the type of transmitter involved may be **excitatory**, that is increasing the chance of the next neuron 'firing', or **inhibitory**, reducing the chance of it 'firing', or passing the pulse on. Each neuron also has mechanisms for the re-uptake of the neurotransmitter, its manufacture, monitoring how much is in the synapse (**autoreceptors**) amongst *many* other processes.

With so many variables affecting the transmission of information at the synapse, it is an area where things can easily go wrong. It is also a highly interactive area of function with neurons communicating with each other from all over the brain. The estimated number of possible combinations of these connections in a human brain is one of the largest numbers known (10 with over 120 zeros following it), this being *many millions of times greater than the estimated number of stars in the known universe*. Synaptic function is readily altered by small biochemical changes in the brain or by the psychological state of the individual; *synaptic activities are the objective units of thoughts, sensations and the initiation of actions*. Clearly, the many synaptic connections in the brain are very important for psychological functioning: they affect it and are partly affected by it. **Psychopharmacology** (the psychological effects of drug action) as a therapeutic approach is the main biological treatment at the biochemical level. Drug treatment is almost entirely dependent on influencing synaptic events. Drugs are described as **agonists** or **antagonists**, depending on whether they increase or decrease transmission respectively at their target synapses. Neuron interaction can be far more complex than can be described here, and the interested reader is directed to the further reading at the end of the chapter.

The following examples illustrate both the synaptic mechanisms and the ways in which drugs can alter them:

▶ Neurotransmitters are made from **precursors**, the 'raw materials'. Drugs can increase or decrease the availability of precursors, and may even be the raw material themselves, thus influencing the final levels of the neurotransmitter in the brain. Because the brain has such a sophisticated biochemical composition, it protects itself from chemicals that are not part of brain function – the so-called 'blood-brain barrier'. Psychoactive drugs either conform to this, or mimic the chemical structure of brain chemicals. **L-dopa** is the precursor for the transmitter **dopamine** and is administered in that form to increase levels of the neurotransmitter in **Parkinson's disease**, in which there is a dopamine deficit.

▶ Once synthesized, the transmitter substance is stored in **vesicles** ready for use. Drugs such as **reserpine** cause some vesicles to leak their contents. Thus when the vesicle is triggered to empty its contents there is nothing to release into the synapse, so inhibiting pulse transmission.

▶ Drugs can stimulate (or inhibit) the **release** of transmitter substance from the vesicles by influencing the 'triggering' chemicals. Black widow spider venom has its effect by increasing the release of **acetylcholine,** a transmitter involved in initiating actions.

▶ **Monoamine oxydase (MAO)** is an enzyme which **breaks down** excess neurotransmitter substances to prevent a build-up at the various stages of its use. A number of drugs inhibit MAO action, called MAO inhibitors (MAOI), and thus have an agonistic effect in increasing the amount of transmitter available. **Tranylcypromine (Parnate)** is a MAOI which increases the availability of **noradrenaline,** countering the effects of depression.

▶ Some drugs prevent the **re-uptake** of neurotransmitter substance into the cell body, which has the effect of maintaining greater quantities in the synaptic cleft, producing an agonistic effect on transmission. **Fluoxetine (Prozac)** acts in this way to increase the amount of the neurotransmitter **serotonin,** also called **5-hydroxytriptamine** **(5HT),** in the synaptic cleft. However, one must consider the action of autoreceptors in this, as described next.

▶ **Autoreceptors** detect the general level of a neurotransmitter in the synapse. If this is high, production of the neurotransmitter is decreased, and if low it is increased. Thus the more complex effect of having an excess of a neurotransmitter may be its depletion in the long term, as production is reduced. Drugs can take advantage of autoreceptors by 'impersonating' the neurotransmitter that stimulates them into reducing production. **Apomorphine** acts in this way to reduce the action of the transmitter **dopamine.**

▶ Drugs may stimulate the action of the **receptors** on the postsynaptic membrane, increasing transmission. However, a common drug action is to block the receptor by mimicking part of the structure of the transmitter that 'matches' the receptor molecule, but does not activate it. The net result therefore is antagonistic to transmission. Some **antischizophrenic** drugs block certain dopamine receptors, reducing the excess dopamine receptor activity which seems to be responsible for some schizophrenic symptoms.

These are just *some* of the ways in which psychoactive drugs act on nerve transmission. These actions at the micro-level are realized by the patient in the **context** of their psychological and physical state, and their environment. Patients should always have *all* the expected effects of drug medication explained fully. This avoids misinterpretation and even panic, which can confound the drug effects, as patients may believe their symptoms have been added to, or reach other disturbing conclusions as to the change in their mental and physical state. There are three other limitations on the effectiveness of drug therapy which need to be considered.

1. From the above examples of drug action, it is clear that it is currently impossible to target *exactly* those neural connections responsible for a **specific abnormality** of behaviour. Given the number of possible synaptic combinations, such a project would dwarf the achievement of time travel! For example, a drug intended to counter depressive thoughts and feelings would inevitably affect other areas of brain function. Although the analogy of 'taking a sledgehammer to crack a nut' would not be entirely fair, *general effects* of drugs intended for specific purposes are often unavoidable. This results in psychological and physical **side-effects**, the unwanted effects of medication, which can be worse for long-term users. Side-effects can drive patients to abandon medication with catastrophic results. However, as medical progress advances drugs become more and more specific in the functions they target. Although critics may view this as damage limitation, it should be remembered that, for some disorders, drug therapy is the *only* relief the patient may have from intolerable distress.

2. The second caveat in the use of drug medication concerns the brain system's reaction to the substance. The body is not a machine. Being organic, it adapts to situations and can grow to compensate for change in function, including chemical change. The term used for this is **tolerance**. The brain becomes used to the presence of the drug and attempts to return to its former state of equilibrium. This has two counterproductive effects, higher doses may be needed to maintain the therapeutic effect and discontinuation of the drug may result in a biochemical imbalance with abnormal behaviour *greater* than that prior to medication (long-term 'hangover' effect). This **adaptation** varies with the type of medication and the responsiveness of the brain system involved. Thus, it is not only *illicit drugs* that result in addiction. For example, **barbiturates**, which have a similar biochemical effect to alcohol, were over-prescribed to elderly people with agitation and insomnia (sleeplessness) in the belief that they were safe for long-term use. Barbiturates are in fact very addictive and withdrawal is far *worse* than that for **heroin**, sometimes resulting in death. The issues of tolerance or compensation for the presence of a drug will also be addressed under substance use disorders (Chapter 8).

3. As with most areas of health provision, **economic profit** and drug production do not combine for the benefit of the patient, as with most drug-dealing, profit often takes precedence. For example, the best medication (to date) for bipolar disorder (formerly manic-depression) is **lithium carbonate**, an unpatented salt available in its **generic**

(unbranded) form. As a result of its low profitability, its benefits were not promoted and its use unnecessarily restricted by poor availability and lack of information. There is no simple answer to this situation. Drug development is extremely expensive and, as with other areas of health, is best considered as a *national service* not a commercial enterprise.

Most therapies in psychiatry came about by accident or while developing treatments for other disorders. For example, the **neuroleptic** drugs which proved so effective as dopamine antagonists in the reduction of schizophrenic symptoms, were previously used as a **pre-medication** to calm patients before surgery. This tranquillizing effect itself was originally a *side-effect* of their first use as **antihistamines** (anti-allergy drugs). **Electroconvulsive therapy** (ECT), a treatment for severe depression, has a similar history, but as can be seen from the box below, this therapy's past is one of controversy.

ECT involves the patient taking **atropine** (to reduce salivary and bronchial secretions) followed by a short-term anaesthetic and muscle relaxant. An electrical current is then administered at about 70–130 volts through one or both hemispheres of the brain, while oxygen is administered. To be successful, there must be a small but detectable **seizure** induced by the current. The therapeutic effect of ECT seems to be proportional to the severity of the seizure, which in turn depends on the size of current and whether it is passed through one (**unilateral**) or both (**bilateral**) hemispheres. Unfortunately, side-effects of memory loss, confusion and in a few cases mania are *also* proportional to the treatment strength, these being additional to the normal risks of anaesthesia. However, the treatment can be dramatically effective in severe, catatonic or drug-resistant depression, as well as catatonic schizophrenic states. It appears to exert its effect by altering serotonin (increase in post-synaptic receptors), dopamine and noradrenaline transmission. In order to achieve this effect, 4–8 treatments are needed if the voltage is given unilaterally and in moderation.

Special topic: ECT, a deserved reputation?

Reports of the therapeutic use of electrical charges across the brain have a long history. In 1792 John Birch reported the use of six electric shocks on a melancholic state (depressed) patient, who rapidly recovered and remained well for a number of years. However, it is the work of the Italian physicians Cerletti and Bini in the twentieth century that led directly to the treatment we have today. It was thought useful to induce epileptic-like seizures in confused and depressed patients, originally by ingesting camphor and later by 'insulin shock therapy'. There was interest in how seizures came about, why they produced a period of calm and better mood afterwards, and a mistaken belief that epileptics were less susceptible to schizophrenia. Cerletti had observed the seizures and unconsciousness produced when 'calming' animals in a slaughterhouse with electric shocks and experimented with these effects. Bini produced a versatile 'electric-shock box', which was sufficiently controllable for use on humans. Once Cerletti was convinced that the voltage needed to create a seizure was substantially less than that required to cause death, he decided to try it on a human patient.

In 1938 Cerletti decided to use a catatonic schizophrenic man, who was confused, incoherent and therefore unable to be identified. He began with a low voltage shock, producing a mild spasm and decided to proceed with a higher voltage. This was met with resistance from his colleagues and a clear, impassioned plea from the patient, who seemed no longer confused but fearful for his life. Cerletti delivered the increased shock and produced the first electroconvulsive seizure.

Since Cerletti's work, a great deal of progress has been made in applying the technique, though less in understanding exactly how it works. Unfortunately for the reputation of ECT, the trial-and-error route to improvement produced unpleasant reports of injury. Patients with burns from the electrodes, bitten tongues, bones broken during seizures, tended to create an image of torture and comparisons with the electric chair! There were also reports of memory loss and patients so confused they did not know which side of a bus stop to stand at. The portrayal of ECT as a punishment for disruptive patients in the film of Ken Kesey's novel *One Flew over the Cuckoo's Nest* added to this negative public image. Dies (1969) even argues that this is how ECT has its effect, by punishing depressive behaviour. Fortunately, the modern procedure does not live up to this image. Refined techniques, technology and sophisticated pre-shock medication have ended the kinds of injury sustained during ECT's development. To be fair to ECT's public image, graphic descriptions of surgery, even dental surgery, would terrify prospective patients and would make early descriptions of ECT seem mild by contrast. Nowadays, the main advocates of the use of ECT are the patients themselves, who feel they have been rescued from the brink of suicidal despair.

Controversy persists regarding evaluating the effects of ECT, especially the use of a true control group. A control group in this case is an equivalent group of real patients who undergo the same procedure but do not receive real electroconvulsive shock, to be compared with those who do. This is fraught with ethical and procedural problems, but in general, 'real' ECT is more effective than 'simulated'. Nowadays, concerns are more focused on economics and overstretched resources. The worry here is that ECT may be seen as a 'cheap alternative' and be administered with inadequate precautions due to time and resource pressures.

Biochemical activity in the brain can be assessed and monitored *in vivo* (i.e. in a living patient's brain) using a technique called **positron emission tomography (PET)**. The patient is injected with a radioactive substance that emits positrons (tiny sub-atomic particles) and then placed in a scanning apparatus, which is able to pinpoint where in the brain the particles are emitted from. If the radioactive substance is a sugar, then the scanner will produce an image of the areas of greatest sugar demand (usually areas of greatest activity) across a 'slice' of the brain. The radioactive substance could be the raw material of a neurotransmitter, in which case activity in the neurons producing that neurotransmitter would be highlighted.

Neuroendocrinology involves endocrine substance (**hormone**) action. There is a great deal of overlap and interaction between endocrine and neurotransmitter systems: they even have some substances in common. Hormones are often stored and excreted into the body in **vesicles**, in the same way as neurotransmitters are emptied into synapses. Hormones are produced by the various **endocrine glands** in the body and are transmitted in the bloodstream to stimulate receptors chemically at various sites in the body and its nervous system The **pituitary gland** is considered to be the 'master gland' of the endocrine system. It sends out specific hormone stimulating hormones that stimulate other glands, particularly the **hypothalamus**, to release the particular hormone in question. The hormones of the hypothalamus primarily affect the following behaviours:

▶ **'Fight or flight'** behaviours, basically those described as controlled by the sympathetic nervous system, which is stimulated by **adrenaline**.
▶ **Feeding** behaviours are stimulated, which includes thirst and more specific appetites.
▶ **Sexual** and other reproductive functions can also be stimulated.

Because the effects of hormones are widespread, they are an imprecise treatment route for abnormal behaviour, restricting their use to rectifying simple deficits in hormonal action. For example, some women suffer severe mood swings and other symptoms when approaching the **menopause**. In some cases, replacement hormones taken orally, or **hormone replacement therapy** (HRT), can help to alleviate this and some of the more serious physical symptoms (low **oestrogen** can lead to cardiovascular problems). However, others taking the replacement hormone may suffer *worse* side-effects than those that brought about the treatment, illustrating the widespread effects and delicate balance of hormones in the body.

The behavioural approach

In Chapter 1, the development of early psychogenic explanations of abnormal behaviour such as those of Freud and Breuer were described. These explanations relied a great deal on **introspection,** considering mental processes in a subjective way. Around the turn of the twentieth century, some psychologists began to reject subjective speculation as unscientific. A major figure in this respect was **John B. Watson** (1878–1958), who repeatedly claimed that a scientific psychology should focus on the observable aspects of objective experiments. This early revolt against introspective techniques marked both the start of the behavioural (or learning) approach in psychology and the birth of its most extreme form, **radical behaviourism.** The rigid position of the radical behaviourist movement almost led to its downfall as psychological knowledge expanded during the twentieth century. However, some of its principles have remained robust, partly due to the fact that they work well and have great practical value, and partly due to the industrious career of **Burrhus Frederic Skinner** (1904–90). Skinner carried the banner of behaviourism through the challenges of the twentieth century, in addition to his more specific achievements described below. The principles derived from the behavioural approach have possibly been the most useful psychology has had to offer in terms of addressing abnormal behaviour.

There are two **elemental** forms of learning: **habituation** and **sensitization.** Habituation is where an organism (including humans) ceases to respond to a stimulus (e.g. a car passing by), when the stimulus has no significant consequences for the organism. However, if a passing car should mount the kerb hitting a pedestrian one day and another day splash muddy water all over you, you may become sensitized to approaching cars, perhaps over-reacting to them. These elemental forms of conditioning form the basic reflexes on which other learning takes place. In abnormal psychology we are mostly interested in the development and application of two types of **associative learning** and the effect of seeing this in others:

▶ **Classical conditioning** (also known as respondent, or Pavlovian, conditioning) involves involuntary responses and is related in principle to sensitization.
▶ **Operant conditioning** (also known as instrumental, or Skinnerian, conditioning) involves voluntary responses.
▶ **Vicarious learning** or **modelling** is where one is influenced by seeing another being punished or rewarded for a behaviour, or providing an example of normal behaviour to be imitated.

Classical conditioning was derived from the work of **Ivan Pavlov** at the end of the nineteenth century. He received a Nobel Prize, not for his contribution to psychology, but for his work on the dog's digestive system. He measured the amount of saliva a dog would produce to a stimulus such as meat powder and in doing this noticed that the dog salivated *before* the food arrived, sometimes at the sight of the food bowl or other inedible objects. Pavlov conducted a series of experiments to investigate how the association between the stimulus of food and the other stimuli was created in the dog.

Pavlov considered the food to be the **unconditioned stimulus (UCS)**, as this did not need to be conditioned to produce an **unconditioned response (UCR)**, food being a 'natural reinforcer'. As a **conditioned stimulus (CS)** he introduced a bell which, although the dog would notice it, would have no reinforcing value for the animal. Pavlov would have the bell sound briefly about half a second before the arrival of the food. He repeated this procedure many times, and later found that sounding the bell without the food resulted in salivation, which Pavlov termed the **conditioned response (CR)**. This procedure is sometimes written thus:

Given responses:	CS	$\longrightarrow$	no response
	UCS	$\longrightarrow$	UCR
Trials 1–100:	CS + UCS	$\longrightarrow$	UCR
Test trial:	CS	$\longrightarrow$	CR

For Pavlov the CS came to substitute for the UCS in producing the dog's involuntary response of salivation. If the test trial is repeated *without* the UCS the response will eventually diminish. This is termed **extinction**. It is important to note that the learned response is not totally lost, merely countered by learning *not* to respond. This can be demonstrated by presenting the dog with a novel stimulus (e.g. a loud noise) or taking the animal out of the experiment for some time: either will result in some **spontaneous recovery** of the response. The CS will also be **generalized** to other, similar stimuli: the less similar the stimuli the less the response. **Discrimination** can be conditioned by reinforcing one stimulus (e.g. a small bell) and not another (e.g. a medium bell), thus having the animal respond to one and not the other and countering generalization. A **secondary reinforcer** is a stimulus which has assumed the reinforcing qualities of a primary reinforcer, e.g. as the bell has come to elicit a similar response to the food. The secondary reinforcer can then be used as a reinforcer, even though it has no intrinsic value to the organism (e.g. money). These are very powerful principles when applied to abnormal behaviour, as will be examined following the development of operant conditioning.

Operant conditioning experiments began with the work of **Edward Thorndike**, who focused on the effect a behaviour's consequences had on its future occurrence. He trapped stray cats in cages, finding that they frantically produced a range of behaviours in their efforts to escape. At some point they would accidentally release the cage door. On subsequently being placed back in the cage, escape became less random and took less time. For Thorndike, the cats' behaviours died out if they did not result in escape (reward) and increased in frequency if they led to escape.

Thorndike termed this principle the **law of effect**, i.e. behaviour followed by punishment will decrease in frequency and that followed by reward will increase in frequency.

B.F. Skinner reformulated the law of effect, emphasizing the consequences of behaviour and introduced the concept of the **discriminative stimulus**. An example of a discriminative stimulus would be a light: when the light is on the behaviour is reinforced, but not when it is off. Skinner produced a specially designed apparatus, a 'Skinner box', adapted for conditioning rats and pigeons. By a process of **shaping**, he was able to reinforce simple or partial behaviours until more complex ones occurred, then by differentially reinforcing these and not the simple movements, he created complex behaviour patterns such as having pigeons play table tennis! Skinner used these principles to explain how human behaviours such as speech are learned, recognizing other factors, but viewing them as unnecessary for the process. He widened the behaviourist view to explain the problems of humanity in terms of reinforcing bad or maladaptive behaviour. Perhaps overstated, his principles are still *very important* when applied to abnormal psychology.

Generalization, discrimination and extinction apply to operant as well as classical conditioning. However, in operant conditioning the *qualities* of the reinforcer and *economies* of reinforcement are important, but of no value in classical conditioning. There are four basic forms of reinforcement in operant conditioning:

1. **Reward** is a positive reinforcer to increase preceding behaviour such as food, though rewards can be diverse when dealing with humans.
2. **Punishment** decreases preceding behaviour, e.g. squirting lemon juice into the mouth of a biting child. What is a punisher depends on circumstances, one person's punishment may be another's reward.
3. **Negative reinforcement** increases preceding behaviour by the *removal* of a punisher. For example, allowing a well behaved child to watch TV following a ban for disruptive behaviour.
4. **Omission** decreases preceding behaviour by the removal of a reward-type reinforcer and is *badly* applied in most families. How many parents have threatened to ban TV watching if bad behaviour continues, then given in for (short-term) peace? Firmly applied this would be omission.

There are ways of economizing on reinforcement (and strengthening learning) in operant conditioning, as alternatives to **continuous reinforcement** (rewarding each response). These involve only reinforcing after a number of responses (**fixed ratio schedule**) or an average number of responses (**variable ratio schedule**), and reinforcing only at the end of a time period in which one response is made (**fixed interval schedule**) or an average time period (**variable interval schedule**). **Secondary**

reinforcers are also used in operant conditioning and in conjunction with schedules, to delay access to primary reinforcement. These can be useful in clinical situations where behaviour change needs to be sustained in the absence of a primary reinforcer.

Vicarious reinforcement refers to the increase in a behaviour as a result of watching *another* individual being rewarded for carrying it out, enjoying it or simply performing it without fear. This **social learning** approach was started by **Julian Rotter**, and later established by **Albert Bandura** in his study showing acts of violence to children and then observing their tendency to reproduce the same actions. Bandura found that learning took place whether the 'actor' was punished or rewarded, but in the case of punishment, the acting out of this learning was suppressed.

Behavioural approaches applied to abnormal behaviour

In 1920, **Watson and Rayner** reported an unethical, but highly influential series of classical conditioning trials. 'Albert' was less than a year old and had no fear of the white rat the researchers presented to him. In fact, he was quite interested in it. However, he was alarmed by the loud noise they made behind him whenever he approached the rat. After a number of trials in which the loud noise (UCS) was paired with the rat (CS) producing fear (UCR), Albert showed fear (CR) when presented with the rat (CS) alone. This would appear to demonstrate that an irrational fear of a specific object or situation, or a **phobia**, can be created by classical conditioning.

This study was carried out at a time when **psychoanalytic** explanations of anxiety problems such as phobias were widespread. By demonstrating a simple behavioural cause for these states, Watson provided a strong argument against complex psychoanalytic explanations that involved early childhood relationships. Further to this, if a phobia could be classically induced, then *extinction* by behavioural means should be possible. However, extinction does not seem to occur naturally; quite the reverse, the **neurotic paradox** refers to the fact that irrational anxiety tends to worsen rather than die out. Thus if a child is trapped in a small dark cupboard with a cat and the intense fear produces a fear of cat fur, a case of **one trial learning**, why does the 'cat/fur fear' worsen in the absence of the cupboard situation (the UCS)? The main explanation is in terms of **negative reinforcement** from operant conditioning. The child is reinforced (relief) for **escaping or avoiding** the feared stimuli (CS), and therefore avoids **exposure** and extinction. Thus any exposure is brief, reinforced with fear and escaped from before fear can subside.

Behaviour therapy is the term given to the use of classical conditioning in therapy, such as the removal of irrational fear by exposure. The principle of **reciprocal inhibition** is central to this and simply refers to certain physiological states being mutually exclusive, e.g. you cannot be relaxed and anxious at the same time, thus relaxation reciprocally inhibits anxiety. This clearly relates to the antagonistic functions of the **sympathetic** and **para-sympathetic** divisions of the **autonomic nervous system**. As mentioned in the previous section, the sympathetic response is intended to *confront* or *escape* danger, not to be sustained as *fear*. Mary Cover Jones (1924) used this principle to reduce a child's fear of animals. She had the child eat a meal, encouraging a parasympathetic response, while keeping a cat at some distance away, which would normally produce a sympathetic response (fear). At succeeding meals she brought the animal gradually closer until the child was able to touch the cat without undue fear. Here, the relaxed response to the cat has replaced the fear response, a process sometimes referred to as **counterconditioning**.

Although clearly effective, behaviour therapy did not have a great impact on clinical practice for another thirty years, partly as a result of a focus on theoretical advancement as opposed to practical application. This may have also been due to criticism from other approaches that it was 'dehumanizing and mechanical' and led to **symptom substitution**. The latter referred to the psychoanalyst's accusation that behaviour therapy simply removed the symptoms of the disorder and left the underlying disorder itself unchecked, then to re-emerge in the form of a different set of symptoms. For the behaviourists, the symptoms *were* the disorder, and they claim that no evidence of symptom substitution has ever been established. Perhaps to bridge the divide, Dollard and Miller (1950) attempted to translate psychoanalytic concepts into behavioural terms. During the 1950s however, **Hans J. Eysenck** made rather scathing attacks on the psychoanalytic approach, at the same time advocating behaviour therapy.

Joseph Wolpe (1958) published an influential book, in which he outlined basic procedures for behaviour therapy, making the early work of Watson and others explicit. There were three major approaches based on classical conditioning, which Wolpe and others helped to popularize in the following years.

1. **Systematic desensitization**, based on the principles of reciprocal inhibition and counterconditioning.
2. **Flooding and implosion**, which were dependent on the exhaustion of the fear response.
3. **Aversion therapy**, where the target stimulus is associated with an unconditioned stimulus which is unpleasant.

In **systematic desensitization**, the therapist first trains the client in an activity that reciprocally inhibits the fear (sympathetic) response. This is usually relaxation in the form of **deep muscle relaxation**, or even borrowing from meditation techniques. There are alternatives to relaxation (as with Mary Cover Jones), although these are less often used, e.g. using **self-assertion training** can give the client this extra skill simultaneously. The next stage is to create a hierarchy of feared situations, usually about ten, from mild scenarios to the most feared situation. This is called a **SUD scale** (subjective unit of discomfort) and can serve a dual purpose, one of which is as a reference scale for the client to indicate their subjective level of fear, e.g. 'I am feeling at about a four'. The main purpose of the SUD scale is to provide a series of situations for the client to work through (usually in their imagination), *while remaining reasonably calm*. Trying to carry on with escalating fear is counterproductive, the process takes a number of sessions and cannot be rushed. The procedure is sometimes carried out **in vivo**, or in real life, although due to practical considerations this is often restricted to occasional checks that the effect has generalized to the real world. Systematic desensitization utilizes the principle of stimulus **generalization**, enabling the therapist to approach the target situation via a distantly similar one, which produces a proportionately smaller response.

In **flooding** the reverse approach to extinction is used, confronting the client with the most fear-provoking situation from the start. **Enforced confrontation** is maintained until the fear subsides and the client enters a **resolution period** (which can be accompanied by euphoria), in which they are imagining (or in) the feared situation but without fear. This paradoxical situation comes about because the sympathetic division of the nervous system is designed for short-term use and after about 20–30 minutes at *full response* the effect dissipates, perhaps to prevent permanent damage or depletion of the organism's resources. A few such sessions can result in long-term relief from irrational fear, and flooding often proves more effective than systematic desensitization and is consequently proving popular in times of restricted resources. However, the ordeal can be quite torturous for the client, who has to be both able and motivated to withstand it. The point about motivation is important as high levels of fear have to be maintained. If the client is able to 'take a break', the autonomic system may recover sufficiently to prolong the procedure greatly. Wolpe himself found it took about four hours of driving an **agoraphobic** (fear of open spaces) girl in a car to achieve resolution. **Implosion** involves using exaggerated imagined imagery, often with the therapist adding to the description of scenarios, thus such situations cannot be experienced *in vivo*. Implosion therapy is less effective than flooding

Aversion therapy is similar in its process to Watson and Rayner's creation of a phobia. An unpleasant UCS is used, such as an emetic, noxious smell or unpleasant imagery – the choice is limited by any potential harm and the need for its effect to be delivered *on time*. This is paired with an undesirable stimulus, such as **alcohol** or an inappropriate sexual stimulus (e.g. picture of serious sexual violence), over a number of trials, in the expectation that the undesirable stimulus presented alone will produce noxious feelings. Ideally, this should lead to the avoidance of the alcohol, etc. in the future, in the manner of the neurotic paradox referred to earlier. However, there is much that can go wrong. The procedure is difficult without the voluntary co-operation of the client, who may be an inmate at a **special hospital** or an out-patient attending an alcohol treatment unit. The treatment needs to be sustained *outside* the clinical environment. The undesirable stimulus is not benign, as in the case of phobic objects, and in cases such as alcohol it is strongly reinforcing, difficult to avoid and socially sanctioned. The principle is sound, but practice is difficult in a less than perfect world. As a result, aversion therapy in cases such as alcoholism has a low rate of success. Its use in sexual disorders involves more complex issues, which will be dealt with in Chapter 7.

Behaviour modification is the term used when applying **operant conditioning** to abnormal behaviour, bringing about a change in behaviour by observing and manipulating its **contingent reinforcers**. This approach has been criticized for treating people as if they were performing circus animals, as it has to be admitted that the same process is involved in both cases. However, behaviour modification has produced humane results in situations where hopelessness was thought to be the only next step.

In Chapter 5 **autism** will be described. This is a very stubborn disorder to treat and for which there is no cure. Half of these individuals grow up with no speech and many of those who do speak do so as a result of behaviour modification methods. **Shaping** speech is very slow as autistic children do not respond well to reinforcers, sometimes only basic ones such as foods. The stages are usually as follows:

▶ Rewarding the child for **looking** at the therapist, attention to the other being a prerequisite for speech.
▶ Reward is then contingent on making **vocalizations** *while* attending.
▶ Vocalizations which approximate to **words** in response to the therapist's initiations are then the only reinforced items.
▶ The process of then differentially reinforcing longer **phrases and sentences** will depend on the responsiveness of the autistic individual.

The shaping of behaviour in this way has been extensively used in the many types of **learning disability** (mental retardation). Prior to the application of behaviour modification, individuals with **profound mental handicap** had been dismissed as being incompetent or beyond therapy. Behaviour modification was not a miracle cure, but it did provide hope and improvement where there was none. Sometimes the behaviours established were simple, such as lever-pulling, but success has also been achieved with toileting, interpersonal communication and basic social skills. There are problems in administering these techniques, with progress being slow and schedules often having to be simple (often continuous reinforcement). **Spontaneous extinction** is where the client suddenly stops responding and the schedule has to be abandoned. Reinforcers are often difficult to establish (as in autism) and the process can benefit from their prior testing. For example, they can be graded for their **approachability** by the client, which is often a good predictor of their effectiveness as reinforcers (Pace *et al.*, 1985). When complex sequences of behaviour are being shaped, a **chaining** of behaviour 'units' may be possible. In chaining, the completion of one behaviour unit (putting on a jacket) can act as both a **discriminative stimulus** (a cue or sign) for the following unit (buttoning the jacket) and a reinforcer (i.e. sense of accomplishment) for the preceding unit (holding the jacket).

Challenging behaviour refers to behaviour that presents a challenge for the clinician or carer. These include **self-stimulatory behaviour (SSB)**, such as rocking or rubbing, and **self-injurious behaviour (SIB)**, such as biting or head-banging. Behavioural techniques have risen to this 'challenge' with a number of methods for reducing such destructive behaviour.

▶ **Punishment** is an obvious choice, e.g. squirting chilli sauce into the mouth of an individual who was screaming. In SIB it is often difficult to establish what would be a punisher.

▶ **Differential reinforcement of incompatible behaviour (DRI)**. A little like an operant version of reciprocal inhibition, behaviour is encouraged which makes the unwanted behaviour impossible. For example, rewarding 'standing behaviour' would make it impossible for the individual to bang her head on the floor.

▶ **Differential reinforcement of other behaviour (DRO)**. Similar to an omission schedule, DRO is the rewarding of *any* behaviour *other* than the unwanted behaviour.

▶ Removing the **sensory consequences** of the unwanted behaviour can sometimes eliminate it. For example, a patient who repeatedly bangs an object on the floor can be discouraged by being placed on a soft surface, thereby removing the sensory feedback.

The reinforcement of desirable behaviour has been applied generally to in-patients on psychiatric wards in the form of **token economies**. Ayllon and Azrin (1968) reported using tokens as **secondary reinforcers** to encourage self-care behaviours among withdrawn and apathetic 'institutionalized' patients. The tokens could then be exchanged for primary reinforcers such as food or cigarettes. However, this change in behaviour is not always maintained after the patient is discharged.

The initial analysis of problem behaviour is an important stage in applying behavioural techniques. Although its application has now widened, the term **applied behaviour analysis** was often used where careful consideration was given to the way the environment supports (reinforces) behaviour. A therapist will often observe abnormal behaviour in its '**natural environment**' unobtrusively noting the triggers (discriminative stimuli) and consequences of a behaviour. An example of the importance of this would be observing that a child's clinging and disruptive behaviour is always followed by a scolding from her mother. It would seem that the child's good behaviour was ignored but bad behaviour gained attention (scolding), which was therefore reinforcing.

Biofeedback refers to a means of combining classical and operant techniques with modern technology. Small portable devices can now give information on a number of autonomic functions such as heart rate, blood pressure, peripheral temperature and galvanic skin response (rate of sweating measured by skin conductance). By feeding this information back about their *involuntary* responses, the client can then modify their *voluntary* behaviour to change these responses indirectly. This technique is increasingly used in the area of **health psychology,** for example, in trying to lower blood pressure in individuals prone to heart attacks.

Early behaviourist views often ignored or diminished the importance of cognitive events. It is surprising, therefore, that the **cognitive approaches** to therapy described in the next section should have emerged from the behavioural paradigm and even form the hybrid, **cognitive-behavioural therapy.** This came about by behavioural psychologists considering mental events in a similar way to behavioural ones and assuming that they can be changed in the same way. **Social learning approaches** (or vicarious learning) are based on these principles and have led to the clinical use of **modelling** behaviour. In this, the clinician or helper carries out a type of behaviour without making abnormal responses, whilst the client observes. Hopefully the client's thinking in approaching the behaviour or stimulus will change having seen someone else do it without adverse consequences. For example, a child that fears cats may watch the therapist playing with one or more cats, without fear and perhaps enjoying their company. The child may then be encouraged to join in. Thus, **mental preparation** precedes actual exposure, which is the point where we need to consider the cognitive approaches in the next section.

A number of criticisms of the behavioural approach have already been mentioned. A selection of these and others are listed below with their associated arguments.

▶ **Ethical considerations.** Like any other scientific tool, behavioural therapies can be used for harm or good. Although for the right reasons, Watson and Rayner (1920) demonstrated this with 'little Albert', whose mother unfortunately removed him before the experimental fear could be countered. People tend to fear the control of behaviour, especially where such control is not readily apparent. A colleague of mine had his behaviour modified by a class of students, who used interest and lack of interest to control where he stood during a lecture. He found it interesting that the 'experiment' had worked, but rather disconcerting that he had no awareness of being manipulated (he had previously explained this was the case for animals in such studies!). In this way, behavioural psychology challenges our notions of free will.

► **Is it mechanistic?** Following from the above, these therapies are accused of creating 'artificial' behaviour, that human nature is somehow being replaced with robotic commands. To some degree, this cannot be denied, but alternatives may be even less acceptable. Drug therapy or psychosurgery must surely be more mechanistic and more humanistic therapies tend to be less effective, or in some cases impossible.

► **Does it last?** A problem with behavioural approaches is sustaining behaviour change in the absence of reinforcers and outside the learning environment. Modern techniques may involve the client more in the process and be combined with **cognitive therapies**, enabling 'homework' to sustain change outside the clinical environment. Behavioural therapies compare very favourably with other approaches having a success rate of around 80 per cent, which is often sustained in the long term.

► **Is it ineffective in some cases?** The simple answer to this is no, behavioural approaches can be applied to most disorders. This is especially the case with biologically-based disorders where there is no way of rectifying the abnormality. Here behavioural techniques may be the only hope of improvement, as in the case of **profound mental handicap**. However, there are disorders which are highly resistant to therapy, including behavioural therapies, such as **psychopathic disorder**, along with other personality disorders (see Chapter 6).

► **Symptom substitution** is part of the psychodynamic school's claim that behavioural therapies address the symptoms, not the 'underlying disorder'. The reply to this criticism, that the symptoms *are* the disorder and that other symptoms do not substitute those treated, would appear to be unopposed. Further to this, the mechanical nature of the behavioural process is thought to leave the client without **insight** into their problem, and there is thought to be a general lack of 'bedside manner' inherent in the therapy. The practice of behavioural techniques is usually the reverse of this, in that the client is normally fully informed of the clinician's intentions and beliefs. This helps to gain the client's full co-operation and gives reassurance that there is no 'serious underlying disorder' or 'emotional conflict from their past' to worry about.

The cognitive and cognitive-behavioural approaches

As mentioned above, cognitive therapies paradoxically emerged from the practice of behavioural therapy, which in its **radical behaviourist** form denied the importance of cognitive events. Following on from the concept of reciprocal inhibition, or mutually exclusive autonomic states, the concepts of mutually incompatible affective and cognitive states were considered by

neo-behaviourists such as Dickinson and Dearing. **Social learning** theorists such as **Bandura,** who considered cognitive change to result from vicarious learning (see previous section), seem still further removed from the radical behaviourists and closer to a **cognitive-behavioural** view of therapy. Thus, rather than clearly separate behavioural and cognitive therapies, there seems to be a continuum of therapies, with radical behaviourism at one end and cognitive approaches at the other. Thus, most of the therapies tend to be cognitive-behavioural.

The term 'cognitive' in this context can be misleading to psychologists, as the original therapies borrow little from **cognitive psychology** as a discipline in psychology. Cognitive psychology views human thought in terms of **information processing,** taking in information through the senses, which is then processed and finally produces a response. Cognitive therapy concentrates on the preconceptions, biases in thinking and limitations placed on responding that colour human cognition and distinguish it from the information processing of a computer. Humans approach situations with **expectations,** a mental 'set' or framework, into which they fit information. This can be helpful in life, but it is sometimes maladaptive and resistant to change.

The central aim of cognitive therapy is to bring about change in maladaptive perceptions and thought patterns, or **cognitive restructuring.** This can be in *addition* to changing behaviour, or as a precursor, assuming that behaviour will follow cognitive change. Cognitive therapists tend to deal with the here and now, rather than examining the historical causes of the maladaptive thinking. Different approaches to this task have followed from the work of individual therapists. Although they share the same overall aim, their approaches differ sufficiently to consider a few of the leading therapies:

Albert Ellis and rational emotive therapy (RET)

Ellis proposed that people feel anxious or behave maladaptively because incorrect, negative and unproductive thoughts or attitudes prevent them from responding in a productive way. His clients would tend to blame their own inadequacies, or blame the situations they were in as not being suited to them. Ellis instructed his clients to think logically about their negative beliefs and question them, seeking out the **illogical basis,** and substituting more **realistic expectations** of themselves. The client needs to address the **self-fulfilling prophecy,** that their negative expectations may lead directly to failure. Here is an example of a maladaptive approach in three stages.

1. **Ordinary situation**: asking someone for a dance at a night-club.
2. **Negative cognitions**: fear of doing something accidentally foolish; fear of being rejected; fear of embarrassment.
3. **Negative outcomes**: failing to ask them; 'freezing' in public; precipitate rejection by nervous negative approach.

The client is asked to work through the negative cognitions and, in Ellis's view, expose the nonsense that is their basis. Substituting more realistic expectations should reduce anxiety and the negative attitude that can precipitate the self-fulfilling prophecy situation. Positive action and a belief in oneself can then produce some positive experiences, increasing the expectation of success.

Ellis identified three groups of ideas which are often rigidly held by disturbed individuals.

1. 'I must achieve and win the approval of my peers; failure means I am incompetent.'
2. 'Other people must always be fair and kind to me, they are worthless if they do not.'
3. 'I cannot tolerate a world of disorder, where I cannot have the things I need immediately.'

These irrational beliefs set absolute standards which cannot be achieved and, in Ellis's reasoning, lead to negative and **masturbatory thinking**.

Donald Meichenbaum and self-instructional therapy

Meichenbaum pointed to the way in which anxious and unsuccessful people make excuses for themselves and engage in self-defeating thoughts. His therapy was simply to have his clients identify the areas in their lives where this occurred and then to produce **scripts** of positive instructions that put the responsibility for success on their own actions. Thus, in place of an alcoholic's thinking 'I have had a bad day, I deserve a drink, I will be anxious if I do not', they would be given phrases for 'self-talk' such as 'I feel well, I do not want to feel ill with drink, I am proud of myself as a sober successful individual'. The self-instructions can be very specific, emphasizing their role as **coping strategies**, and can even reduce psychotic speech. Meichenbaum admits that self-instruction needs a high level of repetition, to be habitual, to be effective.

Meichenbaum (1986) presented his methods of **stress inoculation training** (**SIT**), in which clients use their coping strategies to deal with artificially induced stressors such as gruesome films in a successful way. This can then be generalized to future situations.

Aaron Beck's cognitive therapy

In common with Ellis, Beck's approach also assumes that maladaptive thought patterns lead to his clients' difficulties. However, Beck does not emphasize the client's tendency to exaggerate negative outcomes, but would question the *validity* of the assumptions on which these presumed outcomes were based, e.g. a lack of faith in their self-worth, despite evidence to the contrary. Beck's name has become associated with the advance of cognitive therapy and is responsible for it becoming a major approach in the management of depression.

For Beck, depressed individuals have an unrealistically pessimistic view of the world, a **cognitive triad,** involving a negative view of themselves, their personal future and current experiences. They make errors of information processing, magnifying negative events and overgeneralizing negative outcomes, e.g. if a relationship fails, then 'no one will ever want me'. As with Ellis, Beck also identified impossible goals such as 'I must be liked by everybody', though he saw these as originating in childhood.

Beck's has a highly structured approach to therapy, setting agendas and time limits, although his interaction with the client is warm and enthusiastic. The client's habitual **automatic thoughts** are identified through the client keeping a daily record. These can then be tested as hypotheses, questioning their evidence and looking for alternative views. Beck uses this **Socratic method** of questioning the client's assumptions, rather than arguing or telling the client they are wrong. Beck uses both behavioural and cognitive techniques, using **behavioural approaches** at first if the client is not responsive to cognitive activity.

Evaluations of cognitive therapy by its exponents are predictably good, with professionals such as Ellis claiming a 70+ per cent success rate. Independent studies have not been as favourable, especially in comparison with behavioural therapies. Studies tend to find that cognitive and behavioural therapies fit together well in clinical practice, but this combination does not seem to produce any measurable benefit over and above the use of behavioural therapies alone. Last *et al.* (1984) consider that thought patterns may not be important for change in behaviour, suggesting that change must be *acted out* in the real world (*in vivo*) for it to become long-term. However, studies in this area are subject to limitations, two of which deserve a mention.

Most studies are of the **analogue** type, that is, the participants are not clinical patients, but are 'prepared' by therapy for stressful situations and their abilities to cope are compared. Carefully matched clinical trials are rare, and often experimental considerations, understandably, have to give way to **ethical constraints.** A further problem when comparing approaches that operate on different areas of human functioning is that their effects may be rather specific to that area. Lang (1968) presented a 'three systems model of fear', in which he examined the independence of three levels of therapy and assessment.

1. **Cognitive**: anticipation and verbal accounts of fear.
2. **Behavioural**: resisting escape and avoidance from feared situation.
3. **Physiological**: does the feared situation produce autonomic arousal?

Lang considered that clients may confront a feared situation (behaviour), but still show a marked physiological response and still verbally label themselves as fearful (cognitive). Other outcomes examined in this way produced similar disparities at these three levels. If Lang is correct in the degree of independence of these areas of functioning, studies comparing, say, cognitive with behavioural therapy should not evaluate their results in terms of behavioural change only. Although this model has been criticized for difficulties of definition (see Hugdahl, 1981), it still makes a strong point in favour of multiple therapy approaches.

Cognitive therapies are a rapidly expanding area of clinical psychology practice and are being applied to an increasing number of disorders, including schizophrenia.

The psychodynamic approach

Just as the cognitive approaches from the last section are a rapidly expanding area, therapies based on the psychodynamic approach, essentially forms of **psychoanalysis,** peaked and declined during the twentiety century. This decline has been more marked in parts of Europe, whilst in the United States there is still a flourishing market for psychoanalysis. However, psychodynamic theory remains important in academic and historical terms, being the first psychological approach to gain acceptance. The aim of psychoanalysis is to produce therapeutic change by allowing the client to gain an **insight** into her or his emotional past. These unresolved emotional conflicts from the past are thought to produce **unconscious conflicts** resulting in their symptoms. As a result of the process involved, psychoanalysis is sometimes described as an **insight therapy.**

Although its precursors can be traced back to **Mesmer** and the hard work of **Breuer** (see Chapter 1), psychodynamic approaches to abnormal behaviour truly began with **Sigmund Freud** (1856–1939). Freud formulated the psychodynamic theory of personality based on his clinical experiences. He initially used **hypnosis** to access the early experiences of his neurotic patients, in the manner that his colleague Breuer had done. However, Freud was not satisfied that this route to his patients' past produced the best therapeutic effect. He felt that clients should be allowed to find their own way to their past in normal consciousness. He used **free association,** which became the basis of **Freudian psychoanalysis.** Many of Freud's followers developed their own variations of his approach, leading to the many variations still practised today.

Freud used his clinical experience to produce his developmental **theory of personality,** and then used this theory to explain his clients' problems (such tautological reasoning is very characteristic of Freud's theorizing). In his theory he introduced new concepts to the scientific and lay world, such as **unconscious motivation** and **infantile sexuality,** which were not always well received by his contemporaries.

The term 'psychodynamic' refers to the active nature of the mental structures that form the basis of Freud's theory of personality. There are three of these and they are thought to develop from one another in the early child-hood years.

1. The **id** ('it') is the home of **Eros**, the source of psychic energy or **libido** (Freud later considered **Thanatos** to be an additional, destructive source of psychic energy). This energy was thought to build up and require release in the form of gratification of the id's instinctive impulses. These impulses are all the primitive biological needs inherited by the individual, present at birth and represented by the id. The immediate gratification of these drives is termed **primary process thinking** and is said to be governed by the **pleasure principle**.

2. The **ego** ('I') is formed when the primary processing of the id is thwarted and gratification is delayed. This type of gratification is termed **secondary process thinking** and as needs have to balanced against the demands of reality, operates under the **reality principle**. Part of the ego is in the conscious self and this negotiates between the id's demands and those of the outside world.

3. The **superego** develops when the id and ego have to conform to the accumulated moral rules of adults and society. Part of the unconscious, the superego acts as a kind of 'conscience', imposing high moral demands on the ego, in contrast to the primitive demands of the id.

These three hypothetical structures are expected to work in approximate harmony, balancing their needs. If they are in conflict, or if one is either dominant or underdeveloped, the individual suffers proportionate degrees of disorder. Freud also believed a mentally healthy individual successfully passes through five **psychosexual stages**. It is during these stages that the id, ego and superego are formed. Distortions of personality can occur if an individual is over- or undersatisfied at any stage, or fails to progress and thus becomes **fixated** or stuck at that stage. The characteristics of these distortions are determined by the stage and whether the individual is under- or over-gratified.

1. **The oral stage** lasts from birth for about the first year. Governed by the id, the child uses its **mouth** to explore the world, beginning with reflexes to explore the breast and generalizing the oral gratification to substitutes such as dummies, thumbs and food. Thus the child gains oral gratification, channelling libidinal energy via the mouth, indicating that Freud considered this a form of sexual energy finding its release. Conflict can occur over feeding. Fixation at this stage is associated with overeating, smoking or verbal excess and a number of more general traits.

2. **In the anal stage** the child moves its focus from the mouth to the **anus**. It gains comfort from its bowel movements and may develop a less than welcome (to the parents) interest in them. However, reality steps in during its second year or so in the form of **potty training** and it is the conflict over these demands of reality that leads to the formation

of the ego. Fixation at this stage is associated with untidiness and aggression (**anal-expulsive personality**), and meanness and acquisitiveness (**anal-retentive personality**).

3. **The phallic stage** is important as it contains the **Oedipal** or **Electra** conflict areas, as a result of which the superego is formed. The focus for libidinal energy is the **penis** or **clitoris**. The child is claimed to be four or five years old at this point and being sexual but naive, has problems adjusting to the acceptability of the attractions to their own genitalia. Fixation at this stage can result in inferiority at one extreme, and promiscuity and narcissism at the other.

    Freud's explanation of how the child internalizes the moral codes that dictate their sexual behaviour (including male and female roles) and develops a superego has been greatly criticized. Perhaps this is due to the refusal of his critics to accept having **infantile sexual desires** or due to the unscientific nature of Freud's speculations. This cannot be easily clarified, as Freud would consider the critics to be **repressing** their infant sexuality – another example of the circular reasoning involved in Freud's theorizing. According to Freud, the male undergoes **Oedipal conflict**. In this, the male child desires his mother (sexually) and sees the father as a (large) competitor in this and wishes him dead (as Oedipus). The child believes his thoughts are open to his parents and the father, being thus aware of his intentions, will punish the child with castration. The child resolves this dilemma by **identifying** with the father, not just imitation, but considering himself to *be* the father, thus no longer needing to compete with, or fear 'himself'. In this way the child adopts both sex-specific behaviour and the values of his parent in the form of the superego. Freud's female equivalent, the **Electra complex,** is more vague and has received more criticism. In this the girl envies the father's penis (i.e. **penis envy**), and wishes to posses the father (sexually) as compensation. Her mixed emotions towards the mother result again in identification, though with the mother this time, resolving the conflict.

4. In **the latency stage** the sexual turmoil of previous stages dissipates and the child turns outward to develop other life skills. Hence reference to *latent* sexual development during this period.

5. **The genital stage** begins in adolescence where the focus of sexual energy is the genitalia of the desired sex. Any **unresolved conflicts** from the earlier stages may then re-emerge to create problems during this stage, which lasts through maturity.

For Freud, conflicts in the early stages can distort personalities, which can be further disturbed by threats from the real world creating **realistic anxiety,** conflict between id and ego in controlling urges (**neurotic anxiety**), and **moral anxiety** from fear of violating the demands of the superego. The ego attempts to defend itself against such anxieties and these strategies are termed **ego defence mechanisms**. Some defence mechanisms can be more adaptive than others, although all can be maladaptive if used excessively. Examples of more successful strategies are as follows:

- **Sublimation** is the channelling of repressed unacceptable (often sexual) desires into acceptable outlets such as sport, art or religion.
- **Identification** (as in the phallic stage) with significant others (real or not) can lead to higher achievement, but only in moderation.

Less adaptive defence mechanisms tend to be short-term solutions, resulting in longer-term problems. The main process is one of **repression**, the repression of anxiety provoking conflicts into the unconscious, requiring one of the other defence mechanisms to provide a distorted outlet. Briefly, examples of the other ego defences are as follows.

- **Projection** is the projecting of one's undesirable urges onto others, preventing the recognition of one's own problems.
- **Rationalization**, as it suggests, is to provide a justification for one's desires or fears in terms which deny true feelings.
- **Reaction-formation** is a kind of overcompensation, urges are repressed and expressed in their opposite form as in the terrorist who fights for peace, but really enjoys the process of war.
- **Regression** is the reverting to an earlier stage of development to evade anxiety, 'seeking the comfort of childhood'.

When the ego defences fail or break down, there is a disintegration of the personality, a process called **decompensation**. Freud considered the neurotic, or even psychotic, conditions that result from abuse and failure of defences to be treatable by **psychoanalysis** (though he had reservations about psychotic states).

Freudian psychoanalysis has basic requirements of the client. They have to be able to afford the treatment, which can take many hours a week for three or more years. Freud considered that older clients (45+) were too fixed in their ways to gain full benefit from treatment and clients needed to be reasonably intelligent in order to engage in the verbal process. Giving the clients insight into the source of their distress does not remove it, but enables them to deal with it in a more realistic way, replacing their neurotic misery with common unhappiness.

Analysis typically takes place with the client relaxed on a couch, with the analyst out of view behind them. With as little prompting as possible, the client engages in **free association**, allowing their verbalized thoughts to drift back in time. It is assumed that the drift of the associated material will be slowly drawn closer to the source of the repressed material, but that this progress will be thwarted by **unconscious defences**. Over time the client will reveal clues as to the nature of the repressed material (it is assumed) they are drifting slowly towards. As the source of the repression is approached, defences and symptoms increase. When the repressed material is brought into consciousness, the experience should result in a **cathartic** release of repressed feelings. As this point is approached the client's unconscious **resistance** may result in 'sudden cure' or some other ploy to subvert the therapy. Sometimes repressed feelings are projected onto the analyst instead of the original individual from the past experience: this is termed **transference**. Sometimes, the analyst may have unresolved conflicts which may be projected onto the client: **countertransference**. This is one reason why an essential part of an analyst's training is their **own analysis**. Freud also used **interpretations of dreams** in his analytic process.

Followers of Freud altered his process or emphasis, producing their own form of psychoanalysis. Modern analysis can be selected from a wide variety of techniques, most of which are briefer and subject to more guidance or 'leading' by the therapist.

Criticism of Freud's theory and therapy is not difficult to find, some major points are these:

▶ His methods were **unscientific,** relying on **case studies,** without any testing of hypotheses or other experimental procedures. He generalized his experiences with a small group of (mostly) middle-class, neurotic, female patients, to the wider population. He kept no **empirical** record of his data (patient verbalizations) and used **introspection** (his own subjective speculation) to fill gaps and organize his work.

▶ His theories were 'all-explaining' (**tautological**) and therefore not falsifiable (could not be tested). According to **Karl Popper,** any theory that is *not* capable of being disproved is not scientific.

▶ Some of Freud's explanations of his patients' cases have been openly challenged. Joseph Wolpe examined Freud's 'little Hans' case, in which the child's fear of horses was related to a castration complex from fearing his father, symbolized by the horse's teeth. Wolpe's explanation in terms of classical conditioned fear due to experiences with horses seemed more plausible.

▶ Many critics thought Freud too preoccupied with the importance of **sex** in his theories, and that this reflected his own obsessions. This was often given as a reason for some of his more dubious collaborations with 'fringe theorists'.

▶ The Freudian psychoanalytic movement has been described as being closer to a **religious cult** than a scientific movement. His methods have been labelled as an **'art-form'** rather than a scientific therapy.

Some of Freud's critics were once his pupils (or followers). These **post-Freudians** and later **neo-Freudians** helped to spread psychoanalysis, but unlike the disciples of a religious movement, they altered the original text. Most of the examples below developed their own versions of psychodynamic theory and analysis.

▶ **Carl Gustav Jung** (1875–1961) disagreed with Freud's emphasis on sex and gave more weight to philosophical and religious aspects of experience in founding his **analytical psychology** approach. His view of personality extended beyond the personal to include inherited **archetypes,** formless predispositions that await realization and reside in the **collective unconscious,** the product of common inheritance that connects individuals. He was concerned with the hidden or repressed side of our personalities with archetypal concepts such as the **shadow, animus and anima** (the female and male aspects of males and females respectively), and **persona** (public face or 'mask'). He described psychological types as being along continua: **extravert** or **introvert; thinking** or **feeling; sensing** or **intuiting; rational** or **irrational.** Jung was criticized as being pseudo-philosophical, and perhaps *less* scientific than Freud.

▶ **Alfred Adler** (1870–1939) founded his **individual psychology** emphasizing the individual's struggle to overcome feelings of **inferiority.** He was less concerned with early experience than conscious strivings and the **overcompensation** that may result (e.g. a deaf musician), or **retreat into illness.** He overlapped with **behaviourists** in thinking individuals should face the consequences of their actions.

▶ **Harry Stack Sullivan** (1892–1949) is probably responsible for the survival of psychoanalysis in the US today, in popularizing its use during his industrious career. He is also known for his attempts to use psychoanalysis with schizophrenic patients, which, despite his claims, had limited therapeutic success. Sullivan's non-confrontational style still survives among many analysts in the US.

▶ **Melanie Klein** (1882–1960) helped to popularize the use of psychoanalysis in Britain. Klein focused on early childhood relations looking in detail at their first encounters with 'objects', the primary 'object' being the breast. Her **object relations** view of an infant adjusting to the good and bad aspects of the same object involved mental processes such as **splitting** good and bad aspects, **projecting** bad aspects out, and **introjecting** good aspects inside.

The psychoanalytic movement has altered in its methods during its history. In addition, it has led to other therapeutic approaches that also have insight as a goal of therapy. Some of these will be examined in the next section.

The humanistic, existential and Gestalt approaches

Each of these approaches considers the individual as a **whole person,** with the same potential for growth as any other human being. Abnormal behaviour is thought to result from some failure in the client's past, restricted self-development or failure to face up to life's challenges. Each therapy aims to give the client some insight into the dynamics of their problem and enable them sufficiently to cope and rise above their difficulties. Some aspects of these therapies have similarities to cognitive approaches. These three therapeutic approaches (particularly humanistic) are often adopted by counsellors and tend not to be used with more disturbed individuals.

The humanistic approach

Many of the approaches described so far tend to deny free will in individuals, considering behaviour to have biological, conditioned or unconscious determinants. Humanistic approaches emphasize that people do have choices, and constraints on their free will tend to be self-imposed rather than determined for them.

The main proponents of the humanistic approach are **Abraham Maslow** and **Carl Rogers**. Roger's influence in the area of therapy has been substantial, to the extent that his approach, **client-centred therapy,** can be referred to as **Rogerian therapy.** More detail on Rogers is given below.

▶ **Abraham Maslow** (1908–70) described a **hierarchy of needs,** which all human beings strive to work through. Individuals have to begin by satisfying the lower, physical needs in order eventually to achieve their 'highest' need, that of **self-actualization.** Influenced by such concepts, which can be traced back to Carl Jung, he also based some of his work on studies of self-actualized individuals such as **Einstein.** For Maslow, people have mental distress when influences such as the family block their progress towards self-actualization. In helping the person to understand how these influences block some of their needs, Maslow hopes that their personalities will strengthen as they becomes aware of their potential to satisfy *all* their needs.

▶ **Carl Rogers** (1902–87) produced a theory of personality in 1959, which assumes humanity to be basically good and motivated towards improvement. His personality theory was based on his **client-centred** approach described in his *Client-centred Therapy* (1951). He aims to **actualize** their potential, and by a process of **self-actualization** develop the characteristics of the **healthy personality.** He considered that the need to enhance the 'self' to be genetically programmed like any other need, and perhaps more important than basic needs. Rogers believes that society imposes conditions of worth, which are transmitted by **conditional positive regard.** These are the standards by which individuals are judged, and states of disharmony result when there is a great disparity between the value on the self imposed by those significant in society and that individual's potential. In his therapy he uses **unconditional positive regard** to encourage the client to develop more positive 'selves', believing the attitude and style of the therapist to be more important than specific techniques. 'Client-centred therapy' has since become **'person-centred therapy'**, with the aim of aiding the client's self-worth by referring to them as a person rather than 'client' or 'patient'.

The existential approach

The existential approach also emphasizes that individuals have positive attributes, which can be inhibited or distorted by the environment. However, the existential approach is less optimistic than the humanistic approach, seeing the modern world as **alienating** and dehumanizing. In existential therapy, the client is encouraged to face up to the realities and **responsibilities** of life: self-fulfilment is not enough, they must recognize their responsibilities to others.

There are three principles in existentialism:

1. **Being.** Humans are aware of their existence, their 'being', and have to take responsibility for it. They have the freedom of choice and should not make excuses to evade this.
2. **Non-being.** Humans know they will cease to exist at some point in time and this awareness creates **existential anxiety**. If an individual cannot accept being and non-being as applying to them, their choices become restricted and the self-actualization process becomes distorted.
3. **Being in the world.** Being at one with one's world. Disorder can result from alienation, a feeling that they have lost 'their world'. Such individuals feel estranged from other human beings or isolated from the natural world.

From this it can be seen that existentialism encourages the client to face up to the inevitabilities of existence, life, accidents and death, *at the same time* as taking the responsibility for their own part in this. Further to this, they are taught to face up to an existence which leaves them essentially **alone in the world,** but at the same time encouraged to relate to others in an unpretentious direct way. Though seemingly depressing in its outlook, the existential view is more realistic than that of the humanistic school. The existential therapist attempts to see the world as the client sees it, in order to understand the distortions the client experiences. The client is made aware of her potential for growth and finding meaning in the world. With support and encouragement, the client can take the responsibility for making choices, knowing that she may live with the consequences for the rest of her life. As with humanistic therapy, the attitude of the therapist is seen to be more influential than specific therapeutic techniques.

There are a number of views within existentialism – **R. May** and **R.D. Laing** are just two examples.

▶ **Rollo May** (1905–) studied under Alfred Adler as a psychoanalyst, and moved into humanistic therapy before helping to popularize existential therapy in the US. May saw the threat to the individual posed by the rapid growth in **science and technology** and the reliance on science to solve all our ills. He quotes from existentialist literature (see Schnieder and May, 1995, in Further Reading) and also refers to novels and films which depict the dehumanizing effects of technology. He saw six characteristics of therapy, which mostly referred to the way of relating to the patient and the insights the patient should achieve. For May, the client is responsible for writing the script for their own existence at that moment.

▶ **Ronald D. Laing** (1927–89) was much revered in the 1960s as an **anti-psychiatrist** and 'psychic guru'. As a psychiatrist, Laing brought his existential or phenomenological philosophy to bear on more severe disorders such as **schizophrenia**. Mildly psychotic individuals were related to, and their view of the world was examined for what sense such patients could make of their own experiences. In the context of the 1960s, this seemed admirable: Laing and his colleagues seemed proud of the fact that visitors had difficulty differentiating the patients from the therapists. Such experimental **therapeutic communities** are viewed far more cynically in retrospect. Laing himself was both loved and hated by his own profession, some seeing him as a clever, witty humanitarian, and others seeing only an alcoholic who fell from grace whilst clinging to popularity.

The Gestalt approach

Gestalt psychology focuses on perceiving the pattern of the whole above the detail from which the pattern is made. For example, one hears a song rather than a collection of individual notes, regardless of the key it is played in or the instrument it is played on. **Gestalt therapy** aims to integrate the whole person, including aspects of their personality and feelings that may have been denied.

Frederich Perls (1893–1970) developed the Gestalt approach to therapy after he disagreed with his analyst colleagues over some of their assumptions. As with the humanistic view, Perls saw his clients as basically good in their potential, and that they should be aware of, and accept responsibility for, their needs and fears, in a similar way to the existentialists. There are a number of techniques in Gestalt therapy which mostly involve role-play. Some examples can be found below. However, as with the previous approaches, the resulting attitude of the client is of primary importance.

▶ **The empty chair** is intended to help the client become aware of and address his true feelings. The client imagines he is confronting an individual or an object in the chair opposite, talking directly to the representation of the feeling rather than *about* it.

▶ **Reversal.** The client is asked to role-play the *opposite* of the way they feel. In a Jungian sense this can put them in touch with the 'other side' of themselves and confront repressed feelings.

▶ **Use of metaphor** involves role-playing or symbolizing a situation analogous to a problem, which prevents the client confronting a feeling. In acting out a parallel situation, the same feeling may be stirred and the client recognize the barrier to it.

There are common elements between humanistic, existential and Gestalt approaches – they all emphasize attitudes within therapy and aim to give the patient insight and the means to cope with their difficulties. Their differences tend to be a matter of emphasis and style of interaction between therapist and client.

Group, family and cultural approaches

Some therapeutic approaches recognize that the client is not acting in isolation and that their **social context** may be adversely influencing their behaviour. Taking this one step further, if the social context of the individual can have a negative effect on their mental health, then that context could be considered or even *used* in therapy. Other people, especially those close to us such as our family, are usually the most influential aspect of this context, though all of these individuals may be collectively influenced by their **cultural context**. Therapists are increasingly recognizing these influences on abnormal behaviour and, as far as possible, utilizing them in their therapeutic approaches.

Group therapies

There are many varieties of group therapy and many of the therapy approaches described so far have versions of their therapies for multiple participants. Some groups are large and perhaps directed by a single therapist, whereas others may be small and consist of only clients interacting, perhaps with minimal prior instruction, perhaps engaging in physical contact or other exercises. Although there are positive reasons for involving others, the origins of group therapy were **economic**. It is at times of economic pressure on health resources that the use of group therapy increases. In the current economic climate, there is pressure on the health service and at the same time conditions such as the **adult effects of child sexual abuse** and **post-traumatic stress disorder** are being revealed to be more prevalent than previously thought. Such conditions can benefit from group therapy settings at some stage in the disorder, although individual therapy will also be needed. There are disorders for which group therapy would seem inappropriate and occasions when it has proved harmful (Lieberman *et al.*, 1973). However it is evaluated, the use of group settings will often be driven by the need to help a large number of clients with limited therapist time.

For some clients, group therapy can provide a great deal of support and reassurance. Simply having other clients present often reassures one individual that they are not alone in their condition, and peer support can help a client to persist with a therapy when circumstances are difficult, e.g. substance abstinence. The group setting directly helps those who have difficulty relating to others and can indirectly help, in that clients may pick up tips on coping with their problems. Although there are variations, group therapies can be broadly divided into three types:

1. **Groups led in therapy**. These are really extensions of individual therapies, but with the additional advantages (and disadvantages) of the group setting. These may use cognitive, behavioural or a number of other approaches, and are led by the therapist(s) giving suggestions or comments and encouraging (or allowing) input from the client group.

2. **Self-help groups.** These are groups of clients with similar (or the same) problems, who organize their own meetings in informal or healthcare settings. The activity is often initiated by one or more clients with experience of both the disorder and its therapy, to help and encourage the others to cope and see therapy through, or simply to admit they have a problem in the first place. In some disorders, even highly trained professionals admit the *limitations* imposed by not having first-hand experience of the disorder (much to their credit). For example, self-help groups can be of great value in coming to terms with child sexual abuse.

3. **Activity-based groups.** These go under a variety of names, often specifying the activity used for therapy. These are often viewed with scepticism by some professionals and public alike, sometimes with justification on the (usually rare) occasions when clients suffer adverse effects. Skills may be learned as the focus of activity, such as social skills, self-assertion or the educational function of the long-established **sensitivity training**, or **T-groups**. More dramatic or confrontational activities may be engaged in, such as the emotional and physical interactions characteristic of **encounter groups**.

Irrespective of the disorder concerned, some individuals are more suitable for group therapy than others. Those less suitable individuals can be helped to benefit by **pre-group training** on how to act in the group setting and gain from it.

Family therapy

In one sense family therapy is a form of group therapy. However, the dynamics of the family 'group' have already been established prior to meeting for therapy; indeed, it is often the purpose of therapy to change these fixed patterns of behaviour. Family therapy has a great deal of overlap with **couples therapy** and **marital therapy**, especially where both involve children. Conflict in families, especially with children, is not abnormal. In the **family systems approach**, the family can be seen as a system of complex interrelationships and addressed as such. Family therapy is usually engaged in for two basic reasons:

1. **Extreme conflict.** This is where the dynamics of the family have become so distorted, or conflict so intense, that one or more members present with stress-related disorders. In this case the disorder would seem to be sustained by the family as it is and intervention has to involve the whole family, usually meeting together (or in combinations) with a therapist.
2. **Disorder in the family.** This is where one (or more) members of the family have a disorder, which may not be caused by the family dynamics, but may be adversely affected by them. An example here would be the effects of **expressed emotion** within the family of a schizophrenic individual on the sufferer's relapse rate (see Chapter 9). Addressing the family interactions can thus improve the condition of the disordered family member.

Often the problems are ones of misunderstanding or lack of communication, and these can quite rapidly be identified and addressed by having the family communicate honestly and directly under the guidance of an experienced therapist. Other situations can only be managed rather than resolved, e.g. if there has been a death or serious rift in the family.

Cultural approaches

There are three main approaches to considering cultural factors in abnormal psychology. One is to consider the way in which disorders are **interpreted** differently depending on the cultural context, or **cultural relativism**: some conditions may, or may not be considered disorders, depending on the cultural context. The second is to consider how the effects of a culture can **influence** the occurrence, or shape the type of disorder found in individuals of that culture: so-called **culture-bound syndromes**. The third is a combination of the first two and applies to the experiences of individuals from one culture when living in another. The latter view is confounded by the stress of moving and adjusting to another environment, but the rate and type of disorder is also influenced by **culture-conflict**. Here are some illustrations of these cultural effects:

► **Interpretation** of schizophrenic symptoms has always been influenced by the culture in which it is found. Although it is diagnosed in every culture, symptoms such as hearing voices can be closely associated with religious experience in some cultures and may be seen as a 'gift' rather than a disability. Thus rates of diagnosis may vary, *even though* the same diagnostic criteria are available, as the sufferer may never enter the healthcare system in the first place.

► **Culture-bound syndromes** are usually related to strong beliefs within the particular culture. In Chinese culture the delusion known as **Koro** (Shook Yang) may represent the emphasis in that culture on conservation of spermatic fluids, preserving some balance between yin and yang. In this delusion men believe their penis is retracting into the body or shrinking. The West is not immune to such influence over disorders: **anorexia nervosa** is primarily a western disorder, perhaps related to the pressure on young women to be slim.

► **Immigrant cultures** are generally thought to suffer greater levels of mental illness, though this varies with the degree of alienation experienced. Difficulties of **interpretation** are magnified in this situation, as culturally-specific behaviour may seem more alien contrasted with a different cultural context, and further difficulties arise when clinician and client are from different cultures. An immigrant expressing themselves in a culturally sanctioned way may have their actions misinterpreted by a GP or psychiatrist unfamiliar with their cultural mannerisms.

Cultural effects usually refer to differences between *ethnic groups*. However, *social groups* within the same ethnic division may have very different cultures. Just as a Haitian may experience cultural conflict in settling in Berlin, an individual from a farming community in Scotland may show some difficulties of adjusting to life in inner-city Liverpool. Clinicians need to be aware of these potential effects, which can colour their client's perceptions, or even their *own* expectations.

The problems of paradigms: diathesis-stress and eclectic approaches

Many people are closely related to schizophrenic individuals and do not develop the disorder, perhaps even as a twin with the same genetic predispositions. Others have survived emotional turmoil and severe illness in childhood, or have been caught up in an earthquake as an adult witnessing horror and carnage, and still show no signs and symptoms of mental disorder. Adopting a single paradigm when assessing and treating a client, such as seeing it only from a biological point of view, can be self-limiting. The clinician may be aware of, and treat, *part* of the problem only. Worse still, the abnormal behaviour may be sustained by non-biological factors, relegating biological treatment to an ameliorative role. The following approaches aim to widen the perspective of the therapist or student of abnormal behaviour:

▶ **The diathesis-stress approach** was first proposed by Meehl (1962). As we saw in Chapter 1, the diathesis-stress approach assumes a biological **predisposition** to a disorder (diathesis), rather than the disorder *itself* being inherited. A level of *stress* on the individual is then needed to precipitate the actual disorder, i.e. for the **expression** of the predisposition. Thus, if the individual is subject to great stress but lacks the predisposition, or if he carries the predisposition but meets little stress in his life, he does not go on to develop the disorder. This is often considered to be the approach associated with **behavioural medicine**, where both behavioural and biological therapies are adopted to cope with stress and related physical illness. The growing area of **health psychology** is allied to this and focuses on the physical effects of psychological stress.

▶ **The eclectic approach** involves the use of each therapeutic approach to the extent that it is *useful* to the individual patient, rather than adhering to one paradigm. This integrated approach is not always easy to achieve in practice as therapists often develop bias in their training and there is often antagonism between some approaches, especially the analytic and behavioural approaches. There has also been some criticism of those few therapists who abuse the eclectic label, when their approach would better be described as unsystematic and random. In contrast, some professionals have developed well-defined eclectic approaches such as Lazarus's (1984) description of **multimodal behaviour therapy**, addressing behaviour, cognition and affect. Other therapies illustrate how opposing approaches are becoming less distinct in terms of the actual practice, such as **cognitive-analytic therapy** (**CAT**) – a combination of brief psychotherapy and cognitive-behavioural therapy.

Multiple or eclectic approaches mitigate against the aims of the specialist, who can offer in-depth skills and knowledge beyond that of the therapist with a more general approach. However, this view tends to assume that one single-therapy approach can be superior to another. As mentioned earlier, behavioural approaches tend to do better in evaluations, but often incorporate elements of cognitive or even humanistic approaches as part of their 'bedside manner'. In a well-controlled study, Shapiro and Firth (1987) compared prescriptive methods (cognitive-behavioural) with exploratory methods (insight). Although the prescriptive approach fared slightly better, *both* methods produced good results. Thus, it would seem unreasonable to deny a client the benefits of another approach if differences *can* be marginal in some instances.

Chapter summary

There are theoretical viewpoints within psychology which represent the disciplines on its borders, such as biology. These are also evident in abnormal psychology. These **paradigms** consider the causes of disorders in their own terms, and as a result produce therapies which act on these assumptions and are guided by the theoretical principles of that paradigm.

The **biological paradigm** considers the contribution of **genetics** to disorders, and although genetic codes are not easily changed, **genetic counselling** is available to limit the passing on of detectable, destructive gene information. Errors and damage can occur in the **neurochemistry** and **neuroanatomy** of the brain, and in the **endocrine system**, resulting in abnormalities of behaviour, thinking and emotion. Although their actions are still relatively crude, **drugs, psychosurgery, electroconvulsive therapy** and **hormone therapy** have provided welcome relief from the symptoms of some of the most stubborn disorders.

The **behavioural approach** relies on the principles of **classical** and **operant conditioning**, which provide **behaviour therapy** and **behaviour modification**, respectively. In behaviour therapy methods such as **systematic desensitization** and **flooding** expose clients to feared situations, reducing the anxious response, or as in **aversion therapy,** associate an undesirable situation with a noxious stimulus. In behaviour modification the basics of desired behaviour are **reinforced,** from which more complex behaviours can be **shaped.** Similarly, undesirable behaviour is not reinforced, or is punished if necessary. These learning approaches can be combined in **biofeedback,** where a client learns to control their blood pressure and other internal functions. Learning can also take place **vicariously** and clients can learn appropriate behaviours by observing others – the process of **modelling.** Behavioural methods prove both effective and efficient in comparisons of therapies.

Cognitive and **cognitive-behavioural approaches** developed from behavioural ones and as such, attempt to change maladaptive thinking patterns to be more productive. In **rational emotive therapy,** clients have their irrational beliefs about their behaviour questioned and substituted by more realistic expectations. **Self-instructional therapy** makes use of the client's **self-talk,** giving them corrective phrases to use in this process. The cognitive therapy of **Beck** has mostly been applied to depression. In this, negative **automatic thoughts** are identified and undermined by a **Socratic method** of questioning.

Psychodynamic approaches stem from the work of **Freud,** who developed his own theory of personality and the associated therapy of **psychoanalysis.** His personality theory proposes stages of **psychosexual development,** during which the mental structures of the **id, ego** and

superego are formed. In this, abnormality results from **conflict** between these structures as a result of early emotional experiences, which have become **repressed**. Psychoanalysis uses **free association** to allow the client to access these early experiences and release the repression. Freud's followers often disagreed with some aspect of his explanations, but maintained the same **insight**-oriented approach in producing their own versions of his therapy. Psychoanalysis has been criticized as being unscientific and its followers accused of practising an art-form rather than an empirical therapy.

Other insight-based therapies include the **humanistic, existential** and **Gestalt approaches**. The humanistic approach of **Rogers**, or **client-centred therapy**, involves helping clients to **actualize** their potential and achieve a **healthy personality**. In existential and Gestalt therapy, clients are encouraged to take responsibility for the choices they make in life and realize the potential for improvement these choices can bring.

Multiple-person therapies, such as **group** and **family therapies**, can provide for **economy** in therapeutic practice. In addition, group methods usefully introduce practical support, shared experience and peer pressure into the therapeutic environment. In **family systems approaches** the dynamics of the whole family are considered in therapy, with the members in attendance. Interactions in the family can then be considered in terms of their influence on a client member of the family. **Cultural factors** are now considered when assessing clients from different cultures, especially where the clinician is from another culture, or the client has moved into a culturally alien environment.

Adopting a single paradigm approach can deny a client the benefits of an **eclectic approach**, that is, selecting from a variety of approaches those which are most useful to the individual case. Some approaches assume more than one causal agent, such as the **diathesis-stress approach**. This assumes a **predisposition** to a disorder, but also requires **environmental stressors** to precipitate an episode. Although most modern therapeutic approaches are useful, behavioural approaches do better in studies comparing them.

Self-test questions

▶ What is meant by genetic linkage?
▶ What is the importance of the autonomic nervous system in explaining abnormal behaviour?
▶ What are the costs and benefits of neurosurgery?
▶ Why are events at the synapse important for drug treatments?
▶ How do the therapies derived from classical and operant conditioning differ?

▶ What is meant by reciprocal inhibition?
▶ What is social learning?
▶ What did Beck mean by 'automatic thoughts'?
▶ How did Freud relate ego defences to abnormal behaviour?
▶ Is psychoanalysis scientific?
▶ Can we usefully distinguish humanistic, existential and gestalt therapies?
▶ What are the advantages of using group formats in therapy?
▶ What is meant by the term 'eclectic'?

Further reading

Andreasen, N. (1985) *The Broken Brain: The biological revolution in psychiatry*. New York: Harper & Row.

Barker, P. (1992) *Basic Family Therapy*. Oxford: Blackwell Scientific Publications.

Beck, J. (1995) *Cognitive Therapy*. New York: Guilford Press.

Carlson, N. (1994) *The Physiology of Behaviour*, 5th edition. London: Allyn & Bacon.

Clarkson, P. and Pokorny, M. (1994) *The Handbook of Psychotherapy*. London: Routledge.

Dryden, W. (1996) *Handbook of Individual Therapy*. London: Sage.

Farber, B., Brink, C. and Raskin, P. (1996) *The Psychotherapy of Carl Rogers*. London: Guilford Press.

King, D. (1995) *Seminars in Psychopharmacology*. London: Gaskell Books.

Leff, J. (1994) 'Cultural influences on psychiatry', *Current Opinion in Psychiatry*, 7, 197–201.

Martin, G. and Pear, J. (1992) *Behaviour Modification*, 4th edition. Englewood Cliffs, NJ: Prentice Hall.

Moorey, S. (1996) 'Cognitive-behavioural therapy for whom?', *Advances in Psychiatric Treatment*, 2, 17–23.

Norcross, J.C. (1986) *Handbook of Eclectic Psychotherapy*. New York: Brunner/Mazel.

Pilgrim, D. and Rogers, A. (1993) *A Sociology of Mental Health and Illness*. Milton Keynes: Open University Press.

Plomin, R. (1994) 'Genetics and experience', *Current Opinion in Psychiatry*, 7, 297–9.

Schneider, K. and May, R. (1995) *The Psychology of Existence*. New York: McGraw-Hill.

Scott, A. (1994) 'Contemporary practice of electroconvulsive therapy', *British Journal of Hospital Medicine*, 51, 334–9.

CHAPTER 3

The assessment, diagnosis and formulation of clients

In this chapter

▶ Reliability and validity
▶ Historical problems
▶ The assessment process
▶ Diagnosis: DSM and ICD systems
▶ The importance of the individual: the formulation

Reliability and validity

As recently as 1980, Clare regarded a diagnosis as a hypothesis to be tested and refined, such is its inherently imprecise nature. A useful diagnosis depends on a valid classificatory system of disorders, a reliable method of assessment and diagnosis, and a consensus among the professionals about their reliable use. The two concepts of **reliability** and **validity** are important in the clinical approach to disorders:

▶ **Reliability** is where the same judgement, rating or test result occurs on different occasions, perhaps using different raters or judges (**inter-rater reliability**). Thus, a reliable psychological test should produce a very similar score when assessing the same patient on different occasions (**test-retest reliability**), even if administered by different psychologists. Two psychiatrists reliably diagnosing the same disorder in different patients in different countries can be seen to push the concept (and the diagnostic process) to its limits.

▶ **Validity** refers to something genuinely representing what it claims to be. Thus, an assessment test of memory should give a measure of memory ability and not simply reflect general intelligence or some other ability. Validity of a diagnosis assumes that the disorder to be diagnosed represents a valid construct (i.e. the *constructed* measure) or **construct validity**, which is far more difficult to ascertain than reliability. To apply the label 'schizophrenia' correctly, there has to be a valid set of signs and symptoms reliably recognized as such, an assumption which has been challenged for this disorder.

There is an **asymmetrical relationship** between reliability and validity in that you can have reliability without validity, but not validity without reliability. Thus a 'height' test which consists of weighing a client may produce repeatable results without ever being a valid measure of height. These two concepts have not always been the strongest features of the clinical approach to mental disorder. The author's own research has found **clinical judgement** of behaviour to be at odds with **systematic observation** of the same phenomenon.

Historical problems

The history of psychiatric diagnosis, as with the history of abnormal psychology, is one of error and confusion until the turn of the nineteenth century. During the twentieth century the history becomes one of slowly emerging objectivity and reliability. Before **Kraepelin** produced a comprehensive classificatory system in 1898, there were numerous descriptions of disorders but these were not well organized and tended to be closely related to the historical concepts of mental disorder such as **melancholia** (depression), **mania, hysteria, dementia** and an increasing number of **neurological disorders**. At this time many professionals still considered some of these to be stages of the *same* disorder, i.e. a depression followed by mania and resulting in dementia, conditions which had been treated by letting blood, as had been the historical method for most illnesses. Earlier in the nintheenth century, **Morel** identified the criteria for classifying disorders as being symptoms, course and outcome, but also included the aetiology of the disorder. The latter inclusion later became a source of professional conflict, eventually dividing classificatory approaches into those inferring a cause and those maintaining a more descriptive approach or '**analyzers versus describers**'.

Although less popular classificatory systems were produced earlier in France and England, the Munich psychiatrist **Emile Kraepelin** devised the most widely used and durable system. By 1913, Kraepelin's systematic description of mental disorders had been adopted in a number of countries. However, this was not universal and the use of different systems has caused a persistent lack of agreement between clinicians and confounded research into mental health.

In 1948, the Geneva-based **World Health Organization (WHO)** published an edition of their **International Classification of Diseases (ICD)** (originally in full: *International Statistical Classification of Diseases, Injuries and Causes of Death)* which contains a complete listing of mental disorders. This listing still retained many of Kraepelin's categories. Soon after this (1952), the **American Psychiatric Association** produced the first edition of the **Diagnostic and Statistical Manual (DSM)**. There have since been revisions and new editions of both systems, the DSM being in its fourth edition and the ICD in its tenth. Statistical procedures such as **cluster analysis** are used to refine symptom groupings and determine the boundaries of disorders. At each revision some efforts have been made to bring what are by far the most widely accepted systems in line with one another. However, the ICD has tended to be a listing of disorders with some inference as to causes, with the DSM aiming more towards detailed, somewhat pedantic descriptions of symptom criteria (see below). The development of these instruments did not end the difficulties of diagnosis, even though clinicians may have been using the same listings or even working in the *same hospital.*

For Feinstein (1967), clinical judgement depended on 'patient knowledge' not classificatory systems, which highlights clinicians' reliance on their subjective judgement in the diagnostic process. Such variable judgements led to a difference in the diagnosis of schizophrenia *within the same hospital* of 22–60 per cent (Passamanick *et al.*, 1959). Rosenhan (1973) published a report in which he and others presented themselves at twelve American mental hospitals. They each complained of one symptom – hearing voices – and most were admitted for an average of 19 days with a preliminary diagnosis of schizophrenia. However, their 'voices' were not of the type found in schizophrenia and following admission they behaved normally (e.g. those who were researchers took notes), these activities being recorded as 'behavioural signs' by hospital staff. Rosenhan used this to argue that if schizophrenia cannot be reliably diagnosed, then perhaps the category is invalid. It could also be argued that the hospitals were being correctly cautious in making the error of admitting 'fakes' rather than turning potentially genuine patients away. Would their scheme have worked in England? As Clare (1980) points out, the rate of diagnosis of schizophrenia at the time was about three times greater in the US than in England. Despite the counter-arguments, diagnostic agreement was not one of psychiatry's strengths before the 1980s.

Syndromes such as schizophrenia achieved notoriety at the time of these studies owing to the different forms of the disorder and varying symptoms in individual cases. If disorders were not consistent, how can diagnosis be consistent? These discrepancies became a focus for the **anti-psychiatry movement**, which used such weaknesses to discredit the medical approach in psychiatry, including its ICD and DSM classificatory approaches. The DSM approach was descriptive and, as with Kraepelin's view, avoided the subjective experience of the patient. This was seen as a weakness by anti-psychiatrists such as **R.D. Laing**, reducing the world of the patient to one of description or *form*, without regard for *content* or *meaning*.

The only way of avoiding such criticism was to improve the standard and consistency of diagnosis. To achieve this, the DSM incorporated even *more* detailed description, devoid of inferred aetiology. In addition, more illustrative and careful descriptions of psychopathology were produced by leading psychiatrists, such as Slater and Roth (1969). Although not perfect, the wider use of the ICD and DSM was improving agreement between professionals and encouraging collaborative research, even between countries. Kessel (1960) reduced the number of potential psychiatric cases from 520 to 50 from a sample of 1,000 presenting patients by applying the ICD system. However, such discrimination between cases could indicate that *validity* is being sacrificed for *reliability* and that this may be the way forward for the future of diagnosis.

The assessment process

The historical difficulties in making an accurate and reliable diagnosis are evidence enough that such a decision should be supported by as much information as possible. The assessment process is where such information is systematically gathered and it is far more extensive than would be the case for physical illness owing to these difficulties of psychiatric diagnosis. The breadth of the assessment will depend on whether they have been seen before and the seriousness of the patient's complaint. Although many texts present a **standardized assessment procedure**, in practice these guidelines and procedures are implemented to different degrees and may give differing weightings to subjective judgement and objective tests. This aside, an assessment of a new patient with pronounced symptoms should ideally include the following procedures.

▶ Physical examination
▶ History taking
▶ Mental state examination or standardized interview
▶ Clinical psychology report
▶ Social work report

The last two items are not always available, but are viewed with increasing importance as the use of DSM-style checklists spreads, requiring **life stress** and **global functioning** information. The clinical psychology report may be the only input from a psychologist. History and mental state are usually assessed by a **psychiatrist**, who is responsible for the eventual diagnosis, and who may also carry out routine items of the physical examination. However restricted the role of the clinical psychologist is in diagnosis, all aspects of assessment are important to the study of abnormal psychology. Thus brief details of each component of the assessment will be examined.

Physical examination

The extent of the physical examination will depend on the patient's age and apparent health. However, physical factors can be deceptively influential and it is better to err on the side of caution. Routine blood and urine tests will be carried out. These may reveal physical disorders contributing to the patient's current state, but also provide a check on **alcohol** and **drug intake**. Specific tests are carried out for known physical disorders which mimic psychiatric symptoms, such as **hyperthyroidism** which mimics anxiety symptoms, in order to prevent misdiagnosis. **Autonomic nervous system measures** such as blood pressure will indicate arousal levels and point to psychologically influenced physical conditions such as **hypertension**. Assessment of general physical state and the presence of disease are not only important for their influence on the patient's current psychological state, but also for judging their ability to withstand some types of *treatment*, e.g. ECT or some drugs.

An important part of the physical assessment is the **neurological examination**, which is essential in cases where neurological function may be implicated. Neurological investigations are divided into looking at the 'hardware', the actual physical parts of the brain and 'software' or **soft signs**, of brain function, i.e. inferring neurological problems from psychological and behavioural tests. Soft signs will be described under the clinical psychology report. **CAT scans** (see Chapter 2) are used quite widely as the equipment is based on multiple X-rays. Although **NMR** is safer as it is non-invasive, it is far more expensive and, along with the imaging of brain **activity** in techniques such as **PET scans**, is not normally available for screening patients, only for research. However, **single photon emission tomography (SPET)** is cheaper than **PET** and, despite lower-quality image production, has become more frequently used in the clinical context. These scans can reveal anatomical abnormalities and poor or abnormal metabolism, which can impair cognitive function or even produce psychotic-type symptoms in otherwise normally functioning individuals.

The **electroencephalogram (EEG)** produces a graphical record of electrical activity near the surface of the brain, which can be detected at various points *on* the scalp. Patterns of activity characterize different mental states, and abnormalities can be used to *infer* neurological problems or detect disorders where electrical activity is disturbed such as **epilepsy**. Some inherited traits such as a susceptibility to alcohol tolerance have been associated with abnormal **evoked potentials** or specific areas of electrical activity in response to external stimuli, such as movement across their area of vision.

History taking

A full history needs to be taken when a patient is first seen and updated on subsequent occasions. Some of the patient's history can be taken at the **psychiatric interview**, a very important part of the assessment process. During the interview, aspects of the patient's **manner, presentation** and **attitude** may be noted, in addition to the actual answers to questions. The interview is intended to be *exploratory*, not simply to confirm initial presumptions about the patient's disorder. Other details may more reliably be gained from relatives, documented records or other professionals such as their **GP** or **social worker**. In each case, doubts about the *credibility* of the source are recorded at the time. This information can be vital in determining what may be causing or maintaining the patient's symptoms. The areas of the patient's history usually fall under the following headings.

- ▶ **History of the current illness.** Whilst establishing the duration, symptoms, effects and management of the disorder to date, the patient is encouraged to disclose as much information as possible, e.g. 'Are there things that make the condition worse?'
- ▶ **Medical and psychiatric history.** This may be supplemented by medical records, but it is helpful to get the patient's account even if the illness or its treatment seems to have no bearing on the current disorder.
- ▶ **Family history** (e.g. parents and siblings). In addition to identifying family membership, deaths and disorders among members, the patient's feelings and interactions with members are also explored.
- ▶ **Personal history.** This has various components which help to build a social and psychological picture of the patient's life with the following typical components:
  - childhood: social and developmental problems in infant and childhood stages;
  - school and education: relations with teachers and peers as well as attainment;
  - occupation: again relations at work may be as important as success;
  - sex and marriage: the ability to form and sustain relationships, including sexual ones;
  - forensic: any criminal activity, and what action resulted from this.
- ▶ **Premorbid personality.** Establishing the patient's social and personal functioning prior to the illness is sometimes difficult to assess and can bring into question the true point of onset. It is important to establish the *rate* of onset of a disorder as well as the change(s) it produced.
- ▶ **Current living circumstances.** Whom they live with, in what type of accommodation, and whether there is friction, can help to build a cross-sectional snapshot of the patient's current circumstances.

The picture generated by this information will inform other aspects of the assessment and there will also be areas of overlapping information. However, *conflict* between information sources could be important and worth pursuing.

The mental state examination

This is the main component of the **psychiatric interview** and can take up to an hour. As when taking a history, aspects of the patient's behaviour during the interview are being observed and noted. These aspects *observed* by the clinician are **signs** of disorder, in contrast with **symptoms**, which are complaints the patient mentions. The clinician needs to take account of factors that may confound these observations such as the age, ethnic background or sub-cultural affiliations (e.g. member of a teenage gang). All such factors need to be separated from the effects of the disorder and the clinician needs to provide a *full account*, and not brief comments in the notes taken. The content of the examination is usually grouped under the following headings and in each case an *absence* of such activity should also be noted.

- ▶ **General information**. This concerns the general appearance of the patient, appropriateness of dress, grooming, movement and how he or she reacts to the interviewer.
- ▶ **Speech.** The quantity, continuity and speed of speech are noted, with special note of any abnormality. There may be abnormal features of speech such as rhyme or sudden change of topic; it may be incoherent or disconnected.
- ▶ **Thought.** This has to be inferred from speech. Abnormalities of thinking include loss of boundaries with other's thoughts (thoughts being 'shared', 'broadcast' or interfered with), disconnected thinking, or thinking that returns obsessively to the same topic. Thoughts may be unduly pessimistic or wildly optimistic. **Delusions,** i.e. unshakeable irrational beliefs, may be presented.
- ▶ **Perception.** Abnormalities of perception may be reported such as **hallucinations,** perceptual experiences that have no basis in reality. These should be distinguished from illusions, or misinterpretations of reality.
- ▶ **Mood.** Extremes of mood for the situation, inappropriate mood or sudden changes of mood are important signs. Abnormal autonomic nervous system activity may be inferred from anxious behaviour, sweating or evidence of obsessive compulsive activity.
- ▶ **Cognitive (intellectual) function** is examined in the following five areas:
  - Memory: short-term memory can be checked by **digit span tests** (testing recall for two nine-digit numbers). Long-term memory can be checked using their history information. Other graded tests can move from easy (who is the leader of your country?) to hard (name six scientists from your country).
  - Attention and concentration: counting backwards in threes or fives usually reveals distraction.
  - Orientation: establishing the patient's awareness of where they are can be judged by graded questions such as: 'What is the current time and what is the name of the place you are in?' to 'Is it day or night?'

- Overall intelligence: this is an estimate by the clinician.
- Abstract ability: the ability to deal in abstract thought can be tested by asking the meaning of proverbs or poetic phrases.
► **Insight.** This is basically to establish that the patient knows why they are being seen in a hospital, that they may be suffering from a disorder and that their symptoms are part of that disorder. Each of these can be directly questioned and the patient's level of judgement rated by degree.

It is important to record the clinician's reaction to the patient, a type of **reflexive analysis,** as this could consequently influence the patient's attitude throughout the interview. There may be justification for the clinician's reaction, and this needs to be noted.

Standardized interviews

Rather than relying on the clinician to question and observe the patient in an unstructured way, an increasing number of structured questionnaires have been produced and tested for use when making these assessments. These assessment **instruments** have questions for both signs and symptoms, and usually require the clinician to rate each item on a scale of severity. In this way the interview is standardized and a preliminary diagnosis can be derived by referring to a manual which suggests which specific items indicate the disorder in question. Well-established questionnaires such as the **Present State Examination (PSE)** have been developed to be analyzed by computer. The **General Health Questionnaire (GHQ)** has been developed for general medical patients to complete themselves and enables the detection of psychiatric disorders. The major diagnostic and classificatory system DSM-IV has its own structured interview, the **Structured Clinical Interview for DSM-IV (SCID).**

These structured interviews aim to achieve a general screening of patients. Where a specific disorder is suspected, questionnaires have been devised which are dedicated to the symptoms of that disorder and are intended to measure the severity of the disorder. These instruments can be self-report questionnaires such as the **Beck Depression Inventory (BDI)** or may require a clinician with training to carry out the ratings as with the **Scale for the Assessment of Negative Symptoms (SANS).** Standardized interviews and questionnaires have been used mostly for research where high levels of reliability are necessary, and have since been adopted in clinical practice. Many of these questionnaires are used routinely as the clinical psychologist's tools of trade.

Clinical psychology report

Some minor complaints referred to a **clinical psychologist** (by a GP) may not warrant a full psychiatric assessment. The assessment by the psychologist in this case would be specific to the complaint and lead to psychological treatment as a hospital out-patient or by visits to a health centre. In the case of more serious or less easily identified disorders, the psychologist's assessment will be just one part of the assessment process.

The clinical psychologist historically has been associated with administering tests, and although they are now mostly involved in other procedures, testing is still a major area of expertise. Psychiatrists and neurologists may also administer such tests, but the clinical psychologist usually has more **psychometric** knowledge. This is partly because **psychological testing** is a specialist area of psychology dealing with the construction, validation, correct administration and interpretation of tests. The standardized use of tests and questionnaires is also a major part of the psychological assessment process, giving the psychologist greater experience of them.

The clinical psychologist's report will contain the results of standardized tests such as intelligence and personality tests, which can be **norm-referenced**. Thus, the average scores will be available for groups of normal (the 'norm') and disturbed individuals to enable comparisons. There may also be data from observation of the patient or information on their cognitive functioning. The following aspects are usually assessed by the clinical psychologist.

▶ **Intelligence.** General intellectual functioning is represented by the **intelligence quotient (IQ)**, an estimate based on a comparison with one's age group and can be weighted for (i.e. can account for) other factors. The 'norm' is represented by a value of 100, so a score of 110 is above and one of 85 below average intelligence, though exactly what is meant by 'intelligence' is not easy to define. Some widely used tests such as the **Wechsler Adult Intelligence Scale (WAIS)** have been accused of being culturally biased. The **Raven's Progressive Matrices** claims to be culture-free as it uses only pattern matching.

▶ **Personality.** These tests have been divided into **projective** and **'objective'** types.

  Projective tests assume that internal conflicts will be 'projected' into benign situations and are clearly dependent on the psychodynamic approach. The **Rorschach ink blot test** has been made famous through popular fiction and consists of a number of ambiguous 'ink blot' designs first produced by **Herman Rorschach** in 1912. The patient's interpretations of these patterns are subject to complex analysis requiring dedicated training. The **Thematic Apperception Test (TAT)** is used in a similar manner, but consists of a series of pictures involving people interacting in various settings for which there is no single clear interpretation. In 1935, Murray introduced the TAT interpretation which is also subject to complex analysis (Morgan and Murray, 1935). Projective tests are poor in terms of reliability and validity and as a consequence are little used nowadays. Such techniques are sometimes employed in a forensic setting when exploring the personalities of suspected serious offenders.

Objective personality tests are so called because they are subject to objective psychometric criteria in their construction, testing and subsequent use, and consequently have good reliability and validity values associated with them. However, it should be remembered that the tests themselves are usually self-report questionnaires and as such cannot be truly objective in a scientific sense. The **Eysenck Personality Questionnaire (EPQ)** provides measures along three dimensions of personality described by Hans Jürgen Eysenck as **extraversion, neuroticism** and **psychoticism**. More factors are assumed in the **16PF Questionnaire** by Cattell and as with Eysenck's scale, there are score ranges which can be associated with abnormal functioning. The US-based **MMPI-2** (Minnesota Multiphasic Personality Inventory) is intended for clinical use, but *despite* its numerous subscales, tends to indicate a general level of disturbance in patients rather than helping to identify specific disorders.

▶ **Specific area tests.** The above personality and intelligence tests identify general areas of poor or abnormal function, whereas other tests target specific dysfunctions and abnormalities. The **Maudsley Obsessional-Compulsive Inventory** assesses obsessive-compulsive behaviour and has subscales for such activities as checking or washing/cleaning. There are a large number of such questionnaire or checklist-based assessment instruments available for most disorders and even individual symptoms. For a critical review of a selection of these see Peck and Shapiro (1990) in Further Reading.

Other specific area tests are used by psychologists to assess **soft signs** of **neurological malfunction.** In this, the psychological effects of neurological problems are measured and used to *infer* specific defects in the neurological 'hardware'. Such neurological tests are often assembled into **test batteries** designed to screen for any existing and potential brain abnormality. The **Halstead-Reitan** and **Luria-Nebraska** test batteries are good examples.

▶ **Observation methods** involve the non-intrusive observation of the patient's behaviour, usually in interaction with others. In practice this is achieved by the use of a specially designed room with a **two-way mirror,** behind which the observers (usually psychologists) sit with video and other recording equipment. In some cases, discussion and assessment may occur at the time, or standardized procedures may be used so that recordings can be systematically analyzed later and perhaps compared with those of other individuals. These techniques are important in difficult cases such as those where disturbed parents are being assessed for their ability to care for their children appropriately.

▶ **Cognitive assessments** refer to assessments of the thinking styles of patients and should be distinguished from the current use of the term 'cognitive disorder' to refer to neurological dysfunction. The cognitive assessments carried out by clinical psychologists are usually linked to the use of **cognitive therapy**.

The clinical psychology report will summarize these assessments together with other test information such as memory function, which can provide more detail for the mental state examination.

The social work report

Social workers (usually **psychiatric social workers**) can assess the patient's financial and other circumstances. In addition to a home assessment, the patient's family may be interviewed to ascertain both their effect on the patient and the patient's effect on them. Social support is increasingly seen as important when considering the patient's ability to live at home. Social work reports are more important when a patient is being assessed for discharge from in-patient care than at first admission.

Diagnosis: DSM and ICD systems

The rather lengthy assessment process described above is far more extensive than would be considered for physical illness. Despite the extra information, a psychiatric diagnosis is still less certain than that made in general medicine. The problems of past diagnostic procedures described earlier have illustrated some of the difficulties involved. However, some of the difficulties seem to be inherent in the nature of psychiatric disorders and the limitations of the human judgements made. The inconsistency of symptoms presented in schizophrenia has been mentioned, but even more 'programmed' disorders such as the genetically based **Huntington's chorea** occasionally present widely varying symptoms. Most psychiatric departments keep training videos showing patients with various disorders or illustrating individual symptoms. Even with training, these examples present a challenge to professionals and for the student of abnormal psychology, they could clearly demonstrate the difficulty of translating textbook descriptions of symptoms into the continuous and variable behaviour of disordered individuals.

The diagnostic process is one of pushing **ideopathic** behaviour into **nomothetic** categories, that is, assigning individual behaviour patterns to fixed classifications of behaviour common to all in that category. Even if the causes of a disorder were the same in each case, the physical and psychological differences between individuals can produce unique reactions to those same causes. In addition, many psychiatric disorders are **syndromes**, that is, they have a range of possible symptoms, a selection of which may be presented by an individual patient but none of which occurs in every case. The boundaries between disorders can also overlap considerably (see personality disorders for an example of this), requiring a **differential diagnosis** to examine on which side of the boundary the particular case lies. There are other factors which can confound the diagnostic procedure. The effects of **medication** or **self-medication** (i.e. alcohol or other drugs) distort behaviour, as do the long-term effects of **institutionalization** or an impoverished environment.

With all these factors working against the psychiatrist, making an accurate diagnosis requires skilled training, a knowledge of patients, and is somewhat dependent on the extensive information gained from patient assessment. There are further implications when making a diagnosis which place pressure on the psychiatrist. These include:

▶ **Labelling:** the effects of attaching a label such as 'schizophrenic' to an individual. The stigma that some diagnoses can bring depends on the unsympathetic reaction of others in seeing the label as a reason for **prejudice** and **discrimination**. The sociological view has also described **secondary labelling** where the labelled individual accepts the label and associated discrimination and begins to *act in accord with these expectations.* For these reasons alone, a diagnosis is given *only* if the psychiatrist is reasonably certain of her judgement.

▶ **Legal and financial** implications of a diagnosis also place pressure on the clinician. In the US and elsewhere, health insurance payments may be appropriate for one diagnosis but not another. In law, a particular diagnosis may make the difference between a long prison sentence (or even the death penalty) and treatment in a secure hospital. Psychiatrists need to be able to recognize the very real pressures placed on them to make a diagnosis for other than sound clinical reasons.

▶ **Treatment** implications often follow diagnosis. The treatment for some disorders may be inappropriate or even damaging if applied to another disorder in the event of an incorrect diagnosis. For the same reason, *necessary* treatment may not be given.

▶ **Prognosis** (i.e. expected future outcome) tends to vary greatly depending on the disorder present. Patients' reactions to a bleak prognosis may be understandably negative and this may affect their progress, or even result in suicide. With such serious implications, some diagnoses are not made lightly.

▶ **Professional agreement and research.** Without close agreement between professionals over the criteria for diagnosing different disorders, professional **communication** would be confounded by their terminology having a different interpretation, especially between cultures. The situation for research is more crucial as the necessary agreement is more exacting. For this reason more stringent standardized criteria may be used, such as the **Research Diagnostic Criteria** (Spitzer *et al.*, 1978) when making diagnoses for experimental comparisons.

Thus the combined pressures on psychiatrists to produce **reliable** and **valid** diagnoses lead them to seek all possible assistance and support. In addition to assessment information, extensively researched classificatory systems are available. As described under historical problems, the major diagnostic and classificatory systems for mental disorders are the US-based *Diagnostic and Statistical Manual*, currently in its fourth edition (DSM-IV) (American Psychiatric Association, 1993), and the Geneva-based *International Classification of Diseases*, currently in its tenth edition (ICD-10) (World Health Organization, 1992). These both aim to provide a comprehensive set of disorder classifications with unambiguous criteria for their diagnosis.

The ICD system

Chapter 5 of the ICD-10 contains a listing of 458 types of mental disorder, some of which are discrete disorders and others subtypes of more major psychiatric disorders. The ICD is sometimes referred to as the 'F' scale as this letter is the prefix for the numbering of the disorders. There are ten major categories of disorders:

1. **Organic, including symptomatic, mental disorders:** types of dementia and delirium.
2. **Mental and behavioural disorders due to psychoactive substance use:** alcohol and other substance use, and associated disorders.
3. **Schizophrenia, schizotypal and delusional disorders:** types of schizophrenia and disorders with similar symptoms.
4. **Mood disorders:** types of depression, mania and mixtures of these.
5. **Neurotic, stress-related and somatoform disorders:** types of phobias (fears), anxiety problems and maladaptive reactions to stress, such as physical complaints or psychological attempts to escape.
6. **Behavioural syndromes associated with physiological disturbances and physical factors:** disorders of natural functions, such as eating, sleep and sex, of psychological origin.
7. **Abnormalities of adult personality and behaviour:** distortions of personality, and impulse control disorders, sexual identity and preference problems.
8. **Mental retardation:** degrees of learning disability.
9. **Disorders of psychological development:** difficulties with language and scholastic skills, pervasive developmental disorders (e.g. autism).
10. **Behavioural and emotional disorders with onset usually occurring in childhood and adolescence:** behavioural disturbances,

problems with early relationships and social functioning, and forms of tic disorders, stammering and bedwetting/soiling.

Both ICD and DSM systems have **unspecified** or **not otherwise specified** classifications at the end of each listing for cases that do not conform to specified categories but have the general characteristics of that grouping. Some see these as a great weakness in the exhaustiveness of the systems; others view them as necessary to help prevent clinicians 'forcing' such cases into the existing categories.

The ICD system is descriptive but retains some inference as to the **aetiology** of the disorders. For example, the term **neurotic** has been retained although it has been dropped from the DSM system. There have been many studies researching and checking the validity of both systems. The ICD system is the major system in the UK and much of Europe. However, the DSM system is more prevalent in the (mostly US) literature, and thus may be more familiar to the reader, as mentioned in Chapter 1. In large-scale research, Sartorius *et al.* (1995) found a high degree of agreement between DSM-IV and the **Diagnostic Criteria for Research** for the current ICD system, ICD-10-DCR.

The DSM system

The DSM system differs from the ICD system in that greater effort has been made to remove inference of aetiology, leaving a highly descriptive set of **operational criteria** for diagnosis. For Compton and Guze (1995) the current revisions of *both* systems represent a welcome move away from **psychodynamic** terms and inference, towards a more phenomenological description reminiscent of Kraepelin. In short, they have become more descriptive; however, this is more pronounced with the DSM-IV. The DSM system has tended to acknowledge new disorders fairly quickly and provides an extensive list seeming to provide for every eventuality in diagnosis. Preskorn (1995) has criticized such an approach for 'creating' new illness categories *before* current ones are fully understood.

The DSM-IV is a **multi-axial** system with five 'axes'. Each patient is expected to be rated on each of these axes (independent scales) in order to give a full picture of the individual's pathology and functioning in different areas. This encourages the clinician to consider the possibility of **comorbidity** – the presence of more than one disorder in the same individual at one time. Comorbidity usually takes the form of one diagnosed disorder against a background of an enduring state such as a pervasive developmental disorder or personality disorder. The five axes of the DSM-IV are as follows:

Axis I is a listing of most of the clinical syndromes with their diagnostic criteria, disorders such as schizophrenia and anxiety disorders.

Axis II contains those conditions which are considered permanent states, mainly personality disorders and mental retardation.

Axis III provides a list of general medical conditions that may co-occur with and influence mental disorders.

Axis IV is a checklist of environmental and psychosocial stressors, which are considered in order of severity of effect.

Axis V is a rating scale called the **Global Assessment of Functioning scale (GAF scale)** giving the patient's current ability to function and cope with life. The range extends from superior ability to imminent danger to self and others.

Despite the efforts of many professionals in the production of the fourth edition of the DSM, some critics (e.g. Klein, 1995) claim that little has changed fundamentally beyond clarification of terms, and early problems with reliability remain. Lewis (1994) has criticized both systems for retaining the 'organic disorders' division, implying that all other disorders are non-organic, which is far from the case and therefore misleading. In producing the latest editions of the DSM and ICD systems, efforts have been made to bring them into line with one another to aid diagnostic agreement.

The importance of the individual: the formulation

The formulation is a method of integrating the comprehensive data required to treat that particular individual and reasonably accurately predict the outcome for the case. Clearly there must be *sufficient* data to provide appropriate treatment and a realistic prognosis. The term **nomothetic** (i.e. law-giving) has been used to describe the diagnostic process in 'pigeon-holing' a patient in a particular classificatory category in which the patient is expected to conform to the general 'laws' of that classification. In contrast, the formulation has a more **ideographic** (i.e. individual picture) approach in providing a fuller prescriptive description of the unique case in hand. A possible format for the formulation may be given by the following headings:

▶ **Demographic data** include such information as marital status, age and employment.
▶ **Descriptive formulation** contains a description of the patient's admission and examination, including the salient features, and the circumstances surrounding it.
▶ **Differential diagnosis** will cover the possible alternative diagnoses that could account for the signs and symptoms present, with some evaluation of their relative appropriateness. Consideration can be given to overlapping disorders and comorbidity.

▶ **Aetiology.** Different aspects of possible causation can be examined here. Factors **predisposing** the individual to the condition can be considered, such as family inheritance. **Precipitating** factors such as significant events during the premorbid (before the onset of symptoms) period can add to this picture. It is also important to explore the possibility that there may be factors **maintaining** the condition, such as substance use or stress.

▶ **Investigations.** Relevant information from various sources such as medical reports and observation of behaviour as an in-patient or reports from relatives and friends.

▶ **Treatment.** An important part of the formulation is the recommended type and approach to treatment. Physical and psychological approaches can be considered separately.

▶ **Prognosis.** Another important section, which should examine the factors pointing to good and poor outcomes for this particular patient. (See Goldberg *et al.*, 1994.)

Thus the formulation is not simply a case history or diagnosis, it contains information and recommendations that are helpful to those professionals involved with the management of the individual case.

Chapter summary

Key concepts in assessment are **reliability** and **validity**: the repeatable and genuine measurement of human attributes. The history of psychiatric diagnosis and assessment is one where reliability and validity have been poor, even after **Kraepelin's** comprehensive classification of mental disorders errors have been revealed by studies. As classificatory and diagnostic systems (such as **DSM** and **ICD**) were developed during the latter half of the twentieth century, diagnostic reliability and validity have improved. The **assessment process** for first episode psychiatric patients is lengthy and pedantic and covers: **physical examination, history taking, a mental state examination** (which may use a **standardized interview**), a **clinical psychology report** and **a social work report.** The extensive nature of the assessment is justified by the difficulties faced in making an accurate **diagnosis**, such as the variable nature of these disorders as **syndromes**, the **individual differences** between patients and the fallibility of **clinical judgements.** Legal, financial, **labelling**, treatment and research implications may follow a diagnostic judgement. The European-based ICD diagnostic system can aid this judgement by providing explicit criteria for diagnosis. The system is descriptive, but retains some inference of **aetiology**. Its US counterpart, the DSM system, has removed more of such inferences, giving strict **operational criteria** for diagnosis in a **multi-axial** structure.

Diagnostic and assessment information is integrated with other information in the **formulation**, giving the appropriate **treatment** and **prognosis** for the individual patient.

Self-test questions

▶ What is the relationship between reliability and validity in tests?
▶ What was the historical importance of Kraepelin's work?
▶ Why has psychiatric diagnosis had a poor image during the twentieth century?
▶ What are the main features of the assessment process?
▶ Why is assessment so lengthy and detailed?
▶ What is meant by the term 'syndrome'?
▶ How do the ICD and DSM systems compare?
▶ How does the formulation differ from other case information?

Further reading

American Psychiatric Association (1993) *Diagnostic and Statistical Manual of Mental Disorders, DSM-IV*. Washington DC.

Exner, J. (1995) *Issues and Methods in Rorschach Research*. New York: Lawrence Erlbaum Associates.

Goldberg, D., Benjamin, S. and Creed, F. (1994) *Psychiatry in Medical Practice*, 2nd edition. London: Routledge.

Harding, L. and Beech, J. (1995). *Assessment in Neuropsychology*. London: Routledge.

Kline, P. (1993) *The Handbook of Psychological Testing*. London: Routledge.

Morrison, J. (1995) *The First Interview*. New York: Guilford Press.

Peck, D. and Shapiro, C. (1990) *Measuring Human Problems*. Chichester: John Wiley.

Pilgrim, D. and Rogers, A. (1993) *A Sociology of Mental Health and Illness*. Milton Keynes: Open University Press.

Sartorius, N., Kaeber, C., Cooper, J. *et al.* (1993) 'Progress toward achieving a common language in psychiatry', *Archives of General Psychiatry*, 50, 115–124.

World Health Organization (1992) *The ICD-10 Classification of Mental and Behavioural Disorders: Description and diagnostic guidelines*. Geneva: World Health Organization.

CHAPTER 4

Legal, community and forensic issues in abnormal psychology

In this chapter

▶ The law and abnormal behaviour: the Mental Health Acts
▶ The scope of forensic psychology
▶ The abnormal offender and psychological profiling
▶ Community provision: rehabilitation and prevention
▶ Health psychology

So far, the professionals involved in mental health have been allied to medicine and the caring professions in this text. However, there are areas of abnormal psychology that involve other professions. When legally enforceable decisions need to be made regarding the health and welfare of psychiatric patients, the **police** and **courts** may be involved. When the patient has committed a criminal offence, specialist professions such as **forensic psychologists** and **psychiatrists** may be required to help resolve the challenging issues raised. In the case of community mental health care, not only is a wide range of professionals involved, but each member of that community has his or her part to play. The paths of all these professionals and others are crossing more frequently as more patients are kept in the community. As a result, fewer beds are available for those 'at risk' (of harming self or others) and more patients live outside institutions, increasing the chance of friction with the public or police.

The law and abnormal behaviour: the Mental Health Acts

One tragic consequence of mental disorder occurs when a patient loses **insight** into his own condition. This usually indicates a **psychotic state** (see Chapter 1) in which the patient has lost contact with reality, but may simply indicate that they do not recognize their own behaviour as being abnormal or harmful. When such an individual can be a danger to themselves or others and refuse to be admitted voluntarily or treated, then most countries have laws to enforce these procedures. In the first half of the twentieth century most patients were 'involuntarily committed', but owing to various advances in treatment and education fewer than 10 per cent of patients are currently held under legal orders.

As such legal restraint applies only to mental and not physical illness, moral issues tend to be raised as well as legal difficulties. To illustrate this moral dilemma, consider a fictitious but comparable situation. What would be the reaction to a 'compulsory surgery order', where someone at risk of heart problems is taken into hospital under legal restraint and operated on 'in their own interest'. Outrage is a probable reaction, and such a patient would be unlikely to tolerate the conditions in which psychiatric patients often find themselves. This differential treatment may be a legacy from the past, but it may equally reflect the very different behaviour and attitudes that are experienced by the two groups of patients. Legal difficulties arise from the rigid nature of legislation and the infinite variability of human behaviour. This mismatch is generally resolved by relying on the expertise of professionals such as psychiatrists, and increasingly on **approved (psychiatric) social workers.** The shift in responsibility to a few individuals has led to accusations of abuse of these powers over a patient's liberty. Some of the groups involved in this process include:

▶ **Relatives** can initiate the process of **compulsory admission** and can qualify to sign the necessary forms. It is the nearest relative (in familial terms) that usually carries this responsibility.

▶ **Psychiatrists** usually qualify as having approved status as doctors and their signatures are usually needed for assessment and treatment orders. They are increasingly being required to assess **risk** (of harm to self or others).

▶ **General practitioners (GPs)** often provide the second doctor's signature (though other medical doctors can do this). The GP is often involved as she or he is usually the first 'port of call' for patients or their relatives.

▶ **The police** are increasingly being involved in supporting psychiatrists and social workers in the compulsory admission process. In England and Wales they have their own powers of detainment under section 136 of the **Mental Health Act (MHA)** (see below).

▶ **Approved social workers (ASW)** have specific powers of assessing whether an individual should or should not be admitted, for which they have special training.

▶ **A registered psychiatric nurse** has some powers of restraint over voluntary in-patients under section 5(4) of the MHA.

▶ **The Mental Health Review Tribunal** is a case reviewing body and consists of a legal professional, an independent psychiatrist and a lay individual. A detained patient may appeal to the tribunal within a specified time period to have the detention reviewed. The tribunal may discharge the patient if they agree that the detention is no longer necessary, though they may impose **conditions** (e.g. out-patient attendance). If the patient is a prisoner, discharge may be to prison. Wood (1993) has critically reviewed the effectiveness of the tribunal system.

In England and Wales the **Mental Health Act, 1983** provides for involuntary commitment and treatment in the case of **mental illness, levels of mental impairment** or **psychopathic disorder** (see next section). In the case of alcohol or drugs, intoxication is insufficient: there *must* be additional mental disturbance as a consequence of use, e.g. amphetamine psychosis. The disorder must be of a nature that requires in-patient treatment, and in the case of less severe or longer-term disorders (e.g. psychopathy), treatment must be expected to alleviate or prevent deterioration of the condition. The various powers and the circumstances for their use are detailed in specific sections of the Act. Reference to these sections has resulted in the use of the term '**sectioning**' to mean involuntary detention. Some of the sections that refer to commitment and treatment are listed below:

▶ **Section 2.** This is an **assessment order** allowing detainment in a suitable place for up to 28 days. It requires the signatures of two doctors (one of whom must be approved under section 12 of the Act) and the nearest relative (who also has the right to oppose the order) or an approved social worker (ASW), who will have normally made the initial application.

▶ **Section 3.** This section is a **treatment order** and also requires the signatures of one approved and one other doctor, supported by the nearest relative or ASW. This order can last for six months in the first instance (renewable) allowing the patient to be detained in an appropriate place and treated.

▶ **Section 4.** An **emergency admission order** allowing detention for 72 hours without right of appeal. It is applied for by the nearest relative or social worker and requires the signature of just one doctor who has recently seen the patient. This section is rarely used independently, but is usually an interim measure while waiting for a section 2 order.

▶ **Section 5(2)** is an **admission order** signed by the doctor in charge of the patient within a hospital to retain the patient for 72 hours.

▶ **Section 5(4)** is a **holding order** which can be signed by a psychiatric nurse to retain a hospitalized patient for 6 hours.

▶ **Section 37** is a **hospital order**. It is usually imposed by a magistrate on the recommendation of two doctors, on an offender facing a prison sentence, or by Crown Court sanction. This is a six-month order which often requires secure confinement.

▶ **Section 41** is a **restriction order** and allows an indefinite detention. It must be signed by a Crown Court judge.

▶ **Section 136** allows a **police officer** to detain a disordered individual found in a public place for 72 hours.

All aspects of the Act are under supervision by the **Mental Health Act Commission**.

The scope of forensic psychology

The term 'forensic' comes from the Latin *forensis* referring to the forum (in Rome), and thus relates to the role of the psychologist in the courtroom. The duties of the modern forensic psychologist have extended beyond advising or appearing in law courts, perhaps more so than forensic psychiatrists and those working in forensic medicine. Although some of the distinctions between psychiatrists and psychologists remain, in the forensic field these have been eroded to some degree, with forensic psychologists providing assessments of prisoners and contributing to judgements as to whether individuals are mentally fit to appear in court. Some of the (overlapping) individual roles of the forensic psychologist (and to an extent psychiatrist) are as follows:

▶ **Prison duties.** Psychologists have carried out assessments of prison inmates for many years. Increasingly, clinical psychologists are being involved in psychological treatment in prison medical units modifying the behaviour of violent offenders. They are more involved when the institution is a **special hospital** or a **regional secure unit**, and can have administrative roles in these. A special hospital is a large mental hospital with prison security, such as Broadmoor, Rampton and Ashworth in England, for violent mentally disordered or mentally disabled offenders. Regional secure units provide secure places in the locality to expand the provision for disturbed offenders, leaving places in the remote special hospitals free for more dangerous patients.

▶ **Expert witness.** Expert witnesses are called upon to give opinions in court based on their area of expertise, not as individual witnesses to criminal acts. For the psychologist this can draw on a number of areas of psychology, some of which are listed below. Appearing in court can demand special skills for which training and support are available from specialist groups. The forensic psychologist as expert witness needs to be familiar with the legal process, the effect their statements have on the court and the consequences for sentencing, and learn to present evidence in a clear, concise, jargon-free way.

▶ **Eyewitness testimony.** Two areas of psychology have a function here: one concerns the factors that affect the honest, accurate acquisition, recall and presentation of eyewitness testimony; the other involves the degree of impact statements can have on the court, especially jurors and their collective decisions. Research by **Elizabeth Loftus** and her colleagues has identified some of these influences such as leading statements, which aid the forensic psychologist in judging the validity of evidence (see Hollin, 1989).

▶ **Ability to testify.** Psychologists may be requested to assess the mental state of a witness to ascertain her or his ability to give testimony in court. The status of psychologists in these judgements varies between countries.

▶ **Mental state of the defendant.** In a similar manner, psychologists are involved in assessing the defendant (accused offender) for different purposes, depending on the stage of the legal process. For each of these, they may be requested to produce a **court report** to be considered in evidence. The crucial stages are:

  – *At the time of offence.* In order to be convicted in England and Wales, the defendant must conform to two criteria: **actus reus**, to have committed the act; and **mens rea**, to have guilty intent as their state of mind. Following the trial of **McNaghten** in 1843, the latter criterion has allowed the **insanity plea** – not being responsible for their actions at the time due to unsound mind. This judgement may have to be made retrospectively and conform to the legally accepted definitions of mental disorder. There are degrees of mitigation: **guilty but insane**, the defendant may be thus diverted from the penal system into psychiatric care (until fit); **diminished responsibility**, here the sentence is reduced to reflect the contribution of a disorder to the criminal act.

  – *Competence to stand trial.* This is independent of the above and usually requires only a minimum level of competence, i.e. to understand the charge and court proceedings. The defendant will often be held in custody until fit for trial.

  – *Competence to be sentenced.* Similarly, the defendant must be able to understand the implications of the sentence passed and be mentally fit to serve it in prison if a custodial sentence is given.

▶ **Offender profiling.** A few forensic psychologists are contracted to work with the police to help describe or identify offenders who are usually disordered. Others work full time in **police behavioural units** creating systems and researching this and other aspects of crime detection (see later section).

▶ **Risk assessment.** An increasingly important area for both the psychologist and psychiatrist in the forensic area is to estimate the risk of an offender reoffending, or of a mentally disordered patient causing harm to self or others if discharged. Prediction is generally poor, with only one third of those deemed to be 'at risk' being a real danger. The odds are improving with research, but the context is also changing with overcrowded prisons and a shortage of hospital beds.

► **Criminology**. Some forensic psychologists focus on the theoretical aspects of crime and research into the area. One of these aspects is the abnormal offender.

Some of the above roles are carried out by the same forensic psychologists, who are often qualified as clinical psychologists.

The abnormal offender and psychological profiling

Two areas of forensic psychology that are increasingly important within abnormal psychology are dealing with criminal offenders who are also disordered, and the work of the psychological profiler. These areas are closely connected, as the more serious offender being sought by the profiler is almost always suffering some mental disorder, for which the term **psychopathy** may be used in persistent cases. The issues surrounding the abnormal offender include those of **compulsory detention** and **special hospitals** from the previous section, and those of **patients placed in the community** from a later section. Although to aid organization these areas are being dealt with separately, the student needs to be aware that they are closely interconnected. The detection of psychopathic murderers and patients who do harm in the community are also highly newsworthy issues. The public popularity of these has led to the creation of numerous fictional accounts from Sherlock Holmes to Cracker, which can present a misleading image of the issues and tend to glamorize the offenders. Such high-profile ('popular') offenders are far rarer than is the public perception and often evade detection, *unlike* their fictional counterparts.

The abnormal offender

Within criminology there is a strong connection between criminal deviance and mental abnormality, sometimes referred to as the **mad-bad debate**. There is an area of overlap between these two forms of deviance and the interpretation of behaviour into one or other category can vary. For example, males are more frequently seen as 'bad' and females as 'mad', though their actual behaviour may be the same, and some countries may hospitalize more abnormal individuals whereas others tend to imprison more. However, it is difficult to identify why it is that these different labels can be interchangeably applied in practice. Many factors play a part in the labelling decision. A number of psychological approaches to crime assume that some abnormality **predisposes** individuals to crime in the first place, below are some examples of these.

- ▶ **Personality.** Physiological differences that lead individuals to be 'extravert' or 'neurotic' were thought to hinder the process of socialization in H.J. Eysenck's theory of crime causation (Eysenck, 1964).
- ▶ **The XYY chromosomal abnormality** was thought to lead to increased violence and therefore crime. However, whereas studies have linked this disorder to increased height, acne and some behavioural problems, the abnormality has not been shown to be associated directly with crime (see Hollin, 1989).
- ▶ **Family and other genetic studies** have found crime to run in families and co-occur in twins, as some mental disorders do. The evidence for crime running in families for **non-genetic** reasons is probably more convincing than the genetic argument for mental disorder running in families, for non-genetic reasons (as discussed in Chapter 2), i.e. social and environmental criminal influences also lead to crime running in families. However, there is a proportion of this influence which *cannot* be accounted for by non-genetic factors.
- ▶ **Attention deficit hyperactivity disorder** has been found to be linked to a 'hard core' of offenders who account for a large number of offences, including the more serious ones. Links have been made between this disorder and abnormalities in the frontal lobe regions: the 'planning' areas of the brain. Unlike the other 'abnormality' theories of crime causation, this evidence is recent and the disorder in question is a stronger predictor of crime than social background (see Satterfield *et al.*, 1994).

This type of theoretical link between crime and abnormality has provided one answer to the mad-bad debate. Simply stated, if criminality is **determined** by a disorder, then this would favour a verdict of 'mad', with the attendant possibility of an insanity plea. However, if the offender was acting under his own **free will**, then the verdict would be 'bad', with no such resort to an insanity appeal.

If a proportion of crime *can* be attributed to mental abnormality, then an examination of mentally disordered populations should reveal a higher rate of crime. Studies carried out early in the twentieth century tended to find that rates of crime were similar in mentally disordered populations (usually in institutions) to those in the general population. However, the general population are not in institutions, where detection is easier and living conditions different from outside. Later studies revealed apparently increasing levels of *some* crimes (but not others) among the psychiatric population. The reason for this may lie in the progression towards having only the most **dangerous** or unstable patients admitted to hospital (and therefore the disordered sample), with those less at risk and therefore less likely to offend being supported in the community. According to Hollin (1989), a true estimate of the relative crime rates is difficult to ascertain, as the factors of crime, mental illness and being in institutions interact to confound any attempt to isolate one of them.

The **types of disorder** associated with serious crimes are more easily identified, though these may be simply the disorders most *readily accepted* as **mitigation** in court. The hallucinations, delusions and paranoid idea- tion in **schizophrenia** (see Chapter 9) have led sufferers to harm others, though self-harm is a more frequent outcome. Patients often act on in- structions from hallucinatory 'voices' or false beliefs that others mean them harm. In **mood disorders** (see Chapter 10) symptoms of depression can lead to **'one-sided suicide pacts'**, in which sufferers see only a bleak future in a threatening world for those close to them, their way out being to kill their loved ones before killing themselves. In the **bipolar** form of the disorder, symptoms of **mania** can lead to reckless acts of irresponsibility or even paranoid reactions, as in schizophrenia. **Substance abuse** (see Chapter 8) has a close association with petty crime. In the case of **alcohol**, although violence and serious motor offences are also associated with its use in the 'non-alcoholic' population, rates of crime among alcoholics are very high, varying between 40 and 80 per cent (across a number of dif- ferent studies). **Mental retardation** is associated with crime, that is, many criminals have a below-average IQ, especially those acting as accom- plices. However, when retardation is more profound, a similar approach to that of the child offender is adopted regarding criminal responsibility. Although rare, the lack of empathy and 'people reading skills' in **autism** and **Asperger syndrome** can lead to callous acts by sufferers who do not always react to the distress of others (see Mawson *et al.*, 1985).

Some categories of disorder have their symptoms defined in almost the same terms as criminal behaviour. These are **conduct disorder, antiso- cial personality disorder (dissocial** in ICD-10) and **psychopathy** (see Chapter 6).

▶ **Conduct disorder** is a condition of childhood or adolescence in which there is *persistent* antisocial behaviour such as truancy, lying, theft, absconding and damage to property. Although teenagers are generally associated with rebellious behaviour, this behaviour is consistent and shows a disregard for the rights of others and is associated with adult antisocial personality disorder. Other childhood disorders have some of these behaviours as symptoms such as **attention deficit hyperactivity disorder** which, as mentioned above, also has a close relationship with adult crime.

▶ **Antisocial personality disorder (APD)** includes persistent behaviours which are adult versions of the above, such as offending, impulsiveness and disregard for others, the truth, finances or future plans. A diagnosis also requires conduct disorder to be diagnosed before the age of 15. About half of adolescents with conduct disorder go on to be diagnosed as APD with most of the others shedding such behaviour with maturity. Around 80 per cent of convicted criminals could be diagnosed as APD, which is hardly surprising given the behavioural criteria. Although the criteria for APD creates the stereotype of the imprisoned, drug-dealing pimp, some are less easily criminalized and exist in many professions (see also Chapter 6).

► **Psychopathic disorder.** About 15 per cent of individuals described as APD could be classified as psychopathic. Whereas APD is defined in terms of antisocial behaviours (e.g. incurring large debts), psychopathy tends to include more psychological descriptions (e.g. lacking in emotion). Hare (1986) revised his own version of Cleckley's (1976) **psychopathy checklist**. These checklists have included items such as superficial charm, emotional immaturity, inability to profit from experience, pathological lying, inability to maintain relationships, etc. O'Kane *et al.* (1996) report a comparison of two contemporary psychopathy checklists.

Psychopaths differ from ordinary offenders in their greater *potential* for harm. As Cleckley (1976) has shown, psychopaths offend without apparent purpose, show no remorse, are loyal to no one, frequently indulge in perverse, sexual and harmful behaviour, and these traits permeate all areas of their lives. Many **sexual** and **serial killers** are diagnosed as psychopaths. The disorder is mentioned in the Mental Health Acts and it is one of the disorders for which **compulsory detention** is almost always specified, though many (e.g. Robertson, 1992) have argued against this automatic diversion. It is a controversial disorder as the 'sufferers' rarely suffer, only those near to them, and their traits often make them *more able* in such areas as business, the military or politics. They are often confined for **treatment** under the Mental Health Act. However, Cleckley, among others, believes the condition is *virtually untreatable*. One of the most difficult distinctions to make is that between the psychopathic offender and the non-psychopathic but **dangerous** offender as they share similar characteristics. Oddly enough, given Cleckley's assertions, this distinction has been made on the basis that psychopathy is a *treatable* condition and dangerousness is not.

Individuals with the above disorders tend to account for the bulk of crimes committed due to their recidivist tendencies and, in the case of the psychopath, some of the most notorious and serious crimes. One job of the forensic psychologist and psychiatrist is to **predict dangerousness** among disordered offenders. As mentioned in the previous section, **risk assessment** needs to be carried out for any patient due for discharge or resettlement in the community. With well-publicized accounts of both patients and offenders being released with tragic consequences, assessment of disordered offenders tends to err on the side of caution, with many who would pose no threat being detained. With an increasing shortage of psychiatric beds, secure unit and prison places there is pressure on those making risk assessments to be *less cautious*.

The pathological nature of the crimes committed by psychopathic and dangerous offenders and the tendency to repeat them, have made such offenders special targets for detection agencies. Public outrage at such crimes have also placed great pressure on these agencies to use all possible resources to catch the perpetrators. One resource which is increasingly being used is the forensic psychologist in the role of **psychological profiler**.

Psychological profiling

The media have glamorized and popularized the work of this branch of forensic psychology with dramatic pursuits of **psychopathic sexual serial killers** in films such as *Manhunter* and *Silence of the Lambs*. The concept of the detective who produces the characteristics or a *profile* of the offender from the characteristics of the offence and crime scene has been around in fiction as far back as the tales of Sherlock Holmes. In fact, real-life profiling has a shorter history than this, with one of the first profiles being made of Adolf Hitler in World War II.

The dramatic tracing of Metesky, the 'mad bomber of New York', started a serious interest in the use of profiling in the US. **Brussel** described the offender by personal characteristics, probable residence and proved remarkably accurate, down to his wearing a double-breasted suit on arrest (Brussel, 1968). The **FBI** initiated fact-finding interviews with offenders, which were carried out by their **Behavioural Science Unit (BSU)**. They focused on sexual and serial murderers and discovered that there were characteristic *types* of murders and murderers, especially **sexual homicide** (the killing of a person in the context of power, sexuality and brutality). One of these distinctions which has been supported over time is that of the **organized** versus **disorganized murder**. The organized murder has characteristics, such as evidence of planning, control, use of restraint and removal or hiding of any evidence (including the body), with the reverse being the case at the disorganized murder scene. From accumulated information, the differing characteristics of organized and disorganized murder suspects can be predicted. An *organized* murder suspect would be expected to be of good IQ, socially, sexually and occupationally competent, live with a partner, will have transport, follow crime coverage and will take steps to evade discovery, whereas the *disorganized* suspect should show the reverse of these characteristics, living alone, being less competent and often living near the crime scene without transport. Thus, using these characteristics provided by profilers, investigative officers reduce the search area and number of suspects dramatically.

The success of the BSU agents was limited, even their own estimate was around 40 per cent success, although recent estimates are much higher.

Higher estimates may relate to the fact that their services were all too often required in cases were there was great public pressure either to stop a serial killer or catch the perpetrator of a particularly horrific crime. They are also often called in when there is little or no useful evidence for the police to work with. Pinizzotto and Finkel (1990) compared professional profilers and detectives with novices in a 'profiling test', and found that the profilers showed superiority only for the crime of rape. Holmes (1989), among many others, has pointed out that success in profiling is greater when the degree of **psychological disturbance** in the offender is high.

Although the FBI dedicated significant resources to the work of the BSUs, the use of profiling in other countries did not start till much later. One FBI agent, Ressler, offered the BSU services to police in the UK during the Yorkshire Ripper case, but this offer was not taken up. The first use of a profiler in the UK was David Canter's contribution in the pursuit of John Duffy the 'railway rapist'. This was not successful, although a later profile for a different case by Paul Britton was more useful. In the UK, it is **forensic psychologists** who are asked to produce profiles not investigative agents (as is the case in the US). These psychologists tend to use a **theoretical** rather than a practical approach and have been accused by the FBI counterparts in the US of lacking empiricism in their methods.

The UK psychologists' apparently **'intuitive'** way of analyzing crime scenes and use of psychological methods have given the more famous UK profilers a guru-like image. This image may have led to some in the police force regarding profiling as an equivalent to spiritualism or astrology, as the methods were not accessible to them. This lack of understanding may have led the **Association of Chief Police Officers (ACPO)** in the UK to form a sub-committee to examine the practical aspects of profiling. Paul Britton was commissioned by ACPO to review offender profiling in the UK, and in 1994 the Police Research Group developed the **Offender Profiling Research Program**. Less 'intuitive' profiling methods have also been developed in the UK. In Derbyshire a computerized statistical database, **CATCHEM** (Central Analytical Team Collating Homicide Expertise Management) has been set up and used with some success. Crime details can be input and the computer will output likely offender details. Perhaps it is the *empiricism* of this approach that has led the FBI to set up similar databases in the US.

Although profiling failures are less newsworthy, some cases have made headlines and have tarnished the image of profiling in the UK. Paul Britton's suspect in the Wimbledon Common case was released when Judge Ognall refused to allow the evidence Britton had gained using an undercover policewoman. Britton had been so convinced by his *theory* as to the suspect's identity, he used coercive tactics deemed unfair by the judge to extract a 'confession'. The way that the UK profiler's theory had overridden procedure meant that *other evidence* could not be heard. Clearly, the work of the forensic psychologist and the legal systems they work with are not always in harmony with one another. As profilers and other forensic psychologists become more experienced with the workings of the legal system and gain more understanding and respect from the police, their evidence may carry greater weight. However, the police have a great deal of experience with courtroom procedure and still find *themselves* at odds with it.

Community provision: rehabilitation and prevention

Rehabilitation and community care

As described in Chapter 1, large mental institutions were built in remote locations to house an ever-increasing number of patients, who could not be managed in any other way until effective drug treatments were developed in the 1950s. The long-term effects on the patients of being in institutions (**institutionalization effects**) were quite devastating in themselves. Even patients who had not been very disturbed on admission were not able to survive well on their own after many years in an institution. These effects were marked in the area of self-care and social skills as many things were done for the patients, including institutional 'social activities'. As with institutionalized prisoners, patients would suffer from **social stigmatization** accentuating the difficulties of integrating into a society that they are out of touch with and that might have changed radically during their institutionalized years. Patients who were not able to leave when appropriate pharmacological therapy became available will be increasingly suffering from the long-term effects of their medication. Seligman (1992) has described **learned helplessness**, which can be a consequence of the lack of personal control in institutions, leading to levels of **depression** in many long-term patients. In **Erving Goffman**'s (1968) analysis of total institutions, he identifies other psychological effects on prisoners and in-patients such as a lack of **personal identity**.

The negative effects of institutions have been known for many years, but the issue became more immediate with the advent of drug management in the 1950s and pressure to end 'incarceration' from the 'anti-psychiatry' movement in the 1960s. In the US and other countries, the 1960s also saw the emergence of residential **therapeutic communities**, a half-way stage between institution and independent living, and later developments such as the **Community Mental Health Centre** movement. In the 1970s new in-patient units were built attached to District General Hospitals to provide local services for the immediate population, but were less able to cope with the severely disturbed than the large dedicated institutions. **Day hospitals** also provide interim care, but as Tantam and McGrath (1989) point out, they can also provide another route to institutionalization. The important concepts of **rehabilitation** and **prevention** began to be seen by some professionals as *more* important than those of diagnosis and treatment.

Franco Basaglia believed strongly in the importance of rehabilitation and prevention while working in Italian institutions in the 1960s and 1970s.

He founded the **Psichiatria Democratica** movement in 1974. His convictions led him to change staff attitudes within his own hospitals and to create political pressure through his writings to bring about change on a national basis. By 1978, '**Law 180**' had been formulated and passed in Italy which effectively ended compulsory detention, except for urgent treatment. The Italian health services began a sustained period of discharging patients (and staff!), closing institutions and putting emphasis on prevention. Jones and Poletti (1985) reporting on the Italian experience, observed that by the mid-1980s there was a strong move to reverse this achievement. Few would argue against the principles of deinstitutionalization, community care and prevention on theoretical grounds; it is the *practical* and *financial* aspects of the process that lead to difficulties.

In Italy the **alternative structures** in the community spoken of by Basaglia were slow to emerge, as was the *funding* of any additional community provision, funding which had never been costed out in advance in any detail. However, large institutions were emptied and sold, and many psychiatrists and other health workers were made redundant. Basaglia died in 1980 and so never witnessed the limitations of deinstitutionalization manifest themselves on the streets of the poorer areas of Italy. The police were often left to cope with **street patients**, discharged without adequate preparation or support, and the occasional tragedies that resulted from severe disturbance and inadequate care. The unemployed professionals were quick to protest and make the most of any newsworthy failure of the process, and the politicians had a clear financial incentive to continue with it. The healthcare professionals and politicians blamed each other for the failings of deinstitutionalization. However, the process continued, though with diminishing political support. The difficulties faced in compromising the extremes of institutionalization and 'street patients' are well represented in what Jones (1982) called **Scull's dilemma**. In essence, this simply restates the age-old problem of what to do when 'you cannot keep them in and you cannot let them out'. The answer would seem to lie in the quality of the *process* adopted for moving from one to the other.

In the UK, the deinstitutionalization process began in the 1980s, with planned closures increasing towards the end of that decade. Professionals in Britain arrived at the conclusion that community care would be *more* expensive than the current use of institutions. They also discussed the difficulties and issues involved such as rehabilitation, and then were surprised to find *cost-cutting* at the top of the political agenda, as it had been in Italy. Some of the many problems that needed to be addressed can be appreciated from the following examples.

▶ The **NIMBY** phenomenon, in which no one wants community care in *their* neighbourhood and the public education required to change this. In community care we cannot assume that the community actually *cares*, and social contact is necessary for social rehabilitation (see Dilks and Shattock, 1996).

▶ How some **chronic** and **severely disabled patients** could never be adjusted to independent living and would require permanent institutional care.

▶ How the process of **rehabilitation** needs to begin almost as soon as a patient is admitted, to prevent institutional effects occurring, and ensuring that the difficult, expensive and often protracted transition of the patient into the community is carried out properly to prevent the waste of resources that accompanies failure.

▶ The need for adequate **support in the community**. Outreach services are needed to prevent the **revolving door** phenomenon, in which patients oscillate between hospital and inadequate care, placing an inordinate burden on resources.

▶ How to avoid the **moral blackmail** that is implicit if the system relies on relatives to act as unpaid carers, in order to take some financial strain off the health care budget.

▶ To recognize that **emergency bed provision** is a necessity and that availability should be local. There needs to be enough 'slack' in the system to avoid the risk of 'disaster in the community'. What should clearly be prevented are cases such as that of Ben Silcock climbing into a lion's den for 'company', or Christopher Clounis stabbing to death an innocent passer-by after being refused what could arguably be described as adequate care.

▶ That there is still a place for the **larger hospital**, which in addition to providing for the severely disturbed, allows for the beds in smaller local units to be ready for emergencies and other unforeseen eventualities.

▶ There is a need to avoid the use of privately run **hostels** for patients in the community (especially the elderly), where cheap accommodation for high profits produces conditions that can be *worse* than institutional care and far more *dangerous*.

The move to community-based psychiatric care seems a bleak prospect, but this need not be the case given sufficient funding and forward planning. The achievable aims of safe and adequate care in an understanding and supportive community and with a focus on prevention are worthy of investment. However, these aims were also around at the time of the Greek and Roman empires.

Prevention and community psychiatry

At the heart of community psychiatry and psychology is the concept of prevention. This is often considered at three levels.

1. **Tertiary prevention**. Closely allied to rehabilitation, this concerns the support or aftercare of patients returned to the community in order to prevent relapse and possibly readmission. It is essential that patients are well monitored during the early stages of adjusting to the rigours of life outside and are adequately prepared for this. The **care programme approach** provides care plans for patients who have been assessed. Patients will have a **key worker** responsible for co-ordinating the plan.
2. **Secondary prevention**. This refers to the early detection of possible problems *before* they can develop into conditions that require hospitalization. It is essential that such **outreach** work does not depend on the patient actively seeking help, that problems are detected or *anticipated* by targeting those *most at risk*. In areas of the UK a **supervision register** is to be kept of all the patients judged to be at risk in each locality.
3. **Primary prevention**. This involves examining whole communities rather than the needs of individuals. Thus primary prevention will be concerned with the provision of adequate primary health care in the form of multidisciplinary **community mental health teams** anchored by the GP, with increased use of community psychiatric nurses along with social workers, clinical psychologists and health visitors with the addition of a variety of newer services such as **family support workers**. Primary prevention goes well beyond immediate provision into areas such as **health education, environmental issues** and **epidemiology** (examining the relative incidence of disorders).

Some of the best preventative measures are those that prevent disorders arising in the first place. Influential factors here are health education from an early age, including the importance of mental health factors, improving the general health of the population and promoting awareness of services that are available, especially those adopting a **prophylactic** role.

Health psychology

This is a rapidly growing area of psychology and medicine, which cannot be fairly represented here. The reader is directed to the further reading and many other health psychology texts. Health psychology is often associated with the overlapping area of **psychological medicine**, making a large contribution to the prevention of some medical conditions by identifying the psychological factors that contribute towards them. The rising importance of health psychology is a direct result of the increased knowledge of the *extent* of psychological influence over what were originally seen as purely medical conditions. Some of these **psychophysiological conditions** are as follows:

▶ **Coronary heart disease.** Stress resulting from time-pressured behaviour was found to greatly increase the chance of a heart attack by Friedman and Rosenman (1974). They identified a **type A personality** with characteristic competitive, time-urgent and hostile behaviours, who could be then trained to reduce this tendency and the risk of a heart attack by moving towards the more relaxed **type B personality** characteristics.

▶ **Essential hypertension** is high blood pressure resulting from psychological causes. The condition is one precursor to a heart attack and is also exacerbated by **type A** behaviour. Forms of psychological stress force blood in a central direction (to the heart and lungs) constricting peripheral capilliaries (blood vessels of the fingers and toes), increasing blood pressure. This can be reversed by giving a client **biofeedback** of their blood pressure and allowing them to reduce this by adjusting their behaviour and thinking patterns.

▶ **Asthma** is the constriction of the airways in the lungs, causing wheezing, breathlessness and even death. Asthma is *sometimes* exacerbated by psychological tension or excitement, and this knowledge can be useful in reducing the risk of an attack.

Other serious disorders have been found to be better resisted by including psychological factors in dealing with them such as **cancer** and **AIDS**, as well as everyday conditions such as **headaches**. Psychological states such as **helplessness** have been found to lower the **immune** reactions of the body to invading organisms or weaken resistance to tumours, and 'psychological hardiness' and a sense of **control** have been found to help resist the progress of physical disorders.

Chapter summary

In most countries, patients who are a danger to themselves or others may be detained and treated on an **involuntary** basis. Legislation is usually contained in the respective **Mental Health Acts** to be enforced by the **police** and **courts** at the instigation of **relatives, approved social workers** and **doctors** (usually **psychiatrists**). Various **sections** of the Acts indicate detention, or detention with treatment, for varying time periods, requiring the written consent of proportionately qualified professionals, with appeals being heard by the **Mental Health Review Tribunal**. Some individuals are more appropriately detained in **prison, special (secure) hospitals** or **regional secure units. Forensic psychologists** are involved in the legal process: in prisons especially those designated for those mentally disturbed individuals who are **dangerous; as expert witnesses** in court often passing judgement on the **mental state** of the defendant; judging **eyewitness testimony;**

offender profiling; risk assessment; and examining theoretical aspects of crime as **criminologists**. Criminologists have considered the relationship between crime and mental disorder, the **mad-bad debate,** and have incorporated the idea of disorder leading to crime in theories of its causes.

The actual **level of crime** among the mentally disordered is greater for some crimes, but this relationship is not a simple one and involves other factors. Some **types of disorders** are associated with crime due to the effects of their symptoms. Examples of such disorders would be **conduct disorder, antisocial personality disorder** and **psychopathy.** Psychopathy is an enigmatic disorder which does not conform to the usual view of mental disorder and has been described as **moral insanity,** with only the arguable 'treatability' of the disorder distinguishing the psychopath from the **dangerous offender. Psychological profilers** produce the psychological characteristics of **offenders** from the characteristics of the **crime** in the hope of limiting the search for suspects. Originating in the US, it has spread to the UK in a more psychologically based form, and although it claims some successes there are many failures and much controversy.

The effects of **institutionalization** on patients is well documented. Since the discovery of **anti-psychotic medication,** the possibility of maintaining patients in the community has become more desirable. **Community care** became a strong issue in Italy during the 1970s and was backed by legislation. The **Italian experience** was not always successful with many ex-patients becoming **street patients** and the move to the community being seen as a **cost-cutting** exercise. Other countries have also attempted to **rehabilitate** patients and empty their institutions with mixed results, usually due to **underfunding.** The other side of rehabilitation is **prevention,** which is considered at three levels: **tertiary** or aftercare preventing relapse; **secondary** or the early detection of individuals developing disorders; **primary prevention** or the examination of whole communities in terms of provision, the incidence of disorders and the factors which influence them. **Health psychology** deals with psychological approaches to preventing **medical conditions** such as **coronary heart disease.** Psychological factors are evident in a range of disorders from **headaches** to **cancer.**

Self-test questions

► What is meant by 'sectioning'?
► What leads to an individual being detained against their will?
► What is meant by the term 'expert witness'?
► How does 'diminished responsibility' differ from 'guilty but insane'?
► Discuss the issues involved in the 'mad-bad debate'.

▶ What is the relationship between conduct disorder and antisocial personality disorder?
▶ Are all dangerous offenders psychopaths?
▶ How has the development of profiling differed in the US and the UK?
▶ What are the practical implications of 'Scull's dilemma'?
▶ How can health psychologists prevent physical disease?

Further reading

Bingley, W. (1993) 'Broadmoor, Rampton and Ashworth: can good practice prevent potential future problems in high-security hospitals?', *Criminal Behaviour and Mental Health*, **3**, 465–71.

Blackburn, R. (1993) *The Psychology of Criminal Conduct*. Chichester: John Wiley.

Carrier, J. and Tomlinson, D. (1996) *Asylum in the Community*. London: Routledge.

Exworthy, T. (1995) 'Compulsory care in the community: a review of the proposals for compulsory supervision and treatment of the mentally ill in the community', *Criminal Behaviour and Mental Health*, **5**, 218–41.

Falloon, I. and Fadden, G. (1995) *Integrated Mental Health Care*. Cambridge: Cambridge University Press.

Fennell, P. (1995) *Treatment without Consent*. London: Routledge.

Jones, K. and Poletti, A. (1985) 'Understanding the Italian experience', *British Journal of Psychiatry*, **146**, 341–7.

Jones, R. (1994) *The Mental Health Act Manual*. London: Sweet & Maxwell.

Leff, J. (1997) *Care in the Community: Illusion or reality?* Chichester: John Wiley.

Phelan, M., Strathdee, G. and Thornicroft, G. (1995) *Emergency Mental Health Services in the Community*. Cambridge: Cambridge University Press.

Pitts, M. and Philips, K. (1991) *The Psychology of Health: An introduction*. London: Routledge.

Prins, H. (1995) *Offenders, Deviants or Patients?*, 2nd edition. London: Routledge.

The Mental Health Act 1983 (1983) London: HMSO.

Walker, N. (1996) *Dangerous People*. London: Blackstone Press.

Watts, F. and Bennett, D. (eds.) (1991) *Theory and Practice of Psychiatric Rehabilitation*. Chichester: John Wiley.

CHAPTER 5

Disorders usually first diagnosed in infancy and childhood

In this chapter

▶ Development and disorder
▶ Disorders beginning in childhood
▶ Attention-deficit hyperactivity disorder
▶ Pervasive developmental disorders: autism and Asperger syndrome

Covering the period from birth to 16 years of age, childhood disorders are not always detected at the time of their onset. This may be because children do not possess the same degree of insight that adults have into their own mental functioning and rely on carers (mainly parents) to be their **advocates** in seeking help. There may be a reluctance to admit that a child has a mental disorder, as the carer may feel it reflects on their parenting skills and professionals may be reluctant to place a stigmatizing label on one so young until they are absolutely certain of their diagnosis. Although there is no clear division between the *types* of disorder affecting children and adults, there are **confounding factors** to be considered when the onset is early in life.

Development and disorder

Children do not arrive complete with an instruction manual and few parents are fully trained prior to a child's birth. Child and carer adjust to one another's behaviour and any sudden *change* in the child's behaviour may alert the carer to the possibility that there is something wrong. However, normal children's behaviour can be quite aberrant at times: they may wet the bed or have a tantrum without having developed a disorder. Parents and professionals will also anticipate some behavioural and biological **milestones** as part of normal **maturation**. For example, if a child fails to talk by a certain age the carer will become increasingly anxious about such an indicator of abnormal development and the child may also be disturbed by the carer's anxious state. Thus the interaction between child and carer can amplify (or moderate) the problems of *either*. A child's behaviour may be disturbed by significant *events* in their life, such as a family bereavement, moving home or inevitable hurdles such as starting school. Although most children exhibit adverse reactions to these events, it is *prolonged* or *profound* reactions that indicate underlying problems.

The process of maturation is an interaction between **genetic expectation** and **environmental conditions,** and disturbance in early childhood can have its effect magnified by disrupting or retarding normal development. However, human development is a *resilient* and *adaptive* process designed to survive in adversity, with genetic programming which has a way of guiding development back on course.

The **paradigms** in abnormal psychology described in Chapter 2 apply to both adult and childhood onset disorders, but they are arguably more influential in childhood. Some examples illustrate this view:

▶ **Biological** changes that take place during childhood are far more rapid and profound than those that occur in adult life. Children have to adapt to a changing body-image, hormonal turmoil and neural development, which constantly alter their relationship with the world in which they live.

▶ **Behavioural** learning is at its peak in childhood and many maladaptive behaviours are inadvertently encouraged and fears created. The parent who responds to a child's tantrums with attention and giving in to the child's demands, should also accept the blame when tantrums become a way of life for the child as it becomes older (and larger). An adult carer with a debilitating fear of spiders should seek professional help *before* a child becomes receptive to their fear and acquires the phobia also. There is no period of life when a greater impression can be made on behaviour and being a responsible parent *means* taking responsibility for this process.

▶ **Attachment theory** was developed by **John Bowlby** (1908–90), who used the psychodynamic paradigm and the work of **ethologists** such as **Konrad Lorenz,** in emphasizing the importance of a secure and unbroken *bond* between child and their nearest carer. Humans have a very long childhood and are ill-prepared for survival at birth, in contrast to species that are born independent. Having a secure physical and emotional attachment in the early years would be vital to the survival of an infant human in the wild. Even within civilization, such a bond is necessary, albeit with less intensity. For Bowlby, the disruption of this bond in the early years (from 6 months to 6 years of age), or **maternal deprivation,** leads to greater levels of mental disorder and criminal behaviour in later life. Bowlby's work is not without its critics (e.g. Rutter, 1979), though even his critics accept that early bonds are important. The other problems of attachment concern the overuse of the bond, usually due to a parent's overdependence on the child and a refusal to allow the growing individual sufficient independence to become a secure adult.

▶ **Family systems theory** (see Chapter 2). This approach sees the family as a dynamic and functional unit which is self-regulating and has its own rules and individual characteristics. Change in a relationship within the family affects all its members, and the family unit may remain upset until normal interactional forces return it to a state of equilibrium. According to this approach, a child within a dysfunctional family suffers due to the *inflexibility* of its dynamics, unequal power relationships within it and the family's inability to adapt to changing demands of its membership. Other family approaches are those that consider **family communications theory**, looking at the style of communication between members, and **family structural theory**, examining dysfunctional family structures, e.g. members 'ganging up' on other individuals in the family.

As a species we tend to be *over-protective* of our children, viewing them as vulnerable, innocent individuals surrounded by predatory adults. This view often leads to the child being brought up with little *experience* of dealing with the real world and perhaps suffering as a consequence. This move to over-protection almost always involves children *least* at risk, with those at greatest risk receiving *least* protection. In recent times this protective approach has been incorporated into a **child-centred** policy for dealing with families, which can produce tyrannical, self-indulgent children and lead to some families being governed by a child's *inexperience* and *lack of responsibility*, rather than being led by a responsible experienced adult. On the other side of this failure to empower children effectively, there are the increased numbers of reports of **abuse** of children, who are bullied into silence.

Thus, the background to mental disorders beginning in childhood is somewhat chaotic, confounded by developmental factors and centred on a time of conflict between dependency and the process of becoming independent. In the following sections the current classifications of childhood disorders will be examined in brief and illustrated by detail on the **pervasive developmental disorders** of **autism** and **Asperger's disorder**, and **attention deficit hyperactivity disorder**.

Disorders beginning in childhood

The DSM-IV lists a number of categories of childhood onset disorders, focusing on disorders less likely to begin in adulthood. In this chapter we focus on disorders that are specifically related to childhood, while recognizing that many adult disorders begin at this time. Classificatory systems always include a final 'catch-all' category of **disorder not otherwise specified** for each disorder group. In order to avoid unnecessary redundancy, this category has not been included here but should be assumed for every classification of disorder.

► **Mental retardation.** Where intellectual functioning is *significantly* below the average for a particular age group and there is impairment of adaptive functioning, mental retardation may be diagnosed. The basic criterion for retardation is an IQ score of below 70, with values below this on a scale of **mild, moderate, severe** and **profound mental retardation**.

► **Learning disorders.** In these, academic functioning is *substantially* below age-appropriate performance. The sub-classifications of learning disorders specify the area of academic difficulty, i.e. **written expression, mathematics** and **reading disorder.**

► **Motor skills disorders.** This is diagnosed when specified motor skills are *substantially* below their intellectual performance and that expected for their age. **Developmental co-ordination disorder** is the main disorder specified here.

► **Communication disorders.** Specific difficulties with language or speech are **expressive language, mixed receptive-expressive language** and **phonological disorders,** and **stuttering.** Some forms of 'baby language' are common and may be maintained behaviourally by *carers* accommodating the deviant speech. Communication disorders are usually *more persistent* than 'baby language' deviations.

► **Pervasive developmental disorders (PDD).** The symptoms of this group of disorders pervade most aspects of the individual's life, persisting into later life. The areas of function affected are those of **social** and **communication** functioning and include stereotyped behaviour and restricted interests. The disorders included are:
  – **Autism** and **Asperger's disorder** (see next section).
  – **Rett's disorder.** There are similarities in the deficits of **autism** and Rett's disorder with stereotyped hand movements, expressive and receptive language deficits, poor co-ordination and a lack of interest in social activity, as well as psychomotor retardation. A major difference lies in the fact that in Rett's disorder **development is normal for the first 5 months** of life, following which head growth decelerates and the symptoms, usually including mental retardation, begin to appear over the following years. It is less common than autism with an incidence of about 1 in 10,000 births and appears to affect females only. As with other PDD, the cause is probably biological and there is no cure as such, making it a diagnosis that indicates a poor prognosis.
  – **Childhood disintegrative disorder.** Whereas the period of normal development in Rett's disorder is five months, in childhood disintegrative disorder this period of normal growth is about *2–4 years*. At some point in the years after this (up to 10 years), there is a *loss of the already acquired skills*, resulting in severe deficits in the areas of language, adaptive behaviour and motor skills. The disorder is very rare, occurring in about 1 in 100,000 births, and is more

frequent in males than females. There is no cure for the apparently biologically based progress of childhood disintegrative disorder, with treatment consisting of behaviourally retraining some of the lost skills. It was once termed **Heller's syndrome** after Theodore Heller, who described the disorder at the beginning of the twentieth century.

▶ **Attention deficit and disruptive behaviour disorders.** Some of these disorders have been mentioned in Chapter 4 in relation to crime. Each of these disorders is marked by a degree of behaviour which is disruptive for those around them and detrimental to the sufferer's adaptive and academic abilities. These disorders can be strong indicators of later **personality disorders** and **criminal activity**, but this is not inevitable. These disorders are more common in males than females, though as with criminal activity itself, this bias is subject to criticism (see Hollin, 1989).

  – **Attention deficit hyperactivity disorder.** See later section.

  – **Conduct disorder.** As mentioned in the previous section, conduct disorder often leads on to the adult **antisocial personality disorder** for which it is a diagnostic criterion. Thus, the relationship between the two disorders is such that antisocial personality disorder always has conduct disorder as a precursor, but conduct disorder does not *always* lead to antisocial personality disorder. A key feature of both these disorders is an apparent *disregard for the rights and feelings of others*, including the rules and laws of society in general. There are four main symptom groupings: (1) *aggressive behaviour* that could harm other people or animals, often initiating fights or bullying with the more likely use of a weapon, and stealing during violence, i.e. mugging, or further assault such as rape; (2) *damage to property* or *theft*, sometimes in the form of arson and more frequently as vandalism; (3) *deceitfulness* in the forms of lying, 'conning', petty theft and indifference to debt; (4) *rule-breaking*, which may include playing truant, persistently breaking parental curfews, violating school regulations and running away from home – *all without* any real reason (e.g. former abuse). DSM-IV recognizes two subtypes: onset before the age of 10 years, or **childhood-onset type**, and onset after this age, or **adolescent-onset conduct disorder**. The latter type is less male-biased, has fewer aggressive features and a better prognosis (i.e. less likely to lead on to antisocial personality disorder in adulthood). The context in which the child lives, or has recently lived, needs to be noted in making a diagnosis. For example, a child who has recently arrived from an area where civil conflict or gang warfare is the norm may have some aggressive behaviours that are *adaptive* or normal in that context.

  – **Oppositional defiant disorder.** Most children are defiant at some time or other but to fulfil the criteria for this disorder behaviour such as defiance, hostility and disobedience, must be persistent and well above the level expected for a child of the given age. The areas of behaviour that are of clinical interest are: loss of temper, arguing with adults, non-compliance with adult rules or requests, deliberately annoying others, blaming others for their own errors, and being resentful, touchy and vindictive towards others. Children with this disorder tend to lack the behaviours which *violate* the rights of others that would qualify them as being conduct disordered.

▶ **Feeding and eating disorders.** Many children go through periods of conflict with adults over eating habits, perhaps overeating, refusing to eat, or eating 'junk' food. Persistent peculiarities of eating and general levels of eating that affect health are the areas of clinical concern. The adult disorders of **anorexia nervosa**, a failure or refusal to eat sufficiently, **bulimia nervosa**, bingeing and purging, and **obesity** due to overeating, often have their onset in childhood and adolescence (see Chapter 8). DSM-IV has these disorders in a separate section and lists only **pica, rumination disorder** and the more general **feeding disorder of early childhood** among its childhood disorders.

  – **Pica** is the persistent eating of substances with *no nutritional value* at an age when this would be inappropriate. Infants may chew on various materials, but in pica the infant ingests available substances such as plaster or cloth. The older child may eat stones, worms and soil or any of the possible non-nutritive substances. This is in addition, not as a substitute for normal food and not part of some religious or sub-cultural practice. In some cases the disorder is associated with **mental retardation**.

  – **Rumination disorder** refers to the persistent *regurgitation* and *rechewing* of food, which is often re-ingested or sometimes ejected from the mouth. There is an absence of the nausea normally associated with such activity and the child has no digestive disorders which would otherwise explain this behaviour. The disorder is very rare and affects more males than females, usually in infancy.

  – **Feeding disorder of infancy or early childhood** broadly covers a significantly lower than average intake of food resulting in a failure to gain weight or weight loss. Failure to gain weight is a fairly common reason for carers to bring children to a clinician, but about half of these can be explained by factors other than this disorder.

▶ **Tic disorders.** Tics are sudden stereotyped movements or vocalizations which can be *simple* as in blinks or grunts, or *complex* as in facial expressions or suddenly produced words. These occur many times a day but do not have a rhythmic pattern. Tics are quite common among children, though most disappear with maturity. Although tics seem involuntary and of a neurological origin, they are characteristically modified by social contexts and psychological factors. For example, complex vocal tics often take the form of obscenities (**coprolalia**) and may *increase* in frequency in situations where they would be *least* appropriate. Tics in tic disorders need to be distinguished from abnormal movements found in other disorders such as **Huntington's chorea**. There are three types of tic disorder distinguished by duration and type of tic, motor or vocal:

– **Tourette's disorder** was reported by **Gilles de la Tourette** in 1885. It is more common in males and is distinguished from the other tic disorders by having both *vocal* and *motor tics* for over a year without remission. The sufferer has the task of learning to deal with the consequent social embarrassment and stigma as well as the tics themselves. There is evidence of a genetic basis for Tourette's disorder and a dominant gene(s) has been suggested by Bowman and Numberger (1993). Treatment with the dopamine receptor blocking neuroleptic **haloperidol** has been effective in reducing the tics and more recent drugs such as **clonidine** are also effective and have fewer side-effects (see Chapter 2). Tourette's disorder is about as common as autism, the incidence being approximately 4 in 10,000.

– **Chronic motor or vocal tic disorder** is distinguished by having vocal *or* motor tics but *not* both. The 'chronic' distinction is defined by a duration of at least one year without remission. The disorder is less debilitating than Tourette's, though both disorders are found in the same families and so must have similar genetic origins.

– **Transient tic disorder** is distinguished by its duration of more than four weeks but *less than one year*. Transient tic disorder can include *either* vocal or motor tics *or both* together.

▶ **Elimination disorders** have two forms, each requiring the occurrences to be repeated over a three-month period. A child should be at least *4 years old* for such a diagnosis to be made:

– **Encopresis** is the inappropriate passage of faeces, soiling cloths, bedding or floor and affects about 3 per cent of children over 5 years of age. This can be involuntary or intentional and should not be a result of the use of laxatives or a medical condition.

– **Enuresis** is the inappropriate emptying of the bladder, which is *not* the result of drug action (diuretics) or organic disease, but may be sustained by parental attention. This can be **nocturnal** (night-time bed wetting), **diurnal** (day-time wetting of clothes), or both. Urinary incontinence is quite common among children over 5 years, but only 7 per cent of males and 3 per cent of females persist to meet the criteria of enuresis without a medical condition. Children can be trained to extend the period of time between each urination in stages or be classically conditioned to wake on urinating by an 'enuresis alarm' (a buzzer triggered by damp). Older children can be operantly rewarded for having dry nights.

▶ **Separation anxiety disorder** is diagnosed only if *excessive* anxiety occurs when a child has to be separated from the home environment or the person to whom they are attached. The child may exhibit a range of anxiety-related symptoms such as enuresis, nightmares and somatic (i.e. 'body') complaints, including headaches, dizziness, stomachaches and nausea prior to separation. Bedtime for the child is difficult and various ploys will be adopted to avoid being left alone in bed, in addition to getting up in the night to join the parents. Early behavioural training (slowly extending the separation time) can avoid these problems with most children, but the 4 per cent or so of those in whom it persists can be diagnosed with separation anxiety disorder. The disorder is often associated with a fear of *losing* the person to whom they are attached.

▶ **Selective mutism** (formerly *elective* mutism) is the voluntary and persistent failure to speak in specific (selected) situations in which being mute is *not* usual (e.g. school). They may use gestures or a distorted voice in place of normal speech. The child may be shy but should *not* be suffering from other communication disorders. There tends to be more females with the disorder and affects less than 1 per cent of children brought to clinics.

▶ **Reactive attachment disorder** involves age-inappropriate ways of relating to others. This is a rare disorder which is closely associated with **pathological care** (usually physical neglect or abuse). There are two subtypes reflecting the polar opposites of social relatedness behaviour:
  – **The inhibited type** fails to initiate or respond in social interactions and may become an 'anxious observer' of the situation, rejecting comfort. This should not be confused with the symptoms of disorders such as autism.
  – **The disinhibited type** lacks any selectivity in attachments and is indiscriminate when relating to others in social situations. This indiscriminate social activity should *not* be a result of developmental delay or retardation.

▶ **Stereotypic movement disorder** is characterized by repetitive, non-functional motor behaviour (**self-stimulatory behaviour**) which disrupts normal behaviour. This may also involve **self-injurous behaviour** such as biting or head-banging. It is associated with **mental retardation** and can affect up to 25 per cent of those with profound mental handicap.

▶ **Other disorders beginning in childhood**. There are a number of disorders that can start in childhood that are usually regarded as adult disorders. For example, **mood, anxiety-related** and **personality disorders** are often detected in childhood and the origins of **sexual abuse, dissociative** and **gender identity disorders** are *expected* to be found early in life. Thus, as stated at the start of this chapter, there is no clear cut-off point between the disorders of childhood and adulthood. However, to avoid repetition, the reader is directed to the relevant adult disorders for descriptions which generally apply whether or not the onset was prior to 16 years.

Attention deficit hyperactivity disorder (ADHD)

Phenomenology, diagnosis and prognosis of ADHD

ADHD is characterized by persistent inattention and impulsive hyperactive behaviour. The child will usually shift from one activity to another without completing tasks, exhibiting enormous energy and enthusiasm. Adult carers are rapidly exhausted by the task of monitoring their activity and may find themselves in constant conflict while trying to moderate their demands and behaviour levels. The conflict, damage to property and occasional injuries resulting from this behaviour would imply maliciousness and vandalism, but this is not usually the case. The child is often surprised by the damage and hurt that can result from their actions. Many normal children are very active, curious and energetic but can inhibit this behaviour if instructed or if the situation demands it. In ADHD, this inhibitory ability seems weak or absent. Although the majority are normal in most other respects, including intelligence, school work is disrupted by their inattention and classroom order is threatened by their hyperactivity. About a quarter of affected children have *additional* learning disabilities, which is considered as **comorbidity** rather than part of the same disorder.

CASE STUDY · Attention deficit hyperactivity disorder

Jason's birth was uneventful but he became a very demanding infant, often seeming unwell, crying frequently and sleeping poorly. This placed a strain on his mother, who was left to cope alone as her husband had a demanding job and other relatives lived too far away to help out. Possibly as a result of the strain, his mother wished to return to work and managed to find a secretarial post when Jason was 3 years old. By this time, the child's incessant questions and boisterous behaviour were notably excessive. After the first three weeks, his first childminder claimed that Jason's 'personality' did not fit with the other children in her care and refused to take him in again, but then admitted that he was simply disruptive and upset the other children. After he had been similarly rejected by two nurseries, the GP referred Jason to a neurologist to eliminate the possibility of brain damage, although this referral was also a result of his (now unemployed) mother's distress, concern and fears that Jason might have a progressive condition. No obvious neurological defect was apparent, though some of Jason's brain activity had been judged low when he was given a PET scan as part of a research project. His lack of impulse control and inattentiveness was evident during further testing at which his general IQ was judged normal. His mother was given dietary advice for Jason, which had little effect on his behaviour, though she was not very thorough in its implementation. During this time, the strained relations between Jason's parents had led to divorce. Arguments had often centred on his mother's extreme concern for Jason's health and, in his father's view, being 'soft on him'.

During Jason's second year of school, complaints by the parents of other children made it clear that something would have to be done about his disruptive behaviour. At home his mother was having a relationship with a younger man who viewed Jason's behaviour as endlessly amusing, often buying him new toys and shoes, which were rapidly worn out or broken. The educational psychologist involved with the school arranged for Jason and his mother to be seen by a team of professionals who dealt with child behaviour problems. A careful record was made of his disruptive behaviour in the home and at school as well as the reactions of his mother and teacher. From this, a system of rewards were devised for not being disruptive, as well as negative consequences such as being confined to his room ('time out'). The mother's boyfriend left during this time, somewhat disrupting the treatment process, due to the mother's fears that Jason might also reject her if she was too strict. After a second shaky start, Jason's behavioural treatment began to show reductions in the target behaviours, which encouraged his mother to persist with the programme. Jason's behaviour improved greatly in more general terms, but the disruptive behaviour never disappeared altogether. Jason is now in his late teens and has just been convicted for stealing cars (for the third time) and given a short jail sentence.

As this case study shows, the prognosis for many sufferers of ADHD can be poor with links to later **antisocial personality disorder** and **criminal recidivism** (see Satterfield *et al.*, 1994). However, *not all* those diagnosed with the disorder follow this course.

A diagnosis of ADHD must establish that inattention and hyperactivity-impulsivity pervade different aspects of the child's life, e.g. school and home. A number of these styles of behaviour such as fidgeting, not listening and impulsive speech should also persist over time and not be a reaction to a single event. There are three forms that may be diagnosed: (1) **predominantly inattentive type**, (2) **predominantly hyperactive-impulsive type** and (3) **combined type**, based on the levels of each symptom group present. The disorder is much more prevalent in males, with an incidence of about 4 per cent during the school years.

Aetiology and treatment of ADHD

Feingold (1973) considered the biochemical effects of diet and specifically the action of **food additives** on a child's behaviour. Although such research has shown the effectiveness of removing additives from the diet, this seems to apply in only a small proportion of cases. If the *reward* and *non-reinforcement* of the child's behaviour is inconsistent (or non-existent!), this can exacerbate the problem. However, when behavioural contingencies are correctly in place (see the case study) there are still problems evident, which would indicate that some biological mechanism is operating.

Genetic studies have found evidence for an inherited characteristic that predisposes individuals to ADHD (e.g. Faraone and Biederman, 1994), although that characteristic has not been clearly specified. Neurological investigations have been a focus of research, with some tentative success. The size of parts of the **corpus collosum,** which divides the two hemispheres of the brain, have been found to differ in children with high levels of hyperactivity. Lower levels of brain function have been inferred from **PET scans** of glucose metabolism levels.

Treatments for ADHD tend to be biological and behavioural. Behavioural treatments involve moderating the child's behaviour by the selective reinforcement and non-reinforcement of 'good' and disruptive behaviours. A behavioural assessment will establish the basic level of unwanted behaviour, against which any improvement due to **behaviour modification** techniques can be compared. A focus for behavioural intervention is the continued educational development of the child as good educational attainment is associated with a better prognosis. A biological treatment that is rapidly gaining popularity is the use of stimulants such as **methylphenidate** (Ritalin). Paradoxically these stimulants calm the behaviour of the (*underactive*) brain function of children with ADHD and improve their response to reward. The problems of long-term use of stimulants, including their side-effects and the question of terminating their use, cannot be overlooked as this treatment increases in popularity.

Special issues in ADHD

The status of ADHD as a disorder has been attacked on the basis that it is unfair to put such a label on a child who may simply 'not fit' into the school system or that poor school and home discipline is being ignored by *pathologizing* the child. Recent biological evidence and the pervasiveness of ADHD behaviour have to some degree countered these arguments. Another controversy involves the link between *some* ADHD children and their later delinquent behaviour. Current research tends to support this link and future work may point to the mechanisms involved. A final point of heated debate is the use of stimulant drugs for ADHD, which is spreading to include other disruptive children, with rather emotive arguments from both sides as to the long-term outcome.

Pervasive developmental disorders: autism and Asperger syndrome

Phenomenology, diagnosis and prognosis of autism

Within one paragraph of a review, Wolf-Schein (1996) mentions that autism is one of the most discussed developmental disorders and goes on to give the rate of autism in the general population as 2–5 cases per 10,000 individuals, affecting 4–5 times more males than females. Why should such a rare condition be the focus of so much academic attention? The answer probably lies in the intrigue that autistic symptoms create for non-autistic people: the selectivity of disrupted function in a child who outwardly appears to be so normal.

The term autism was used by Bleuler (1911) when referring to the withdrawn behaviour in some cases of schizophrenia. Kanner (1943) adopted the term to describe a group of children who 'have come into the world with innate inability to form the usual, biologically provided affective contact with people' (Kanner, 1943, p. 250). Kanner initially used his own name to label what he saw as an undiscovered disorder, substituting '**early infant autism**' only later. The confusion caused by name changes and the use of the term beyond Bleuler's meaning was exacerbated by autism being labelled as a '**childhood psychosis**' (some authors still do) and its not being differentiated from **childhood schizophrenia** in early classificatory systems. Thus, some early publications have *erroneously* referred to autism as 'childhood schizophrenia', whereas the two disorders are different, e.g. there are no hallucinations or delusions in autism. In 1980 autism was recognized as a distinct disorder in DSM-III and is currently (DSM-IV and ICD-10) listed as a **pervasive developmental disorder**, along with the very similar **Asperger's disorder**. Szatmari (1992) has considered the evidence for an **autistic spectrum disorder** to cover *non-autistic* diagnoses that are within the pervasive developmental disorder category.

Autism is usually diagnosed at 2–3 years of age, although the child has often seemed '*odd*' from birth (Rutter, 1974). For a diagnosis, onset should be before 3 years of age, which may need to be a *retrospective diagnosis* due to the difficulties in making such a serious decision about one so young. Wing and Gould (1979) identified a **triad of impairments** which characterize autism. These are the major areas used for diagnosis. Briefly, the child will show deficits in social interaction, communication and flexible thinking:

▶ **Social interaction.** The child withdraws from social contact and fails to form relationships even in the absence of mental retardation, which is present in 75 per cent of cases. The child is indifferent to others rather than shy and *can* be dangerous in circumstances where they may be indifferent to the suffering of, or harm done to another. They lack the empathic ability to recognize fear or pain in other's faces (see Tantam *et al.*, 1989). In one tragic case, an Asperger boy killed an elderly lady and, when asked why that victim had been chosen, he stated that 'she was old, so it would not matter'. It must be emphasized that such occasions are rare (see Mawson *et al.*, 1985). The autistic infant does not 'engage' when being held, avoids eye contact and does not seek attention. They often form attachments to inanimate objects, which are far removed from the cuddly toy of the normal child, instead items such as bricks or mechanical parts become their 'attachment objects'. Kanner observed an '**extreme autistic aloneness**' in these children, an isolation that extends into adulthood. However, as Tantam (1988) observed, when the older autistic individual *does* show any interest in others, they drastically lack the social skills needed to maintain relatedness. They tend to relate to 'people as objects' rather than as human beings – what have been called 'cat-like' attachments as opposed to the 'dog-like' attachments of non-autistic people (see Hobson, 1986). The autistic individual is usually happiest when alone.

▶ **Communication.** Mutual attention is a basic requirement for communication. The autistic infant avoids *eye contact* and *shared attention*, and usually shows severe deficits in *verbal* and *nonverbal communication development*. Only half of autistic people learn to speak, and those that achieve language use often fail actually to use it, or use it abnormally. Clearly, if the child lacks any interest in others, he or she also lacks any interest in communicating with them. The development of some speech by the age of 5 years signifies a *good prognosis* in terms of autism, but the language they do develop often has unusual features:

– **Echolalia** is the phonologically accurate repeating of sounds, usually speech. This provides a key to other language peculiarities in autism, as the form of echolalia resembles 'digital sampling' of sound. They repeat words and phrases parrot fashion rather than constructing them, with the same intonation and phrasing. In **delayed echolalia** the repetition may occur hours or weeks after the original sound.

– **Pronoun reversal** is common, the autistic individual will refer to themselves as 'he', 'she' or 'you' instead of 'I' or 'me'. This is probably a product of echolalia, i.e. they refer to themselves in the exactly the same way they hear others talk to them.

– **Neologisms** are 'new words' or words with a novel application. In autism this again is related to echolalia in that the new words are often synthesized from others' speech when referring to the thing they have now come to represent, as with 'golead' in the next case study (pp. 111–12).

– **Nonverbal deficits** are evident in their verbalizations as well as their movements. Speech may be monotone, repetitive and will often form a monologue, ignoring the attempts of others to interrupt. They are poor at understanding the nonverbal communications of others (see Tantam *et al.*, 1989).

▶ **Flexible thinking** is restricted in autism, especially in childhood at the time when it is well developed in normal children. This is very evident in play, which requires **second-order thinking** (see Frith *et al.*, 1991) such the use of pretence, e.g. pretending a plate is a hat, for the autistic child it will always be *a plate*. In the same way *jokes*, which require flexible imaginative thought and the use of metaphor, are not understood by the autistic child. They tend to understand things in very literal terms, e.g. the autistic reply to 'take a seat' may be 'take it where?' Leslie (1990) has related this to what he terms their lack of a **theory of mind**, meaning that the autistic child lacks a theory as to what is in another person's mind. Thus they are very poor at *reading people* which is fundamental to social relatedness. Baron-Cohen *et al.* (1985) devised a test for this, the 'Sally doll experiment', in which autistic children demonstrated deficits in comprehending that the understanding of another may differ from their own, when compared with carefully matched controls. Frith *et al.* (1991) see this cognitive deficit as the basis for most of the characteristic features of autism, though some have argued with this (e.g. Tantam, 1992; Hobson, 1990).

In addition to these major deficits, there are other features that are common in autism:

► **Obsessive ritualistic behaviour** which must be adhered to or tantrums may result. The autistic individual may also react with tantrums to any sudden noise, change in their environment or routine. They often have a rigid insistence on sameness, which pervades most aspects of their behaviour, e.g. eating the same foods, at the same time and in the same setting *every day*. This rigidity affects their play, often creating repeated patterns or endless lines of objects such as building bricks, and also their thinking (see above).

► **Mannerisms** such as hand-flapping or walking on their tip-toes are common, as are **stereotypies**, or **self-stimulatory behaviour** (e.g. rubbing) and **self-injurious behaviour** (e.g. head-banging). These activities are socially limiting and can stigmatize the autistic child in public. Thus they seem to have three functions: (1) to increase social avoidance; (2) immediate self-comfort; and (3) compensation for rigid, controlled behaviour and lack of social reward.

► **Objectification**. The autistic individual avoids people and emotion and may gravitate towards a more *mechanical* view of the world. They often reduce human characteristics to objective ones such as describing people in terms of height or weight instead of more personal aspects such as 'sensitive' or 'friendly'.

► **Emotional deficits** have been mentioned, but some professionals see their inability to recognize or relate to emotion as fundamental to autism (see Hobson, 1990).

► **The autistic savant** (once referred to as 'idiot savant') is an autistic individual who displays one or more 'special abilities', which seem out of keeping with the level of functioning of the sufferer. These abilities are a rare 'by-product' of autism which seem to relate to their mechanical, impersonal and obsessive interests. Examples of these are exceptional mathematical abilities, musical performances, meticulous reproduction of complex geometric shapes as artwork or the ability to memorize large lists, e.g. dates, names or numbers. It has been suggested that specialist areas of the brain that fail to be fully developed for language, are utilized for such interests.

CASE STUDY Autism

Charles was a very 'good' baby – he very rarely cried and did not demand attention. His mother thought this may have been some sort of compensation for the painful and complicated birth that heralded his arrival. As Charles grew, his apparent indifference to others became a source of worry to his mother, though his father thought this was just his 'personality' as the father's own brother had been unsociable as a child and quite eccentric as an adult. By the time her friends' babies had been putting two-word phrases together, Charles had not shown any interest in speaking or in his mother's numerous attempts at creating some rapport. Despite having had his hearing tested at a clinic, his mother returned to her GP twice claiming Charles must be deaf, while secretly fearing he might be brain-damaged. Her GP explained that Charles did not react normally to sound but was not deaf. The experienced family doctor became concerned that Charles might be developmentally delayed and that the cause might be neurological, but did not reveal this to the mother, trying to allay her worries. Working on his experience of similar problems, the GP made an appointment with a psychiatrist known for his research into infant disorders – a 'specialist' as he told the mother. Charles's mother was at last satisfied that 'something was being done', but had reservations about attending a psychiatric out-patient unit and occasionally muttered 'but he's too young to be mad', loud enough for his father to hear. After a few follow-up appointments, the decision was made that Charles was autistic and his mother and father were given information on what the disorder was, what to expect and how to cope in practical terms. They were put in touch with a number of organizations that could offer support and advice, and Charles was also placed on a (rather long) waiting list to attend a special day school.

Charles was a very attractive boy with a strange aloofness, always seeming 'distant' when in company. This 'distance' could be literal when they had guests, Charles would enter the room and sit by the door watching the seconds hand of the clock (as he often did) never making eye contact. His mother was thankful that Charles was an exceptional case of autism in not being notably retarded and having gained the use of one or two words by the time he was 5 years old. He rarely used these words, one of which was entirely his own. For Charles, 'golead' was the family dog, possibly a contraction of his father's words *to* the dog, 'Go get your lead!' Charles would stare at his hands for long periods of time but still showed little interest in other children, or others in general. He was never sociable unless he wanted something, and then would stare fixedly at the object without speaking or looking at his mother. For about a year, life became very difficult for Charles's mother as a result of sudden tantrums in public (for reasons known only to Charles), a similar reaction to any change in routine, and a number of odd mannerisms and embarrassing 'comfort motions', as his mother called them. At one point his mother felt she was a prisoner within her own home and his father began to 'work away' more often. A clinical psychologist introduced a number of behavioural measures to moderate these behaviours which were reasonably successful, though his mother felt they went against her 'instincts'. When Charles finally entered special school his tantrums at home worsened, but almost disappeared when his mother fully complied with the school professionals' suggestions.

Charles did not have much interest in girls as a teenager and never had a girlfriend as such. However, he did develop an obsession for a few months, in which he noted down his estimate of bra sizes of girls he saw and kept these records carefully with girth and cup size but no other detail, seeming to use the numbers to identify girls he thought 'important'. The 'hobby' came to an abrupt end when Charles made a sudden attempt to check his estimate physically. It took a letter from his psychiatrist to assure the poor girl that prosecution was not the best course. Since his mother's illness, Charles has lived in a hostel and supplements his keep by putting junk mail in envelopes, slowly folding each one and placing them into neat piles of exactly eleven envelopes.

Aetiology and treatment of autism

Early views of autism could not equate the appearance of these children with their social deficits and so **psychogenic** causes were popular, i.e. the child was assumed to be normal at birth and disturbed by some environmental experience. Parents, particularly mothers, were thought to be 'cold' and 'unresponsive' to the child's needs, and the child withdraws into what Bettelheim (1967) called 'an empty fortress'. However, research has not supported this (e.g. Rutter, 1983), finding that autistic symptoms cannot simply result from social withdrawal and that the parents of autistic individuals do not differ from other parents. It would seem that any parental 'coldness' must *result* from bringing up an unresponsive child and that such theories simply add blame to the worries of already stressed parents. Another psychogenic approach was that of Ferster (1961), who considered that lack of parental attention made the parents 'poor reinforcers' (i.e. a *behavioural* explanation), leading to the behavioural and communication problems in autism. Such an explanation would be limited by the same research undermining Bettelheim's explanation.

The current view of autism is one of a biologically based disorder, although the specific biological mechanism is elusive. Clearly, the problem occurs too early in life to be a result of life-events and is closely associated with mental retardation, which occurs in the majority of cases. Autism is associated with **perinatal complications** (problematic births) (see Gillberg and Gillberg, 1983), which often result in neurological damage and also nervous system disorders such as **encephalitis** can result in autistic-like symptoms. Some prenatal disorders such as **rubella** are associated with higher rates of autism. All these factors suggest that autism results from some form of neurological abnormality, which interferes with normal infant development.

Actual neurological abnormalities found in autism involve a number of brain areas. Bauman and Kemper (1985) have found differences in the **cerebellum** in autism and Jacobson *et al.* (1988) identified increased **third ventricle** size, implying a reduced brain mass (in that region) in autism. As Prior (1987) has stated, the evidence for a neurological basis to autism is very strong, but the findings are diverse and inconsistent. This would suggest that *different abnormalities* may be involved in combining to produce *different forms* of the disorder. Bailey (1993) has reviewed the evidence for a biological basis to autism, and draws attention to that which shows the involvement of the **frontal cortex**. The importance of this brain area in an overall biological explanation of autism is that it may link biological explanations with the cognitive explanations of how the symptoms may arise from such neurological abnormalities.

One such cognitive explanation is the **theory of mind** approach of Frith *et al.* (1991). These authors have suggested that their cognitive explanation has such a neurological abnormality as its cause. Tantam (1992) does not argue with any of these authors regarding the assumed organic basis, but does take issue with the primacy of the lack of 'theory of mind'. In normal children this ability does not develop until after the age when some of the social deficits of autism have become evident (see Tantam *et al.*, 1993). Tantam proposes that a failure to develop the **social gaze response** is a more fundamental disability, leading on to the other deficits *including* that of 'theory of mind'. By social gaze response Tantam means the inherent tendency to focus gaze on social cues and learn to follow the gaze of others, which can develop into the social use of gaze and attention. It may be possible that an even more fundamental deficit in **figure-ground** perception may precipitate the failures of both social gaze response and theory of mind (see Holmes, 1994). The figure-ground distinction is the ability to distinguish a central 'figure' against a background or 'ground', and is one of the earliest cognitive abilities to develop. This probable weakness in development would make it difficult for the autistic infant to distinguish *what was important in the general and social environment*. It is possible that this is what Frith (1989) is considering in describing a deficit in finding 'central coherence', which she has supported by showing that autistic children are less distracted by 'central coherence' in performing on an embedded figure test (Shah and Frith, 1983) (i.e. finding geometric shapes hidden in complex figures), a measure of **'field-dependence'**. A failure of the figure-ground ability is almost *certain* to be neurologically based – again, an explanation of autism based in the area of cognitive neuroscience.

Abnormalities of **neurodevelopment** are likely to be a product of early neural damage or genetically based neural abnormality. The evidence for a genetic contribution to the aetiology of autism is strong, despite the difficulty in determining this in a rare disorder that results in sufferers rarely marrying or having children. There is about a 4 per cent risk of having a second autistic child, as compared to a 0.0003 per cent risk for births in the general population. Evidence from **twin studies** (see Chapter 2) is also convincing. Steffenburg *et al.* (1989) found concordance rates of 91 per cent for monozygotic (identical) twins against 0 per cent for dizygotic (non-identical) twins. An **autosomal recessive inheritance** (a recessive gene on the 'body' or non-sex chromosomes) has been suggested by Smalley (1991) for autism. As the occurrence in identical twins is not 100 percent, there must be other factors involved. However, as mentioned above, there may be different causal mechanisms producing different forms of the disorder. Further along these lines, it has been suggested that different *genetic disorders* contribute to varying forms of autism, i.e. **genetic heterogeneity**. Unfortunately, the diversity of the genetic and other factors clearly implicated in autism does not lend itself to any obvious treatment approach. Indeed, the prospect of reversing neurodevelopmental abnormalities is daunting for even the most optimistic professional.

Other factors that may lead to autistic symptoms have been examined and some have led to experimental treatments. Levels of the neurotransmitter **serotonin** have been found to be high in autism (Freeman and Ritvo, 1984). This has led to attempts to reduce these levels using **fenfluramine**, with some resulting improvement in behaviour and IQ, but these were complicated by the side-effects of the drug. This was also the case when using **neuroleptic** drugs intended to calm the autistic child. **Megavitamin** treatment resulted in very limited and inconsistent improvement.

As with irreversible conditions such as mental retardation (often present in autism), behaviour modification techniques simply target problem behaviours and try to change them, a more practical approach. Autism presents unique difficulties for this approach. Normal individuals respond to basic reinforcers (see Chapter 2) such as food, but can then be 'weaned' on to social reinforcers (e.g. praise) and eventually will perform required acts for the sense of achievement. This is not the case with autistic individuals, who do not find people or social rewards reinforcing. Often the whole process seems unrewarding to the therapist. An example of this is the progressive conditioning of speech production using basic reinforcers to shape attention, sounds, words and then phrases, only to find that the autistic individual has no interest in developing, or even using, their language skill. Behavioural approaches are useful in reducing **challenging behaviour**, such as **self-stimulatory** or **self-injurious behaviour**. Occasionally punishment, such as squirting lemon juice into the mouth, may be required in the case of biting or screaming (part of tantrum behaviour) if other methods fail. The most successful behavioural programmes are intensive, sustained and extend the learning environment to the home and school. Lovaas (1987) reported remarkable global improvements in applying such a scheme for 40 hours a week for over two years, using terms such as **'normalization'** to describe the outcome. The goal of 'mainstreaming' the children so they could further benefit from a normal social and educational environments was mostly achieved. However, this success was *not* a cure and the autistic children chosen for the scheme did not include 'low functioning' cases.

Quill *et al.* (1989) have reported favourably on **'Daily Life Therapy'** (from **Higashi**, Japan) as practised at the Boston Higashi School in Massachusetts. As with the work of Lovaas, this is also an intensive regime but with a focus on

▶ group oriented instruction
▶ highly structured routine activities
▶ instruction centred on learning through imitation
▶ reducing self-stimulatory and self-injurious behaviour by rigorous physical exercise
▶ the use of movement, music and art

In the US, **Martha Welch** has used the term 'cure' in relation to her **holding therapy** for autism. 'Holding' involves the parent forcibly holding the autistic child with eye-to-eye contact, regardless of the child's (often violent) protests. The emotional drama is intense and often frightening to witness, eventually reaching a **'resolution'** when the child will sometimes accept comfort and seem less emotionally distant. There is little empirical research on this approach and it is omitted from most literature. This may be because Welch claims that 'holding' repairs the damaged bond between the autistic child and its immediate carer and through them, other people (see Welch, 1989). The 'neo-Bettelheim' explanation tends to blame the parent and is subject to the same criticisms as the original theory. However, the holding procedure is identical to the behavioural technique of **flooding**, where enforced exposure to a feared stimulus (in this case human social and emotional contact) results in a 'resolution period' when these fears subside. If this is the underlying mechanism and it is effective in some cases of autism, then it is worthy of immediate empirical research.

Autism is both a fascinating and tragic disorder, and almost all aspects could be considered **special issues**. It is true of many disorders that we can understand some of the traits in the normal population by studying these extreme forms. Perhaps our *disproportionate interest* in autism reflects some recognition of the changing human condition in this increasingly impersonal, mechanical and unemotional world.

Asperger syndrome (Asperger's disorder)

Around the time Kanner was describing autism, Hans Asperger (1944) wrote a description of a group of children who had many of the social deficits of autism but differed in significant ways. Many professionals like to think of the **pervasive developmental disorder** of Asperger syndrome as a 'pure form of autism', lacking the severe retardation and language complications, or even 'mild autism' (Wing, 1981). Klin *et al.* (1995) have carried out a neurological assessment of both Asperger individuals and a sample with 'higher-functioning autism', finding distinctions on some tests. Some have considered whether the separate Asperger category should exist at all, as it overlaps considerably with autism and **schizoid personality disorder** (see Kay and Kolvin, 1987), concluding that there are reasons for Asperger's syndrome as an independent classification (see Tantam *et al.*, 1993). For Asperger (1979), the differences between autism and his syndrome were substantial. In order to avoid repetition of the description of autism, the following deals in the similarities and differences between the two disorders only.

The *similarities* between the disorders include:

▶ They use **language** in an inflexible pedantic way, not reciprocating but engaging in monologues, both showing the speech peculiarities described for autism, e.g. pronoun reversal. They have poor nonverbal skills, but tend to 'mimic' well.

▶ **Flexibility of thought** and **imaginative play** is lacking and both are obsessive in wanting sameness in the environment, displaying **stereotyped behaviour** and may be very sensitive to sounds, smells, etc. They show rigid, mechanical, impersonal interests, e.g. astronomy or archaeology, and may have specially developed abilities in their *chosen* interests. They are withdrawn and socially isolated regarding people as objects, and may be indifferent to the emotions of others (see Tantam *et al.*, 1989).

▶ Both disorders show a **male bias, physical clumsiness** and **aggressive, restless behaviour**.

Asperger syndrome *differs* from autism in the following ways:

▶ They develop **language** *early*, in contrast to the delay or absence in autism. Although language use is abnormal, they sometimes seem in advance of normal children in terms of 'adult-type' speech. Asperger syndrome is thought to have a *later onset*, is diagnosed later and has a *better prognosis* than autism.

▶ They *rarely* show the **mental retardation** evident in most cases of autism and have an awkward, 'eccentric' or poorly presented appearance in contrast with the 'inherent attractiveness' attributed to autistic individuals.

▶ They more frequently have **special interests** and develop these, providing they do not involve human intimacy. This applies to the development of motor skills, e.g. if they 'take to' walking at an early age they overtake others in this ability, otherwise it may be delayed in development.

▶ Although they have the indifference to others seen in autism, Asperger individuals are more aware of the presence of other people.

Although Asperger individuals have better developed language and other abilities, the causes are thought to be similar to those of autism and treatment approaches share many of the same limitations.

Chapter summary

Disorders of childhood are confounded by **developmental factors,** with biological and behavioural influences being greater. The child's position in the **family** is also important, as is the **bond** with its nearest carer, and it is better to consider all involved parties rather than just the child. Childhood disorders include **mental retardation, learning, motor skills** and **communication disorders; pervasive developmental disorders,** including **Rett's** and **childhood disintegrative disorders; attention deficit** and **disruptive behaviour disorders,** including **conduct** and **oppositional defiant disorders; feeding** and **eating disorders,** including **pica, rumination disorder** and **child feeding disorder; tic disorders,** including **Tourette's, chronic motor or vocal tic** and **transient tic disorders;** the **elimination disorders** of **encopresis** and **enuresis; separation anxiety disorder; selective mutism; reactive attachment disorder; stereotypic movement disorder.**

Attention deficit hyperactivity disorder (ADHD) is highly disruptive and has been linked to later delinquent behaviour. ADHD responds to both behavioural and drug treatments, though the latter is controversial.

Autism is a pervasive developmental disorder for which there is no cure, although **behaviour modification** has helped to manage the difficult behavioural features. Autistic individuals show severe deficits of **social interaction, communication** and **flexibility of thought.** The latter deficit has been linked to a failure to appreciate the different thinking of others, or a **theory of mind.** They also display **obsessive behaviour, mannerisms** and a **lack of emotion,** but sometimes have special abilities of a **mechanical** type. **Speech** develops only in 50 per cent of cases and then it is abnormal. This feature distinguishes autism from the similar **Asperger's disorder,** in which language develops normally but is used in an abnormal way.

Self-test questions

▶ In what ways do childhood disorders differ from those of adulthood?
▶ Why are pervasive developmental disorders so called?
▶ How can conduct disorder and oppositional defiant disorder be distinguished?
▶ What is involved in pica?

▶ Why is the concept of attachment important in childhood disorders?
▶ How can ADHD be treated?
▶ Which childhood disorders carry a risk of later criminal behaviour?
▶ What is meant by 'autistic savant'?
▶ How does a 'theory of mind' relate to autism?
▶ How does Asperger syndrome differ from autism?

Further reading

Aarons, M. and Gittens, T. (1991) *The Handbook of Autism: A guide for parents & professionals.* London: Routledge.

Bailey, A. (1993) 'The biology of autism (editorial)', *Psychological Medicine,* 23, 7–41.

Barkley, R. (1996) *Taking Charge of ADHD.* New York: Guilford Press.

Baron-Cohen, S., Tager-Flusberg, H. and Cohen, D. (1994) *Understanding Other Minds: Perspectives from autism.* Oxford: Oxford University Press.

Frith, U. (ed.) (1991) *Autism and Asperger Syndrome.* Cambridge: Cambridge University Press.

Gillberg, C. (1995) *Clinical Child Neuropsychiatry.* Cambridge: Cambridge University Press.

Mandel, H. (1997) *Conduct Disorder and Underachievement.* New York: John Wiley.

Murray Parkes, C. and Stevenson-Hinde, J. (1993) *Attachment across the Life Cycle.* London: Routledge.

Rutter, M. (1995) *Psychosocial Disturbances in Young People.* Cambridge: Cambridge University Press.

Seigel, B. (1996) *The World of the Autistic Child.* New York: Oxford University Press.

Tantam, D. (1992) 'Characterising the fundamental social handicap in autism', *Acta Paedopsychiatrica,* 55, 83–91.

Weiner, J. (ed.) (1996) *Diagnosis and Psychopharmacology of Childhood and Adolescent Disorders,* 2nd edition. New York: John Wiley.

Wolf-Schein, E. (1996) 'The autistic spectrum disorder: a current review', *Developmental Disabilities Bulletin,* 24, 33–55.

CHAPTER 6

Personality disorders

In this chapter

▶ General issues in personality disorders
▶ Paranoid, schizoid and schizotypal personality disorders
▶ Antisocial, borderline, histrionic and narcissistic personality disorders
▶ Avoidant, dependent and obsessive-compulsive personality disorders
▶ Development and management of personality disorders

General issues in personality disorders

A **personality disorder** (**PD**) is a maladaptive pattern of behaviour, which begins in *childhood* or *adolescence* and becomes an *enduring* and *salient trait* during adulthood. Bernstein *et al.* (1996) have identified some of the childhood characteristics that seem to predict later PDs, a prediction that was better for girls than boys (Cohen, 1996). This maladaptive trait becomes less influential as middle-age approaches, although it is *resistant* to attempts to change it at any stage of life. In DSM-IV, PDs are located on Axis II, indicating that they are relatively *permanent* disorders which should be considered *in addition* to and diagnosed *separately from* any other mental disorder from Axis I. Unlike the Axis I disorders, PDs are characterized by these **durable traits** rather than transient symptoms or recurrent episodes. Personality disordered individuals may suffer difficulties, but it is usually *others* around them who suffer most from their behaviour. They are common disorders, affecting around 10–13 per cent of the general population (Weissman, 1993).

Students of psychology will be familiar with the **state–trait** debate over the causes of behaviour. **Trait theorists,** who believe that the fixed personality characteristics of the individual predict how they will react in any situation, disagree with **state theorists** (situationalists, e.g. **Walter Mischel**), who consider that people react differently depending on the situation in which they find themselves. With normal individuals *some* traits are carried with the person, but potential for change exists if situations facilitate this.

However, PDs are resistant to change and, when these exaggerated traits enter a situation, the situation changes in a predictable direction – a kind of *self-fulfilling prophecy* of personality which follows the individual through life. Occasionally, they may find employment or relationships that 'suit' their personality distortions and cause less disruption to all. For example, the **obsessive-compulsive** type may adapt to work as a cleaner in a fast-food restaurant, or the **schizoid** personality could be content as a computer operator working in isolation.

There are a number of specific categories of PD, each deriving its name from the prominent trait, which significantly disrupts the individual's occupational and social functioning. Having categories in abnormal psychology creates the illusion that they are clearly differentiated, with definite boundaries between them. However, 'carving nature at the joints' is not a simple matter, and the boundaries in PDs are *far* from clear. Morey (1988) has demonstrated the remarkable *overlap* between the different PDs, with most sufferers qualifying for two or more PD diagnoses at the same time. Many professionals have suggested using a **dimensional system** of diagnosis and classification for PD, giving a score on each of a number of personality traits (e.g. obsessiveness). Current personality research suggests five dimensions, the so-called **five factor model** (for an overview, see Deary and Matthews, 1993). Widiger (1991) believes that if *both* dimensional and categorical methods are used, there would be more information, flexibility and fewer arbitrary decisions involved when applying the existing categories of PD.

Table 6.1 shows the slight differences between the equivalent DSM-IV and ICD-10 PDs. There are more divisions in the DSM-IV system, although there are two subtypes of emotionally unstable PD in ICD-10 (**impulsive** and **borderline**). This leaves no major ICD-10 category for schizotypal PD.

Table 6.1 *DSM-IV and ICD-10 classifications of personality disorders (PD)*

DSM-IV	ICD-10
Paranoid PD	Paranoid PD
Schizoid PD	Schizoid PD
Schizotypal PD	
Antisocial PD	Dissocial PD
Borderline PD	Emotionally unstable PD
Histrionic PD	Histrionic PD
Narcissistic PD	
Avoidant PD	Anxious (avoidant) PD
Dependent PD	Dependent PD
Obsessive-Compulsive PD	Anancastic PD
	Also included with this ICD section are:
	Mixed PD
	Troublesome PD

However, the ICD-10 system *does* provide a category of **schizotypal disorder** in its section for schizophrenic disorders.

There are apparent gender biases among the PDs, with more males being diagnosed as having **antisocial PD** and a predominance of females with **borderline PD**. However, this bias could be seen as an extension of the '**mad-bad**' **debate** (see Chapter 4), with male deviance being seen as 'bad' (antisocial PD is associated with criminal behaviour) and female deviance as 'mad' (borderline PD involves emotional instability), perhaps reflecting an *inherent bias* in the diagnostic and classificatory process. Akhtar (1996) has refuted the notion of a female bias in borderline PD, but confirms the existence of a male bias in antisocial PD.

The DSM-IV PDs are divided into three subgroupings or **clusters**. These share general features, which can also be viewed as **dimensions** of these disorders. The clusters are as follows:

- ▶ **Cluster A** PDs are characterized by *odd* and *eccentric* behaviour and possibly represent mild features of schizophrenia such as paranoia, withdrawal and fanciful thought. However, there are *no* psychotic symptoms, and these individuals are *not* schizophrenic. This cluster includes **paranoid PD, schizoid PD** and **schizotypal PD**.
- ▶ **Cluster B** disorders have *dramatic, attention-seeking, emotional* and *selfish features*, with a tendency towards *reckless* and *impulsive behaviour* in some of these PDs. Individuals with these disorders tend to make others victims of their behaviour, although they can be destructive to themselves. **Antisocial PD** is an important and controversial category here (see also Chapter 4) along with the more restrictive concept of **psychopathy**. The other disorders in this cluster are **borderline PD, histrionic PD** and **narcissistic PD**.
- ▶ **Cluster C** PDs tend to show traits such as *anxiety, apprehensiveness* and *fearfulness* traits and tend to be the *victims of circumstance*. The disorders in this cluster are **avoidant PD, dependent PD** and **obsessive-compulsive PD**.

Paranoid, schizoid and schizotypal personality disorders

Paranoid personality disorder

As its name suggests, this PD has persistent and unjustifiable suspiciousness of others as its central feature and sufferers seem to *anticipate* being exploited and abused. They are very *jealous* and can be prone to the delusional disorder, **morbid jealousy** (or delusional jealousy). This usually proves highly destructive to their sexual relationships, in which they are constantly testing their partners, making unwarranted accusations with the most implausible evidence and often engaging in spy-like activities to 'catch them out'.

This determination to *prove themselves right* and others wrong also leads to viewing themselves as infallible, tending to look down on others or ridicule them in a sarcastic manner and blaming others for their own mistakes. They are argumentative, complaining and competitive in an 'unhealthy' way. Paranoid individuals may work hard to maintain a façade of superiority and the self-esteem that it justifies. They tend to be preoccupied with testing the *loyalty* and *trustworthiness* of other friends and work colleagues. This often leads to their feeling that there may be a conspiracy against them, or that they are the *victims* of discrimination or vindictive campaigns (similar to the ones they try to orchestrate). There is often hostility as a result of their interpreting the actions of others as being *threatening* towards them, e.g. neighbours *deliberately* play loud music to annoy them. Paranoid individuals can bear a grudge for extended periods, rarely forgiving others.

There may be a genetic relationship with schizophrenia, and paranoid behaviour often occurs as part of the **prodromal syndrome** (i.e. behaviour preceding the onset) in schizophrenia. Paranoid PD overlaps with **borderline** and **avoidant PD**.

Schizoid personality disorder

Schizoid individuals are withdrawn and do not seek the company of others. They tend to avoid social events, which make them uncomfortable, and have few close friends, preferring solitary or impersonal pursuits such as computing. They live in an unemotional world, seeming 'cold' and aloof, and have no real desire for sexual experiences, or intimacy of any kind. They are **anhedonic**, that is, they lack pleasure-seeking behaviour and would not understand much of the motivation for a beach holiday.

In contrast to paranoid PD, schizoid individuals seem indifferent to criticism or praise. Their indifference to others extends to their self-presentation, making no concessions to fashion or taste in clothes. They present a 'bland face' to others, being poor at reading or expressing nonverbal information or other social cues (see Tantam *et al.*, 1993; Holmes, 1994).

Schizoid PD overlaps with paranoid, schizotypal and avoidant PD. It also overlaps considerably with **Asperger syndrome,** to the extent that Kay and Kolvin (1987) considered the schizoid label possibly redundant.

Schizotypal personality disorder

Schizotypal PD lies somewhere between normality and schizophrenia and has been thought of as **'attenuated schizophrenia'**. However, schizotypal individuals have *illusions* (e.g. sensing an 'aura') rather than hallucinations, and *odd beliefs* (e.g. the supernatural) and *magical thinking* (e.g. telepathy) rather than the delusions of schizophrenia. They are eccentric, and this extends to their appearance and adds to the overall 'Mystic Meg'- type image they *live* (not act). There are other *mild* versions of schizophrenic symptoms such as unclear or peculiar speech, ideas of reference and some restriction or flattening of emotion.

There are genetic links with schizophrenia (Siever *et al.*, 1990) as well as other biological similarities (e.g. Baron *et al.*, 1984). There are large overlaps with other PDs, i.e. **schizoid, paranoid, avoidant, narcissistic and borderline PDs**.

Antisocial, borderline, histrionic and narcissistic personality disorders

Antisocial personality disorder

Antisocial PD is four times more common in males than females and characterized by a *persistent disregard for the rights and feelings of others*, impulsive behaviour and antisocial acts. The *DSM-IV* criteria for antisocial PD requires a diagnosis of **conduct disorder** before the age of 15 and adult behaviour such as irresponsibility towards self-support and debt, reckless behaviour, lack of empathy or remorse for misdeeds, deceitfulness (e.g. compulsive lying), impulsivity (i.e. a failure to plan ahead), and general irritability and aggression. The majority of prison inmates would qualify as having antisocial PD as it has a close relationship with criminality. In Chapter 4 the criminal context of this PD was identified, along with a description of the minority of antisocial individuals who could be labelled **psychopathic** using more psychological traits (see Hare, 1986) rather than behavioural acts associated with antisocial PD. See Chapter 4, and consider the case study of Andy.

Psychopathic and antisocial individuals tend to be identified among 'caught criminals', but not all are found on the wrong side of the law. Those escaping criminalization may be less aggressive (e.g. homeless drifter), more 'creative' (e.g. unethical experimental scientist), or may use their insensitivity to others to advantage in business, politics or the military.

CASE STUDY ## Psychopathy

Andy was the younger of two brothers. Born at the start of his father's one-year prison sentence, his mother was able to wean him 'in peace'. By the age of two his father would randomly strike Andy when drunk or annoyed with his mother – 'to make a man of him' was his excuse. During his third year, his mother found herself screaming at Andy to make him stop beating the tin drum his father had bought him, but Andy's shrieks of laughter indicated that he enjoyed his mother's shouts as much as the drum. A month later the pet budgie was found floundering on the carpet mortally injured, having paid the ultimate price for failing to 'sing along' with Andy's drum. As soon as he was able, Andy joined in with the neighbourhood 'gang' and although he was the youngest, was soon leading the more disreputable faction in 'adventures'. One 'adventure' consisted of throwing burning newspaper over the rear walls of houses, which eventually led to near-disaster when fire spread from a shed to the rear of a house. The other boys were terrified, but Andy's eyes lit up at the chaos and he looked gleeful when the police and fire services arrived. Although only 7 years old, Andy convincingly lied, placing blame on an older boy and not fearing reprisals. His father beat him anyway, but one week later, Andy was repeating the behaviour and included his own house.

By the time he was 11, Andy had added theft, taking and driving, and truancy to a growing list of wrongdoings, often stealing worthless items for the 'thrill of it'. Although one of the smallest boys in the neighbourhood, he was established as the local bully, and never seemed to experience fear. He expressed interest in becoming a butcher when he grew up, perhaps because the local butcher was the only person who would employ him. During his delivery rounds, he would use his undeniable charm and confidence to con extra money from customers, and occasionally force his attentions on girls as young as 12 who may have answered the door. One girl claimed Andy had raped her and, during his subsequent convincing denial, Andy paused and suddenly admitted guilt, but claimed 'It didn't matter, she was only a girl'. By the age of 30, Andy had spent more time in prison than out and was finally given a ten-year sentence for killing, then sexually assaulting a young girl. When asked why he killed her before having sex, he smiled and replied: 'It would have been illegal otherwise, wouldn't it?' Andy was moved to a special hospital.

Borderline personality disorder

Borderline PD has a close association with **mood disorders,** being characterized by *unstable mood,* with emotional swings from child-like dependence to intense and uncontrolled anger. Although borderline individuals frantically avoid being alone, either through real or imagined abandonment, their unstable relationships are usually short-lived. Their sense of self-identity is disturbed, leaving them uncertain as to what *they* really want in life. They are prone to impulsive *self-damaging behaviour* such as drug abuse (including medication), casual sex, shopping sprees and gambling. Self-harm extends to self-mutilation, **parasuicide** (non-serious attempts) and actual suicide.

Although there is a likely genetic component to borderline PD, it is also associated with physical and sexual abuse in childhood (Ogata *et al.,* 1990). The original name meant 'on the border of schizophrenia', but it has *little* relationship with schizophrenia, and is better thought of as related to mood disorder with which it is frequently comorbid.

Histrionic personality disorder

Individuals with histrionic PD have an overwhelming need to be the focus of attention and engage in overly *dramatic, attention-seeking behaviour.* Theatrical displays of emotion hide the poverty of emotion actually *felt* by these self-centred people, who are attracted to acting and similar professions. They carry their performances into their personal lives, where they fail to 'live' their lives and consequently have impoverished, short-lived relationships, often further undermined by sexual provocativeness and seductiveness, and exacerbated by impulsiveness. Histrionic individuals are easily influenced by others and are preoccupied with *attractiveness* as a very important attribute, often being attractive themselves.

The histrionic individual's concentration on the superficial and child-like attention-seeking suggest some retardation of emotional development. Histrionic PD overlaps with **borderline PD** and has a high rate of comorbidity with **antisocial PD**, with which it may share some causal elements.

Narcissistic personality disorder

As the name suggests, narcissistic PD individuals are highly *self-centred*, having an unrealistically *high opinion of themselves* and their position in life. This view is often tinged with fantasy or what normal people would consider the material of day-dreams and they also believe they can only relate to people with high social status (i.e. how they see themselves). Those with narcissistic PD require constant attention and compliments, but lack genuine empathy for others and thus take advantage of those around them. This is highly destructive to relationships they may have, which also suffer from their *jealousy* and an arrogant sense that they deserve superior treatment.

This disorder has been thought to be on the increase *as a result* of society being more selfish in general and, as with **histrionic PD**, may reflect a failure to grow out of a childish, self-centred way of regarding others.

Avoidant, dependent and obsessive-compulsive personality disorders

Avoidant personality disorder

Avoidant individuals are very *sensitive to criticism* and fearful of causing social embarrassment for themselves. This anxiety leads them to exaggerate the potential difficulties of exposing themselves to public scrutiny in order to avoid such situations. Similar anxieties about rejection lead them to *avoid relationships*, or even the attention of others. In describing this disorder, Theodore Millon (1981) stressed that the avoidance of social relationships was *not* a result of indifference (as in schizoid PD), but as a result of the *anxiety* caused to avoidant individuals by entering into relations with very **low self-esteem**. The belief that they are inferior can make avoidant individuals strive to achieve perfection, in the hope of gaining a 'safe' response.

Avoidant PD overlaps with **borderline** and **dependent PDs**.

Dependent personality disorder

As its name suggests, individuals with this PD are highly *passive* in relations with others, allowing partners to make all decisions and *agreeing* with decisions they know to be wrong. They lack confidence and suffer high degrees of anxiety if they have to request anything of others or initiate any activity. They cling to inappropriate relationships or rapidly rush into them, desperately afraid of being left alone.

Many dependent PD individuals seem to have failed to detach from their childhood bonds and cling to others as substitutes for their lost parental security. Sudden disruption of the maternal bond is thought by some to lead to these behaviours (e.g. Stone, 1993) in a similar manner to Bowlby's concept of **maternal deprivation**.

Obsessive-compulsive personality disorder

Obsessive-compulsive PD is *not* the same as the **anxiety disorder** obsessive-compulsive disorder (see Chapter 10), there are *no* obsessions *or* compulsions in the PD. The main traits in obsessive-compulsive PD include an undue focus on *detail*, sticking to routines and an unnecessary adherence to rules. Such over-control of behaviour is usually self-imposed and coun-terproductive. This overly pedantic approach to life's tasks constantly aims for *perfection*, but this is usually in some minor detail and is very costly to the task as a whole. The attention to detail leads the obsessive individual to find great **difficulty** in *making decisions* and although they prefer work to pleasure (especially males) and seem industrious, their overall performance is poor due to bad time-management. Their lack of 'warmth' and their serious, anhedonic approach to life make them poor partners in relationships, though some find their reliability and predictability reassuring. They also show **rigidity of thought** and attitude and tend to *hoard* objects rather than consume them, especially money.

Many of the obsessive traits are those described by Freud in his writings on the **anal-retentive character** (see Chapter 2). People with obsessive-compulsive PD are also prone to episodes of **obsessive-compulsive disor-der**, the latter being a much rarer condition.

Development and management of personality disorders

This is a weak area of abnormal psychology, with little certainty about the causes of PDs and most treatments being relatively ineffective. Hence the use of the terms 'developmental and management' rather than 'aetiology and treatment'.

Clearly, abnormalities in the behaviour of adults with PDs can be traced back to childhood (Bernstein *et al.*, 1996) and are not usually due to later life-events. This would point to possible genetic predispositions for traits or early disturbances of development, as proposed by the psychodynamic school. There is evidence for inherited traits in many of the PDs and some neurological explanations of how these are expressed have been attempted (see Further Reading). There is some acceptance that disrupted emotional bonds can lead to later personality deficits, such as the many descriptions of '**affectionless psychopathy**' by John Bowlby. However, there have been cases of abrupt personality change, without other deficits, following *neurological damage*. For example, in 1848 Phineas Gage suffered severe damage to his frontal lobes and rapidly developed marked antisocial traits in the absence of other impairments. The extreme nature of the traits and resistance to treatment would suggest a part is played by abnormal neurodevelopment in PD. However, abuse, neglect and inconsistent discipline have all been found to lead to antisocial behaviour in later life. The exact combination of factors in PD is uncertain and may vary between individual PDs.

In addition to a general difficulty in altering behaviour in PD, some PDs are highly *resistant* to treatment approaches, particularly borderline, antisocial and obsessive-compulsive PD. It is difficult to set up a **therapeutic relationship** with a borderline individual, a problem exacerbated by their tendency to change therapist and threats of suicide which often occur during mood disturbance (Isometsa *et al.*, 1996). Failure to learn by mistakes is a common feature of antisocial PD, and antisocial individuals will frequently *manipulate* the therapeutic relationship to their short-term advantage. Some specific approaches can help, such as assertion therapy with dependent PD. Black *et al.* (1996) have found cognitive therapy superior to drug therapy and placebo (no treatment) in changing traits, and cognitive therapy has been found generally useful in managing the more amenable PDs. Given the fact that PDs are lifelong propensities that weaken after middle age, self-sustaining approaches (e.g. cognitive change) are preferred to more short-term remedies (e.g. drug therapy).

There *may* be some 'clustering' of PDs in subgroups of society, in which their traits may be less troublesome, e.g. antisocial individuals in prisons and 'criminal haunts', schizotypal personalities joining 'new age travellers' and even schizoid individuals 'gathered in isolation' within computer-based companies. However, a word of warning to students of abnormal psychology: the '**medical student syndrome**' refers to the tendency for students falsely to believe they have many of the disorders they study – a kind of *academic hypochondriasis*. Although PDs are relatively common, they do represent *extreme* traits, and although you may be a little obsessive or jealous, it is unlikely that this debilitates you to the degree of qualifying as a disorder.

Chapter summary

Personality disorders (PDs) are characterized by **persistent exaggerated personality traits**, which can be traced to childhood or adolescence, but weaken in middle age. There are three groups or **clusters** of these disorders in DSM-IV. **Cluster A** PDs are characterized by odd and eccentric behaviour and possibly represent mild features of schizophrenia such as paranoia, withdrawal and fanciful thought. However, there are *no* psychotic symptoms and these individuals are *not* schizophrenic. This cluster includes **paranoid PD, schizoid PD** and **schizotypal PD**. **Cluster B** disorders have dramatic, attention-seeking, emotional and selfish features, with a tendency towards reckless and impulsive behaviour in some of these PDs. Individuals with these disorders tend to make others victims of their behaviour, although they can be destructive to themselves. **Antisocial PD** is an important and controversial category here (as outlined in Chapter 4) with the more restrictive concept of **psychopathy**. The other disorders in this cluster are **borderline PD, histrionic PD** and **narcissistic PD. Cluster C** PDs tend to show traits such as anxiety, apprehensiveness and fearfulness traits and tend to be the victims of circumstance. The disorders in this cluster are **avoidant PD, dependent PD** and **obsessive-compulsive PD**. The development of PDs seems to involve genetic, neurodevelopmental, and early attachment and learning experiences, but their durability and other features make single explanations difficult. Management is troublesome, although **cognitive therapy** is useful in less 'resistant' PDs.

Self-test questions

► What is meant by the personality-situation debate?
► Are individual personality disorders clearly distinguished?
► Contrast the categorical and dimensional approaches to personality disorders.
► What distinguishes the three clusters of personality disorders?
► What key features distinguish schizoid and schizotypal personality disorders?
► How does psychopathy differ from antisocial personality disorder?
► Why are obsessive-compulsive personality disorder and obsessive-compulsive disorder different?
► Give reasons for the difficulty in treating personality disorders.

Further reading

Bernstein, D., Cohen, P., Skodol, A., Bezirganian, S. *et al.* (1996) 'Childhood antecedents of adolescent personality disorders', *American Journal of Psychiatry*, **153**, 907–13.

Blackburn, R. (1988) 'On moral judgements and personality disorders. The myth of psychopathic personality revisited', *British Journal of Psychiatry*, **153**, 505–12.

Clarkin, J. and Lenzenweger, M. (1996) *Major Theories of Personality Disorder*. New York: Guilford Press.

Cleckley, H. (1976) *The Mask of Sanity.* St Louis: C.V. Mosby.

Deary, I. and Matthews, G. (1993) 'Personality traits are alive and well', *The Psychologist*, July, 299–311.

Derksen, J. (1995) *Personality Disorders: Clinical and social perspectives.* Chichester: John Wiley.

Dowson, J. and Grounds, A. (1995) *Personality Disorders: Recognition and clinical management.* Cambridge: Cambridge University Press.

Millon, T. and Davis, R. (1996) *Disorders of Personality: DSM-IV and beyond.* New York: John Wiley.

Paris, J. (1996) *Social Factors in Personality Disorders.* Cambridge: Cambridge University Press.

Raine, A., Lencz, T. and Mednick, S. (1995) *Schizotypal Personality.* Cambridge: Cambridge University Press.

Stein, G. (1992) 'Drug treatments of the personality disorders', *British Journal of Psychiatry*, **161**, 167–84.

CHAPTER 7

Sexual and gender identity disorders

In this chapter

▶ General issues in sexual and gender identity disorders
▶ Sexual dysfunctions
▶ The paraphilias
▶ Gender identity disorder
▶ Aetiology and treatment of sexual disorders

General issues in sexual and gender identity disorders

In 1938, **Alfred Kinsey** looked in vain for information on sexual activity to aid his teaching about marriage. Kinsey was thus motivated to produce extensive survey information on the various sexual activities of the public (Kinsey *et al.*, 1948; 1953), who were in turn shocked by the extent of the diversity revealed. This was a time when 'normal sexual behaviour' was for procreation not for recreation, and homosexuality was considered a disorder requiring treatment. With little idea of what was 'normal', even professionals were unsure of what constituted a disorder. In addition, individuals with sexual difficulties felt a great deal of embarrassment and shame in asking for help.

By the 1960s sexual knowledge had increased, sexual liberty was seen as a *right*, assisted by the arrival of oral contraception. Masters and Johnson (1966; 1970) produced observation data on sexual activity and disorder, which began to be widely disseminated in popular magazines. The public became less inhibited about seeking advice and sought treatment to increase **sexual enjoyment**. By the 1990s, **rationality** had replaced both the repression and enthusiasm of former years. The advent of AIDS inhibited promiscuity and limited resources began to restrict treatment to that which **causes distress** or **suffering**. This latter criterion reduces the need to define explicitly what is normal from the vast range of sexual behaviours, but creates legal problems over the issue of **consent** in sado-masochistic, paedophilic and incestuous acts. Potts and Bhugra (1995) have argued that the current diagnostic systems, ICD-10 and DSM-IV, both fail to demarcate clearly between normal and abnormal behaviour in their coverage of sexual disorders.

Sexual disorders are classified by DSM-IV into three main groups: **sexual dysfunctions, paraphilias** and **gender identity disorders**.

Sexual dysfunctions

Most sexual dysfunctions are **hypophilias,** i.e. *less* than normal sexual activity. **Hyperphilias** (more than normal sexual activity) receive far less interest, although they can be damaging to relationships if the partner does not enjoy the level of activity. Apart from the disorder classifications themselves, sexual dysfunctions are divided in other ways, as follows:

▶ **Primary** dysfunctions have *always* affected the sufferer, whereas
   secondary dysfunctions are problems that have only developed
   recently.
▶ A **complete** dysfunction is one that occurs in all situations, with
   partial dysfunction only pertaining to *some* situations, e.g. a man may
   only have erectile failure when having an affair.
▶ **Males** and **females** may suffer the same problems, but clearly other
   dysfunctions are sex-specific, e.g. erectile disorder.
▶ The **stages** or phases of the sexual act are often used to subdivide the
   disorders, i.e. the **desire, arousal** and **orgasm phases,** in addition to
   more general problems, i.e. **sexual pain.**

In addition to these, it is *very important* to identify dysfunctions that arise directly from the consequences of medical conditions, substance use or the natural process of ageing, *before* assuming other aetiologies. The specific sexual dysfunction disorders, by sexual stage, are as follows:

▶ **Desire dysfunctions.** This sexual phase is the initial interest in
   having sex, not simply caring for a partner, but actually wanting to
   become erotically aroused, initiate or accept a sexual advance. The
   two disorders listed for this phase *must cause significant distress to be
   diagnosed as disorders* and can apply to males and females.
   – **Hypoactive sexual desire disorder** indicates an absence of desire
     for, or very little interest in, sexual activity. This also applies to
     fantasy situations and it may be important to know if the lack of
     desire is restricted to one partner. As with most disorders, it is not
     diagnosed if the lack of desire is the product of drug or alcohol use
     or some other known medical condition.

- **Sexual aversion disorder** indicates *active avoidance* of sexual contact. The individual has an *aversion* to genital contact, rather than a lack of interest in having sex.
▶ **Arousal dysfunctions**. Physiological changes prepare both males and females for sexual activity, some of which are similar (e.g. vasocongestion) and others are sex-specific (e.g. vaginal lubrication). The *paradox* of the sexual act relates to the need for *both* arousal *and* relaxation (i.e. *opposing* **sympathetic** and **parasympathetic ANS** activity), oddly enough sexual *arousal* (e.g. penile erection) requires a level of *relaxation*. For whatever cause, failure of these reactions can have severe psychological effects on esteem and future behaviour.
  - **Female sexual arousal disorder** concerns the failure to become physically aroused (i.e. blood flow to the pelvic area, vaginal lubrication and the vaginal and clitoral expansion), or for this arousal to dissipate before the end of the sex act. Historically, this disorder has received little research as it is **'non-fatal'**, i.e. it does not *prevent* intercourse and procreation. Fortunately, such disregard for the female's enjoyment is disappearing.
  - **Male erectile disorder** is a common source of complaint, involving the failure to achieve or maintain a sufficiently erect penis to complete the sex act. Different degrees of dysfunction can indicate differing causes from a vast range of factors, ranging from previous failure, inability to relax or guilt, to a wide range of medical conditions, all exacerbated by the 'fatal' outcome, i.e. intercourse and procreation are prevented.
▶ **Orgasm dysfunctions**. A failure to achieve a sexual orgasm or an unreasonable delay in this affects both males and females. Again there has been a research bias as a result of past 'procreationist views', i.e. failure of a female to orgasm did not prevent conception.
  - **Female orgasmic disorder** is a common complaint and could clearly be linked to male premature ejaculation. About 15 per cent of females have always been **anorgasmic**, i.e. never have orgasms, and this tends to become a lifelong condition. In many cases, education as to *how* to achieve orgasm is needed (**vibrators** have helped here) as well as discouraging the female from being passive with regard to her orgasmic needs.
  - **Male orgasmic disorder** is the absence of, or greatly retarded, ejaculation. The male's efforts (which often become pleasureless and 'mechanical' during the act) can be painful to the female and distressing if orgasm is easily reached by non-vaginal means.
  - **Premature ejaculation** is the male's inability to delay orgasm for a 'reasonable period' *after* vaginal penetration. What is reasonable is up to the individual couple, with most surveys producing population averages of around 2 minutes (note this includes *all* occasions). As

with female orgasmic disorder, education helps, but there are also techniques, e.g. the **'squeeze technique'** (firmly squeezing the base of the penis several times early in intercourse).

▶ **Dysfunctional sexual pain.** Pain or severe discomfort associated with the sexual act can lead to *sexual avoidance* by classical conditioning (see Chapter 2).

– **Dyspareunia** is genital pain of variable intensity associated with intercourse in males or females.

– **Vaginismus** is the involuntary contraction of the outer perineal muscles of the vagina. This occurs when penetration is attempted and may prevent the insertion of objects such as tampons as well as sexual penetration, which may be attempted with painful results. Progressive insertion and acceptance of objects of increasing size while relaxing can help to reduce this spasm.

The paraphilias

Paraphilia (literally 'preference for that beyond') is taken to mean sexual desire for that which is inappropriate, replacing the term 'sexual deviation'. 'Inappropriate' desire is usually directed at non-human objects, suffering, humiliation or children. These sexual targets are usually necessary for arousal or are the preferred targets of sexual activity, either in life or fantasy. These preferences range from the bizarre, such as being aroused by sneezing (King, 1990), to the unacceptable, such as the sadistic and forceful use of children. The vast range of paraphilic targets cannot be fully represented by the disorder classifications in this section, which tend to reflect traditional categories. Most *prostitutes* are familiar with at least some of these paraphilias and will indulge their clients within limits.

Many of these activities have been *criminalized*, which few would argue with, but unfortunately this has often exacerbated the paraphilia and made treatment difficult. Further to this people with paraphilias tend *not* to seek treatment, partly through embarrassment, but in many cases because they do not want to change their behaviour. For example, surveys have revealed that only 15 per cent of sadomasochists wanted to be rid of their problem and 76 per cent of transvestites had never sought advice. Arousal may be gained by *actual or fantasized* paraphilic activity, which usually begins in adolescence (with signs in childhood) and declines with old age. The main classifications of paraphilias are as follows.

▶ **Exhibitionism** involves the exposure of the genitals to a non-consenting other, almost always a stranger, often while masturbating. **Anonymity** and the ability to shock are key factors for the exhibitionist, who *rarely* pursues the interaction further. Although the least potentially harmful of all paraphilics, exhibitionists are the most likely to be criminally prosecuted as they are easily caught. Some have speculated that they have a desire to be caught. They are usually male, but this may be due to the acceptability of female exposure (e.g. exotic dancers).

▶ **Fetishism** is the use of inanimate objects during sex, or as a substitute for a sexual partner. Often orgasm is not achievable without the fetish object, e.g. ladies' underwear. Fetishism overlaps with **sadomasochism** and **transvestism**, but cross-dressing only should not be considered a fetish. Also many non-disordered individuals adopt the symbolic appearance associated with these disorders, but purely as a fashion statement and should not be confused with behavioural fetishism (Snowden, 1996). Rubber is a very common fetish material, leading to the *Mackintosh Society* for enthusiasts.

▶ **Frotteurism** is the rubbing of body parts (genitals or hands against buttocks, genitals or breasts) against non-consenting strangers, usually in crowded places such as lifts or public transport. Although the frotteurist may fantasize about having a relationship with their victim, *anonymity* is usually maintained. Acts of frotteurism are not always disapproved of by the victim. Curious observations have been made by Stern and Stern (1981) of anonymous sexual acts, including intercourse, on public buses in the old Soviet Union. This breaks the 'non-consenting' aspect of the definition of frotteurism, but a tacit agreement to anonymity between these participants was also reported by the authors.

▶ **Paedophilia** covers a spectrum of behaviours. In DSM-IV it is given as sexual acts with a pre-pubescent child by an individual who should be 16 years old and at least 5 years older than the victim (there is flexibility in these ages to cover young paedophiles). However, the blanket term covers behaviour ranging from the coercive fondling of a child, who is not disturbed by the act (*at the time*), to forceful, repeated intercourse, and sadistic acts, with intimidation. The latter would be better distinguished as '**sexually sadistic paedophilia**', but as no child of this age can be considered to give 'consent', in law and psychiatry all cases must be assumed to be by 'force'. Sub-classifications of paedophilia are concerned with whether the individual is attracted to children only, preferred gender(s) of the victim and if the act is also one of **incest**.

▶ **Sexual masochism** is to seek *suffering*, such as humiliation, restraint or violence, as part of sexual gratification. The name is derived from **Leopold von Sacher-Masoch (1835–95)** who wrote about sex acts involving pain, including *Venus in Furs*. One particularly dangerous form is the **autoerotic** practice of self-strangulation or suffocation (**hypoxyphilia**), which may result in death as the masochist has no one to come to their rescue.

▶ **Sexual sadism** is complementary to the above in that the sexual sadist seeks to *inflict suffering* or humiliation on their partner or victim, and thus takes a dominant role to the masochists subservient sexual role. This term is also derived from a writer, **Donatien-Alphonse-François de Sade (1740–1814)**, who wrote about **and performed** acts of sexual sadism on women and children. Although sadism with non-consenting partners can result in **rape** or **sexual homicide**, consenting partner activity can occasionally result in tragedy, especially where **restraint** is involved (it is thus unwise to let *anyone* put you in *total* restraint). **Sadomasochistic** relationships are thought to be a gross exaggeration of the dominant–subservient male–female sexual roles from human history and the biting, pinching and slapping of sex play may represent the acceptable elements of sado-masochistic activity.

▶ **Transvestic fetishism** is gaining primary sexual pleasure from, or during **cross-dressing**, usually males dressing as females. The males in this case are usually of heterosexual orientation, but if the behaviour leads to a gender identity disorder (i.e. transsexual behaviour) then the subtype 'with **gender dysphoria**' may be diagnosed.

▶ **Voyeurism** is gaining sexual pleasure from the secret watching of other people who are in states of undress or engaging in sexual acts. This is usually an anonymous activity, with no contact being sought with the victim, except in fantasy.

Fetishism

Paul's relationship with his wife Ann had become strained and Ann had convinced him to join her on a visit to a counsellor. Neither was forthcoming about what their 'bedroom problem' was, other than that Paul preferred Ann to keep most of her clothes on, and she wanted children but Paul wanted 'something else'. On the counsellor's recommendation Ann saw a sex therapist on her own. During the meeting Ann burst into tears confessing her worst fears that Paul did not love her, but seemed to prefer her underwear and had discovered boxes of old stockings and tights in the garage, some of which were clearly not her own.

The therapist managed to interview Paul on his own, but only after Ann had threatened to leave the marriage. At first Paul claimed he was frightened to have children. However, when faced with the 'evidence', confessed to being sexually aroused only by nylon hosiery, preferably tights, and that this had gone back as far as he could remember to early masturbation experiences. He even remembered running around in his mother's stockinged legs as a child, while she served in a shop. Paul agreed to undergo some sexual reorientation therapy, which included talking through his difficulties, relaxing with Ann *without* her wearing underwear, and aversion therapy for tights. In time, Paul responded well to sexual relations with Ann, but still had an uneasy relationship with underwear, occasionally crossing the road to avoid lingerie shops.

Gender identity disorder

Individuals with a persistent conviction that they should be of the **opposite gender** and feel significant discomfort with their assigned sex, in the *absence* of physiological factors (e.g. hormonal disorders), qualify as being gender identity disordered. Although explanations of this disorder include reinforcement of sex-inappropriate behaviour in childhood, some biological disposition or imbalance may underpin this. Gender inappropriate behaviour should be apparent from an early age, excluding that *encouraged* as a result of 'modern sex-role modelling'. For example, the male child will always adopt and identify with female roles in play. Initial treatment may consist of cross-sex **hormone treatment**. If the condition causes sufficient distress, the label **transsexualism** may be used and **sex-reassignment surgery** considered once the respective legal age is attained. This is a drastic procedure in which the current sex genitalia are removed and those of the opposite sex fashioned, within the limits of surgical technology, supplemented with hormone therapy. The final result often disappoints those who have the unrealistic expectation of *becoming* the opposite gender. Applicants are thus rigorously tested for their conviction and realistic view of the outcome.

Ego-dystonic homosexuality (unwanted homosexuality) is a disorder in the catch-all category **gender disorders not otherwise specified**. Although ego-syntonic homosexuality (i.e. homosexuality the ego is content with) is *not* considered a disorder, sexuality of **any orientation** that causes sufficient distress can be considered a sexual disorder.

Aetiology and treatment of sexual disorders

The causes of sexual disorders are chiefly faulty learning experiences often with biological abnormalities as a catalyst, although Kinzl *et al.* (1995) draw attention to family dysfunction as well as sexual abuse in childhood in the aetiology of sexual disorders. Some sexual disorders are exclusively a result of biological factors or secondary to other disorders (e.g. **diabetes** or **depression**) and should be diagnosed as such. Individuals with paraphilias are thought to have neurological abnormalities which predispose them to early erotic attachments during infancy or childhood, or their earliest sexual experiences are associated, in a classical conditioning sense, to bizarre stimuli.

Many sexual dysfunctions are a result of anxiety and may be treated as anxiety disorders. **Cognitive-behavioural therapy** is most successful here, especially when the disorder results from a 'self-fulfilling prophecy' following a previous failure.

One explanation sees **female orgasmic disorder** as not being a true disorder but a product of evolution (see Cole and Dryden, 1988). Females of a number of species have the clitoral 'equipment' and can be stimulated to orgasm, but this *rarely* (if ever) happens during intercourse as it is usually too brief. In humans 50 per cent of females have orgasmic problems, but only a minority of females see orgasm as important in sex, seeing it secondary to intimacy or penetration. One answer to the female orgasm falling into evolutionary disuse is that not experiencing orgasm places the female in *control* of exactly *who* she may conceive by and *when* she may conceive. This is an extension of the **sperm wars** view of natural selection, which assumes that females are *subconsciously* seeking the best 'material' for their offspring.

Sexual disorders demonstrate almost the complete range of therapies available, and in many cases a number of therapies are applied in treating the same disorder. Clients are usually carefully assessed first, with initial examinations to eliminate biological abnormalities or diseases, and alcohol or drug complications (often the result of **self-medication** for anxiety). Fedoroff (1991) has emphasized the importance of taking a sexual history for these and other disorders. It may be important (especially with paraphilias) to measure sexual arousal to varying stimuli, which is achieved by using a **penile strain gauge** for males and **thermisters** (vaginal temperature) or **photoplethysmography** (measuring vaginal opacity, i.e. blood engorgement) in females. An appropriate therapy may then be indicated. The following are only a selection from the wide range of therapies appropriate to sexual disorders.

▶ **Biomedical therapies** are on the increase (Rosen and Leiblum, 1995) and include:
  – **Surgery** to correct physical abnormalities, surgical implants (e.g. for erectile problems), sex reassignment surgery and castration (for paraphilias).
  – **Drug therapy** can be for anxiety, to produce erections and the various hormone therapies including those for paraphilic offenders (e.g. **medroxy-progesterone acetate** or MDA).
  – **Mechanical devices** such as vibrators and vacuum tubes for arousal dysfunctions.
▶ **Cognitive-behavioural therapies** are highly effective for dysfunctions, but often have different titles. In their **conjoint therapy,** Masters and Johnson (1970) dealt with couples, attempting to take their client's attention away from their dysfunction and instead focus on their relationship. Their **sensate focus** technique removed the anxieties producing dysfunction and refocused their attention on the giving and receiving of pleasurable *sensation* with one another. This involved *banning* intercourse, thereby removing the fear of failure, its anxieties and also making intercourse 'forbidden', therefore attractive. The couple are then given non-genital touching exercises (i.e. while relaxed), which become more erotic over the weeks until they 'break the ban', often cured of their problems. Clearly this is **systematic desensitization** (see Chapter 2) with added cognitive and educational instructions.

► **Surrogate partners** are a controversial, but effective means of treating *individuals*. Trained therapists (often ex-patients or their partners) engage in progressive sexual activity with clients, while educating and instructing. Thus the client is freed from performance anxiety or fear of failure, this being a relative stranger (see Cole, 1982). **Thomas Szasz** has criticized this as being little more than prostitution. However, better prostitutes have often provided this therapeutic function for many years, either knowledgeably or inadvertently.

► **Helen Kaplan** has used a psychodynamic approach to dysfunctions with some success for a number of years, producing a number of variations and combinations of techniques (e.g. Kaplan, 1983).

► **Aversion therapy** is still an effective treatment for paraphilias, providing it is combined with skill creation and the *encouragement* of more normal sexual activity. The association of the paraphilic object with noxious stimuli, either *in vivo* (nausea-inducing drugs, shock or pungent smells) or cognitively (imagining discovery or the consequences of their actions), produces aversion. There are many variations on these techniques which are useful for offenders such as paedophiles, who are willing to participate. For example, in **masturbatory satiation** the client masturbates to orgasm with a *non-deviant* fantasy, then attempts to masturbate to their deviant fantasy, and is frustrated, unable to orgasm. Thus, satisfaction comes to be associated with normal images and discomfort with deviance.

Some sexual disorders are particularly difficult to treat, such as paedophilia, but are better treated than ignored in prison, where decaying social skills may worsen their deviance. The benefits of the successful treatment of dysfunctions can also have positive effects on personal relationships, occupational functioning and self-esteem in general.

Chapter summary

Sexual disorders have only recently been considered for therapy as a result of ignorance and embarrassment. They are now split into three broad groups, **sexual dysfunctions, paraphilias** and **gender identity disorders**. Sexual dysfunctions are failures in the process of intercourse. At the desire stage there is **hypoactive sexual desire disorder** and **sexual aversion disorder** affecting both males and females, and at the arousal stage, **female sexual arousal disorder** and **male erectile disorder**. Dysfunctions of the orgasm phase are **female and male orgasmic disorders**, and **premature ejaculation** in the male. **Dyspareunia** is sexual genital pain and **vaginismus** is a spasm of the vaginal muscles which causes pain and may prevent penetration. The paraphilias are sexual responses to preferred but inappropriate stimuli including **exhibitionism, fetishism, frotteurism, paedophilia, masochism, sadism, transvestism** and **voyeurism,** many of which are criminalized and may be treated with **aversion therapy. Gender identity disorder** is the belief that one should be of the other sex, but treatment with hormones and transsexual surgery has a limited outcome. **Biological** and **behavioural** causes for most of these disorders result in treatments from the same paradigms. Some sexual therapies have specialized terminology, such as **sensate focus therapy,** but these have a cognitive-behavioural basis.

Self-test questions

▶ What problems existed for sex research in the 1930s?
▶ In what ways are sexual dysfunction disorders subdivided?
▶ What are the phases of sexual intercourse used to group its dysfunctions?
▶ How does male and female sexual arousal fail?
▶ Why is frotteurism a paraphilia?
▶ What is the relationship between the paraphilias and sex offenders?
▶ Can gender identity disorder be successfully treated?

Further reading

Bancroft, J. (1989) *Human Sexuality and its Problems.* Edinburgh: Churchill Livingstone.

Cole, M. (1985) 'Sex therapy: a critical appraisal', *British Journal of Psychiatry,* **147,** 337–51.

Cole, M. and Dryden, W. (1988) *Sex Therapy in Britain.* Milton Keynes: Open University Press.

Eskapa, R. (1987) *Bizarre Sex.* Glasgow: Grafton Books.

Howitt, D. (1995) *Paedophiles and Sexual Offences against Children.* London: John Wiley.

Kaplan, H. (1995) *Sexual Desire Disorders.* New York: Brunner/Mazel.

Masters, W., Johnson, V. and Kolodny, R. (1986) *Masters and Johnson on Sex and Human Loving.* London: Macmillan.

Rosen, I. (1996) *Sexual Deviation,* 3rd edition. Oxford: Oxford University Press.

Spence, S. (1991) *Psychosexual Therapy: A cognitive-behavioural approach.* London: Chapman & Hall.

CHAPTER 8

Substance-related disorders

In this chapter

▶ General issues in substance-related disorders
▶ Alcohol- and nicotine-related disorders
▶ Other substance-related disorders
▶ Issues in the aetiology and treatment of substance-related disorders

General issues in substance-related disorders

There is a great deal of ignorance, hypocrisy and misinformation surrounding the problem of substance misuse and this is further complicated by issues of legality. Whenever a substance enters the body it is broken down, some is absorbed and when metabolized it may affect our mental state, i.e. is **psychoactive**. Humanity has been quick to identify the most psychoactive substances, especially if the effect is pleasant. Even if the effect is less than pleasant, it offers a change of state which can be seen as a 'mental holiday' or escape from boredom.

With repetition, the body learns to **tolerate** some psychoactive substances, i.e. compensate for its presence. This means that larger doses will be required to produce the same psychological effect and abstinence will leave the body still physically compensating for some time, i.e. **withdrawal effects**, which can be avoided by continued use. Thus, **physical dependence** is a process of taking sufficient to avoid withdrawal symptoms (a **maintenance dose**) and **psychological dependence** is the anticipation of the mental change or 'high' (which would require *more* than the maintenance dose at this stage). Where dependence is detrimental to adequate functioning the label **addiction** is appropriate. The term **substance abuse** refers to taking an amount which will produce a *substantial change* in mental state, usually beyond any 'normal' dose (i.e. a 'binge'). This sporadic behaviour does not usually involve dependence, just an inability to moderate intake once started.

So far the reader will have probably formed a picture of a heroin addict or perhaps someone on a drinking binge. In order to counter these stereotypes, it may be useful to consider one of the most commonly abused substances to illustrate some of these processes: food. This is not a trivial example. The three most medically damaging substances of abuse are **tobacco, alcohol** and **food,** in that order. The deaths or serious illness resulting from *all* the rest of the substances, including all illicit drugs, would seem *negligible* in comparison to those directly resulting from tobacco, alcohol and food abuse.

Most classification systems have **obesity** (related to overeating or binge eating), **anorexia** and **bulimia** under **eating disorders**, but it may be enlightening to consider them in the context of food abuse. Though influenced by other factors, obesity is usually taken to be a medically dangerous form of overweight resulting from excessive eating, with a prevalence of around 50 per cent in some developed countries. Such individuals are addicted to high levels of food intake, in order to feel physically 'full' and mentally less anxious or relaxed. In seeking psychological comfort from food they may target **simple carbohydrates,** especially chocolate. The pain of feeling 'empty' and agitated *as well* as experiencing natural hunger, makes it difficult to moderate intake or to diet, leaving a destructive cycle of inactivity and increased intake. In anorexia there is *overcontrol* of the eating impulse and the reverse physical consequences to the above begin a destructive cycle in the opposite direction, i.e. overactivity, reduction in digestive capacity and reduced food intake, *in addition* to any psychological motivation for starting the cycle. In bulimia food is abused in *high-calorie binges,* after which the sufferers **purge** (vomiting or use of laxatives) themselves to avoid weight gain and causing physical damage as a result (e.g. from digestive acid). At the physical level, each of these disorders involves the abuse of food in addictive behaviour cycles. Some research is also beginning to establish links between eating disorders and substance disorders (Grilo *et al.,* 1995).

Clearly, food is not dangerous within the limits of normal intake and this may be partly true of a number of substances, but this raises the issues of **toxicity, purity** and **collateral damage.** Our bodies are built to deal with reasonable levels of toxins, indeed if we had 'purified intakes' we may become hypersensitive to impurities, similar to lacking immunity to disease. However, some substances have an unknown toxicity (e.g. **designer drugs**), some have impurities which cause widespread damage (e.g. smoking to obtain nicotine), others are so pure as to be easily overdosed (e.g. pure heroin). For example, **cannabis** has a pronounced psychological effect, but very low toxicity (it is almost impossible to have a lethal dose), little if any potential for physical addiction and has been used for thousands of years, so its long-term effects are documented. However, when mixed with tobacco and smoked, it takes on all the (considerable) risks of smoking and introduces the user to nicotine addiction. Cannabis use may also introduce the user to another risk: it is illegal.

An important issue in substance use is the fact that in most countries a wide range of substances are *illegal* and this exposes the user to further problems. Failure of a 'user–dealer' contact (who usually has little other contact with crime) may bring the user into contact with criminals, for whom drugs are just *another* source of criminal income. Such individuals prefer to sell profitable, addictive substances (e.g. heroin or crack cocaine) and will 'convert' customers from bulky, easily detected, unprofitable, non-addictive substances (e.g. cannabis). The user may even be drawn into other criminal activity, and is liable to blackmail if they hold a vulnerable position in society. Thus the user's social and occupational functioning can be undermined by many factors beyond the simple drug-use cycle, including possible arrest for possession and consequent **criminalization**. In England the **Misuse of Drugs Act 1971** divides illicit substances into **class A, B and C drugs**, A carrying the highest penalty. Conviction does *not* lead to treatment orders, but usually *imprisonment*, which often exacerbates the problem. The prevalence of drug use in prison is very high due to the boredom inherent in secure confinement and it has often been easier to maintain discipline by allowing a level of 'self-medication' among prisoners. However, recent measures such as **urine-testing** have led to unrest in prisons and a move from easily detectable drugs such as cannabis to less detectable ones such as heroin.

Thus there are many arguments for **decriminalizing drugs**, especially the less medically dangerous substances. This would remove the criminal link between 'soft' and 'hard' drugs preventing 'progression'. It would also consider drug use as a medical treatment issue, not a criminally punishable issue and could drastically cut levels of crime and its cost, and remove the drug income to organized crime. Arguments against tend to rely on the need to punish and control users, and often play on unrealistic fears of 'the spectre of mass drug use'. More rational arguments against legalization centre on the need for forceful control when dealing with addictive substance use and the loss of market control and profit for the legal drug producers (i.e. medicines and alcohol), although *any* reduction in alcohol use will reduce crime. Some societies (e.g. parts of the Netherlands) are experimenting with partial decriminalization and have seen some long-term signs of success. **Designer drugs** have taken advantage of the slow and specific nature of the law by designing drugs to be similar enough to existing psychoactive substances to have an effect, but sufficiently different as to escape the letter of the law. These drugs can be very dangerous, as they are new, untested and their long-term effects are unknown.

There are many types of abused substances, both legal and illegal, and their characteristics vary vastly. They can be roughly grouped by their effects on the nervous system into: **CNS depressants** such as alcohol, opioids (e.g. heroin), barbiturates and benzodiazepines (e.g. Valium), which *reduce* inhibitions, control and sophisticated thought; **CNS stimulants** such as amphetamine, caffeine, cocaine, nicotine, cannabis, methylenedioxymethamphetamine (MDMA or ecstasy), d-lysergic acid diethylamide (LSD), phencyclidine (PCP or angel dust) and psilocybin (from 'magic mushrooms'), which increase inhibitions, vigilance, controlled action and thought. Many stimulants *also* have **hallucinogenic** properties, e.g. LSD, cannabis, MDMA and psilocybin, producing intense or distorted perceptions, hallucinations, insightful or pseudo-creative thought and users often seem quiet and introspective, sometimes fearful.

Many abused substances act on or near the **nucleus accumbens** in the brain. This produces a sense of pleasure as it is *part* of our **endogenous reward system**, which is why we feel good if we accomplish something useful. It is nature's way of **operantly conditioning** us to increase useful behaviour and, along with a punishment mechanism (producing fear and a 'sense of failure'), to help us avoid danger. Some drugs, especially **heroin** and **cocaine**, interfere more directly with this mechanism and the **endogenous pain gating** system in the body, powerfully triggering the reward mechanism without the user 'achieving' anything *and* reducing pain, making such drugs more addictive (see Wise, 1987). Thus the user may prefer the drug to sex, or lack the need to be productive or accomplish and instead will attach great importance to the procedures immediately prior to a 'fix', as this is the 'behaviour' bringing about the synthetic 'reward'. These are behaviours typical of the '**junk culture**' described in the books of William Burroughs. Most hallucinogenic drugs *lack* this reward stimulation, which is possibly one reason why they lack addictiveness.

Alcohol- and nicotine-related disorders

Alcohol and tobacco (the main source of nicotine) are legal in most parts of the world, which does not reflect on their dangerousness: they are the most dangerous substances of abuse in these societies today. Both substances cause massive **collateral damage** in the body, leading to cancers, cardiovascular and lung disease, liver failure, brain damage and many other serious or fatal conditions. In addition, alcohol users are prone to fatal overdose (especially with spirits) as alcohol *disinhibits* and *impairs judgement* in addition to being toxic. These characteristics of alcohol also lead to accidents (e.g. drunk driving), violence and crime, at a heavy cost to society. However, very moderate use of alcohol can assist some biochemical processes, reduce stress and anxiety, and help inhibited individuals to socialize. There is, however, *no* safe level of tobacco use.

Alcohol

Ethyl alcohol has been around for 5000 years, and as a **CNS depressant** has been used for relaxation and anxiety reduction. Because it is cheap and easily available it is readily abused, with around 5 per cent of adults in the UK having a drinking problem. Alcohol use confounds many medical conditions and psychiatric disorders, especially **antisocial personalities** (e.g. Kwapil, 1996) and **depression** (where it co-occurs in 50 per cent of

suicides). Many patients **self-medicate**, with alcohol potentiating medication and undermining their treatment. The larger dose effects of alcohol, i.e. insensitivity, aggression, staggering and slurred speech, are common in casualty units as alcohol contributes to many accidents. High-dose effects include impairment of mental and physical functioning, and eventual death from choking or vital function failure. Long-term excessive use is commoner amongst some professions (e.g. journalists and even *doctors*) and can lead to cirrhosis, gout and **Wernicke-Korsakov's syndrome** (a serious form of memory deficit). Even small regular amounts of alcohol during pregnancy can lead to '**foetal alcohol syndrome**', with possible premature birth, and mental and physical problems in the child (e.g. Baroff, 1986). Women and some races (e.g. Asians) have less **alcohol dehydrogenase**, the enzyme that breaks alcohol down, and are thus far more susceptible to its effects.

Evidence of *genetic factors* in some alcohol problems is fairly strong, including that from adoption studies (see Cloninger and Begleiter, 1990). Other factors affecting the rates of alcoholism are availability, cost, peer pressure and the presence of anxiety and mood disorders. Alcoholism is difficult to treat in the long term. In the short term, **detoxification** involves two weeks of severe physical withdrawal (longer and more dangerous than for heroin, but less difficult compared with barbiturates). These withdrawal symptoms such as **delirium tremens** (hallucinations and feverishness) can be reduced with **benzodiazepines** (though secondary dependence to these is possible). Following this, alcohol avoidance can be maintained by the *supervised* administration of **disulfiram**, which reacts to make the individual ill if they take alcohol. This and any form of **aversion therapy** can only be short-term measures, as supervision is difficult and alcohol is socially ubiquitous. *Cognitive approaches* can help the individual avoid the self-deception and cues that lead to use, or even to cope with moderate consumption. Peer group support, e.g. **Alcoholics Anonymous**, can help in the case of those that stay with the group (many drop out).

Nicotine

Nicotine is an addictive stimulant found in tobacco, which can be sniffed, chewed or smoked. Smoking is its most addictive and deadliest form, being responsible for around *one in every six* deaths worldwide. It results in permanent lung damage, bronchial complications, and is closely linked to a number of *cancers*, some of which become many times more likely if *combined* with **alcohol**.

The major causes of smoking are **modelling** of the behaviour and **peer group pressure**, the fact that smoking is dangerous merely *adds* to its appeal for children and adolescents. These are the very people who have the greatest chance of avoiding the habit *by not starting*. Smoking is initially very unpleasant and requires *persistence* to acquire the habit, so not starting is *easy*. Perhaps *real* cinema heroes need to be shot while fumbling for a cigarette or lose fights while wheezing with bronchitis. Giving up can be helped by **nicotine patches** to remove the initial withdrawal, but greater determination and positive thinking is needed to conquer the smoking **habit**, with all too many people 'giving up giving up'.

Other substance-related disorders

There is a vast range of substances used, each with very different characteristics. The following is a brief selection of substances and reflects *some* of the categories in the classificatory systems.

▶ **Opioids** are alkaloids extracted from opium. They are **CNS depressants** sometimes referred to as 'narcotics' or 'junk', producing sedation and pain relief, which has been utilized medically in the case of **morphine**. **Heroin** was extracted from morphine in 1874 and used in cough mixtures and *children's remedies*, but heroin has proved the most addictive of the opioids as it produces an instant and sustained euphoria, absent in the others. Some individuals seem to use it sporadically, usually smoked, or develop an intravenous habit which they maintain (*without* increase) for years with few ill effects. These are usually middle-class individuals, who maintain employment and health, and avoid criminalization and contaminated drugs. Far more individuals fall prey to the cycle of increased need, loss of employment, crime and ill health. Withdrawal is brief, but psychologically painful. However, heroin undermines the body's **reward** and **pain gating systems** and has a very powerful psychological hold on susceptible individuals who enter its subculture, as William Burroughs wrote, 'Junk is the ideal product, the ultimate merchandise. No sales talk necessary. The client will crawl through a sewer and beg to buy' (Burroughs, 1959, p. 9).

▶ **Cocaine** is a **stimulant** with anaesthetic and short-term euphoric effects, producing confidence and mental stamina similar to **hypomania**, which has made it popular in 'sniffed' form with those who can afford it. Cocaine is addictive, but less so than the opioids. However, when free-based with ether, the resulting lumps, or **crack** produce a *highly* addictive *brief* euphoria when smoked.

▶ **Amphetamines** are **stimulants** (e.g. **methedrine**) that increase alertness, energy and stamina, and produce subjective mental acceleration – hence the street name, '**speed**'. They are highly addictive and prone to 'weekend abuse'. They place dangerous strain on the cardiovascular system and can lead to confused paranoid states that mimic psychosis. **Caffeine** produces similar but weaker effects and is used as a stimulant in the form of coffee. It is also added to soft drinks, which may increase later use of *both* soft drinks and coffee, and *may* partly explain an increased preference for amphetamines in the young.

▶ **MDMA** and **MDA** are stimulants with hallucinogenic properties, which were first synthesized around 1910, but became associated with the electronic dance culture of the 1980s and had their illegal status reinforced as a consequence. Currently *millions* of young people take **ecstasy** (as the drugs are known) every week, with its effects of hallucinations, increased empathy, energy and repetitive movement, being inextricable from the dance environment (the effect is far 'calmer' in a relaxed setting). There are very rare fatal reactions, complications from dehydration and anxiety, but few short-term ill-effects have been observed. However, long-term effects are relatively unknown and regular users are acting as an 'uncontrolled drug trial' in this, with potential damage to the **serotonergic** transmitter system.

▶ **LSD** was synthesized in 1938 and is a very powerful **hallucinogenic**, with as little as *50 micrograms* producing profound disturbance of time, visual and other sensory perception, and consciousness change lasting up to 12 hours. Expectation, the presence of a 'guide' and pre-existing anxiety or mental disturbance can affect the experience, with anxiety and apprehension leading to **panic** or **paranoia** – a 'bad trip' requiring tranquillizers. Hidden mental disturbance may be precipitated with the possibility of **flashbacks** (recurring experiences long after the substance has left the body) or attempts to 'fly'. Most normal individuals enjoy a profound, sometimes spiritual experience (in which they would not *dare* go near an open window), but usually *never* want to repeat the experience. The use of LSD to ease the spiritual and physical pain of **terminal illness** has ended due to its criminalization. There is no potential for physical addiction as it requires exhaustible endogenous substances, though anxious and disturbed individuals keep trying to have a 'good trip'. Similar experiences are found with **mescaline** and **psilocybin**.

▶ **Cannabis** comes in many forms ('grass' or 'hashish'), but its active ingredient **delta-9-tetrahydrocannabinol (THC)** has **stimulant** and **hallucinogenic** properties. It can be eaten or drunk with coffee, etc. in which case it is very safe in relative medical terms, but the effects can be unpredictably timed and powerful. When smoked, the effects are shorter, more controllable, but carry the very *serious* health risks of **smoking**. The effects are mild euphoria, time and perceptual distortion, with users tending to be quiet and introspective (the *opposite* of alcohol). THC collects in areas of fatty tissue producing a **reverse tolerance**, i.e. regular users need *less*, and is thus not *physically* addictive. It is thought to mimic the endogenous brain chemical

anandamide. Further to the above arguments regarding decriminalization, calls have been made to allow the medical use of cannabis to relieve nausea in **cancer treatment**, eye pressure in **glaucoma**, suffering in **multiple sclerosis** and improvement in **AIDS** cases (e.g. Salan *et al.*, 1975).

▶ **Prescribed medications** are frequently abused (often by females) or sold on the black market. **Barbiturates** were used to produce sedation (**CNS depressants**), but are less frequently prescribed now as they are *highly* addictive with *very severe* withdrawal effects, including death. They potentiate with alcohol and have a very **high toxicity** (more lethal than heroin). **Benzodiazepines** (**anxiolytics**) were widely used for anxiety as they had a very **low toxicity**, but have proven to be **addictive** in the long term due to an insidious rise in anxiety on withdrawal. The antidepressant selective serotonin reuptake inhibitor, **fluoxetine** (**Prozac**) has been greeted in a similar way, but as yet without firm evidence of serious side-effects.

Issues in the aetiology and treatment of substance-related disorders

In a perfect world, no one would try a drug or abuse a substance, and the behavioural cycles would not begin. However, we live in a world with rapidly increasing substance use and abuse. Surviving the situation may be a matter of tolerance and **education**. Propaganda and repression may simply be **amplifying** the situation as it did during Prohibition in the 1920s in the US, when alcohol was prohibited. Some individuals may be at greater risk for addictive behaviour by inheriting a greater tolerance, having associated mental disorders, a high conflict environment, poor stress tolerance, greater exposure or simply being impressionable. These individuals may need targeting. In detecting those with a biological disposition to substance abuse, some abnormalities in **event-related potentials** (particularly P3) have been researched for alcohol and now other substances (see Brigham *et al.*, 1995). With regard to risk factors such as exposure, stress and modelling, it is clear that society should *not* be putting **commercial interest** before the health of future generations, nor confusing the concepts of danger, glamour, crime and abuse, especially in the young.

Treatments for substance disorders usually include detoxification, with counselling and peer group support. However, the full catalogue of treatments have been tried in these disorders with various claims of success, e.g. **methadone substitution treatment** or **portable shock machines** for heroin. The only highly successful remedy for substance disorders is the sustained determination to enjoy life without abuse on the part of the sufferer.

Chapter summary

There are many **psychoactive** substances and the body can develop a **tolerance** to some, leading to **withdrawal** which motivates continued use, or **dependence**. When continuation disturbs functioning it is termed **addiction**, which is distinguished from **abuse**, or sporadic excessive use. The three most medically dangerous substances are **tobacco, alcohol** and **food**. Food abuse is one way to examine **eating disorders**. Most substances differ in their **purity, toxicity** and the **global damage** they cause, and the issue of **legality** can confound treatment for some substances. Psychoactive substances broadly fall into **depressants, stimulants** and **hallucinogens**, with the first two affecting the human **endogenous reward system**, making them physically addictive in contrast to hallucinogens.

Both alcohol and nicotine cause many deaths and are highly addictive. Other substances of abuse include **opioids, cocaine, amphetamine, MDMA, LSD, cannabis** and **prescribed medications** (e.g. **barbiturates**). Although there may be **biological predisposing factors**: exposure, media influence and availability all contribute to substance use, and treatment depends greatly on the will of the abuser.

Self-test questions

▶ How does substance use become addiction?
▶ How may eating disorders be related to substance abuse?
▶ Discuss the conflict between legal and health approaches to substance disorder.
▶ What is meant by the endogenous reward system?
▶ What distinguishes alcohol and tobacco use from that of other substances?
▶ Why is MDMA use of particular concern at this time?
▶ In what ways do opioids and hallucinogens differ?
▶ What are the confounding issues in the cause and treatment of substance disorders?

Further reading

British National Formulary (1997 – revised biannually) published by the British Medical Association and the Pharmaceutical Society of Great Britain.

Drummond, D.C., Tiffany, S., Glautier, S. and Remington, B. (1995) *Addictive Behaviour: Cue exposure theory and practice.* London: John Wiley.

Edwards, G., Strang, J. and Jaffe, J. (1993) *Drugs, Alcohol and Tobacco: Making the science and policy connections.* Oxford: Oxford University Press.

Fals-Stewart, W., Schafer, J., Lucente, S., Rustine, T. *et al.* (1994) 'Neurobehavioural consequences of prolonged alcohol and substance abuse: a review of findings and treatment implications', *Clinical Psychology Review*, 14, 755–78.

Gordon, R. (1990) *Anorexia and Bulimia.* Oxford: Basil Blackwell.

Jarvis, T., Tebbut, J. and Mattick, R. (1995) *Treatment Approaches for Alcohol and Drug Dependence: An introductory guide.* London: John Wiley.

Legg, C. and Booth, D. (1994) *Appetite: Neural and behavioural bases.* Oxford: Oxford University Press.

McMurran, M. (1994) *The Psychology of Addiction.* London: Taylor and Francis.

Nace, E. (1995) *Achievement and Addiction.* New York: Brunner/Mazel Publishers.

Orleans, C.T. and Slade, J. (1994) *Nicotine Addiction: Principles and management.* Oxford: Oxford University Press.

Schlaadt, R. and Shannon, P. (1994) *Drugs*, 4th edition. Englewood Cliffs, NJ: Prentice Hall.

Strang, J. and Gossop, M. (1994) *Heroin Addiction and Drug Policy: The British system.* Oxford: Oxford University Press.

Schizophrenia and other psychotic disorders

9

In this chapter

▶ Phenomenology, diagnosis and prognosis of schizophrenia
▶ Aetiology and treatment of schizophrenia
▶ Special issues in schizophrenia
▶ Other psychotic disorders

Schizophrenic disorders (along with mood disorders) were once classified as **functional psychoses**. The status of schizophrenia as a psychosis has never been under question. However, the term 'functional' (i.e. having no known organic cause) has been undermined by much evidence of **organicity** in schizophrenia (Cutting, 1985) and is now little used. Some disorders have been usefully differentiated from schizophrenia in the DSM-IV and are included in this chapter, although the main focus will be schizophrenia, which is considered to be the 'heartland of psychiatric science'.

Phenomenology, diagnosis and prognosis of schizophrenia

Schizophrenia is synonymous with the lay view of 'madness', featuring psychotic symptoms such as **delusions** and **hallucinations**. Affecting around 1 per cent of the world's population at some point in their lifetime, it is still something of an enigma for psychiatry, lacking a clear definition and aetiology.

Morel (1852) identified bizarre and withdrawn behaviour, which was described systematically by Kraepelin (1919) using the label **dementia praecox**, believing that it involved inevitable cognitive decline. Bleuler (1911) gave it the name schizophrenia to emphasize the 'loosening of associations', which he saw as the basic symptom. Literally meaning 'split mind', schizophrenia is *not* to be confused with a Jekyll and Hyde-type split personality. Bleuler's concept of the disorder was broader than Kraepelin's and many professionals (e.g. Kety, 1974) see it as a **syndrome**; i.e. a cluster of related symptoms of uncertain aetiology.

The symptoms are not all of equal practical value in diagnosis. Schneider (1959) identified three '**first rank symptoms**' to be the primary focus of any diagnosis. Diagnostic agreement was greatly improved (WHO, 1973) by focusing on these psychotic symptoms:

▶ **Delusions** are unshakeable, faulty beliefs which can influence the person's behaviour. **Primary delusions** (**autochthonous delusions**) are held with extreme conviction regardless of counter-argument or conflict with reality. 'First rank' forms of these delusions vary in content, but usually involve inappropriate meaning being attributed to everyday events; e.g. shops closing mean 'the world is about to be destroyed'. Delusions of reference are 'first rank' delusions in which such misattributions are directed towards the individual themselves; e.g. TV news items are direct communications to and about the schizophrenic individual. Delusions may be **paranoid** (e.g. people are plotting to kill one) or **grandiose** (e.g. belief that one is God), though these are usually considered to be 'second rank' delusions.

▶ Delusions usually follow a period of confusion and a sense of slight change in the individual's perception of the world which is referred to as '**delusional mood**'. There are a number of specific **delusional disorders** (see later sections) that do not display the other features of schizophrenia, however such specific delusions can also be part of schizophrenic symptomatology. In **Capgras's syndrome**, for example, the person believes someone close has been replaced by an exact double.

▶ **Hallucinations** are false percepts. In schizophrenia these are mostly **auditory** (hearing voices), however hallucinations of the other senses, e.g. visual and olfactory, also occur but are considered to be '**second rank**' hallucinations. Auditory hallucinations are usually voices discussing the patient in the third person (or second), often in a very *critical* way. As far as the patient is concerned, they are outside the head, not just inner speech. The voices tend to be very persistent and can be distressing to the individual, especially if they are commanding the person to carry out something unpleasant (e.g. committing suicide).

The patient's ability to cope with the illness is improved if they realize that the voices, however clear, external and separate from their own thoughts they may seem to be, are hallucinatory and part of the disorder. Non-schizophrenic individuals have also been reported to have similar hallucinations and self-help groups have been set up to reassure sufferers that such experiences may not *always* be confirmation of schizophrenia (e.g. **Hearing Voices Network**).

▶ **Thought disorder** can take the forms of disturbance of thought processes or thought content. Thought disorder symptoms which are central to the diagnosis of definite schizophrenia, or **nuclear**

symptoms, tend to be those of 'alien' control of, or interference with, thoughts. **Thought insertion** is the belief that thoughts are being put in one's mind by others, and conversely, in **thought withdrawal,** thoughts are being taken from one. The belief that thoughts are available to others is termed **thought broadcasting** and in **passivity of thought,** that one's thoughts (also emotions) are under external, or 'alien', control. Other forms of thought disorder or non-nuclear symptoms include: **thought block,** or sudden loss of train of thought; over-inclusiveness in thinking; over-generalization; knight's move **(asyndetic)** thought, or **derailment in thinking** – moving to unrelated topics; racing, **pressured thought; poverty of thought;** and **distractibility.**

Thought disorder often leads to peculiarities of speech or writing. **Neologisms** (new words) are used or formed from idiosyncratic combinations of words. Words or phrases may be repeated over and over (**verbigeration**) and be echoing the words of others (**echolalia**). **Perseveration** is where a redundant train of thought or conversation persists, and **incoherence** refers to where the train of thought is frequently lost or disconnected. '**Word salad**' refers to a jumble of words that lacks sense or structure, where this approximates to sense it is termed '**telegraphic**'. **Clang association** uses rhyme to replace sense in speech or writing, for example, 'can I have a cigarette? a bet? wet, going out, go without.' Though speech *production* is clearly disturbed, comprehension remains largely unaffected. The term thought disorder has been criticized as being too broad by some (e.g. Andreasen, 1979) and has led to confusion over its definition among professionals.

In addition to the rather strict 'first rank' symptoms of delusions, hallucinations and thought disorder, there are other symptoms of schizophrenia. The importance of many of these further signs and symptoms is more closely related to **poor prognosis** (future condition) than reliable diagnosis. They are usually grouped under the headings of emotion, motivation and social activity and motor function.

▶ **Emotional disturbance** tends to one of two extremes. There can be a loosening of emotion, moving from laughter to tears without apparent cause, often showing emotion which is inappropriate to the situation, e.g. laughing in tragic circumstances. Another form of disturbance is a **flattening of affect,** a marked absence or poverty of emotion.

▶ **Motivation and social activity** can be secondary disturbances, that is, as a consequence of other symptoms, but also occur as primary symptoms of schizophrenia. Lack of energy, drive and pleasure-seeking behaviour (**anhedonia**), and a **progressive withdrawal from social**

interaction are characteristic features of some sufferers, even occuring before the onset of the disorder. In other schizophrenic individuals, these symptoms are more evident in the later phases of **chronic** forms of the disorder. **Lack of decision-making** and **ambivalence** are also characteristic. Such withdrawal has been illustrated by Clare (1980) in describing two patients, who had not spoken in the *fifteen years* they had shared *adjacent* beds.

▶ **Motor disturbance** can take a number of forms. Most pertinent to schizophrenia is **catatonic stupor**, an immobile state, in which the sufferer may maintain an effortful awkward posture for hours and can have their pose altered by another person, giving rise to the description of '**waxy flexibility**'. Schizophrenic individuals exhibit **stereotyped movements**, e.g. repeated rocking or rubbing, and behavioural mannerisms. There may be increased activity, agitation, restlessness or decreased movement, with the most extreme case being catatonia. Some characteristic movement disturbances, e.g. facial grimaces, can be exacerbated by the **Parkinsonian side-effects** of medication (i.e. the uncontrolled movements seen in **Parkinson's disorder**).

A **diagnosis** of schizophrenia carries a great deal of stigma and has had a history of unreliability. This has led some critics to question the validity of such a diagnosis (e.g. Rosenhan, 1973). Thus, the current criteria for diagnosis are rather stringent and focus on the more salient 'first rank' symptoms. Criteria vary between diagnostic systems, those for DSM-IV include the following.

▶ At least one of the **'first rank' symptoms**, i.e. delusions, hallucinations or thought disorder, in addition to one other characteristic symptom must be present. However, only one symptom may be acceptable if it is a severe form of delusion or hallucination.
▶ **Occupational and social functioning** should have markedly deteriorated from their premorbid levels.
▶ Overall presence of the disorder must exceed **six months** (one month in the ICD-10 system).
▶ Onset of symptoms must be **before the age of 45.**
▶ The diagnosed disturbance must rule out mood disorders, and organic (i.e. non-schizophrenic) or substance-induced symptoms.

Subtypes of schizophrenia have existed since Kraepelin suggested **catatonic, hebephrenic** and **paranoid** types, characterized by their most prominent symptoms; i.e. movements; disorganized hallucinations, delusions and emotions; 'organized' paranoid delusions, respectively. An important addition of **simple schizophrenia** was made by Bleuler, to indicate a slow, progressive deterioration with no prominent symptom.

The current subtypes listed in DSM-IV have changed little from these early divisions, though there are now five subtypes:

1. **Paranoid type** schizophrenia is characterized by a preoccupation with fairly 'organized' delusions or hallucinations, in the absence of disorganized behaviour or emotional disturbance.
2. **Disorganized type** schizophrenia has the features of disorganized speech and behaviour, and flat or inappropriate emotional responses.
3. **Catatonic type** schizophrenia has various forms of motor disturbance, e.g. stupor, echopraxia (imitation of others' actions), mannerisms or grimaces, physical resistance, agitation.
4. **Undifferentiated type** schizophrenia cannot be classified as another subtype, but still features prominent psychotic symptoms.
5. **Residual type** schizophrenia is usually found later in the progress of the disorder (i.e. after at least one episode) and is characterized by a lack of prominent psychotic features and the presence of emotional blunting, social withdrawal and odd beliefs and behaviour (not bizarre).

The integrity of schizophrenia as a single disease entity has always been under question, as can be seen from the above subtypes the symptoms can vary from one patient to another. Also, no one symptom unequivocally identifies the disorder, and symptoms may change over the course of the disorder, illustrating Bleuler's use of the label **the schizophrenias** indicating a group of related disorders.

Further attempts have been made to subdivide schizophrenia so the component syndromes correspond to differences in symptoms, prognosis, treatment or underlying pathology. Four of these **dimensions** of schizophrenia are listed here as: **process-reactive**; **paranoid-non paranoid**; **positive-negative**; and **Liddle's three subtypes**. The latter two are at this time current paradigms in schizophrenia research.

1. The **process-reactive** division relates to distinctions in the progress of the disorder. In 'process' schizophrenia there is poor premorbid functioning, slow deterioration and a poor prognosis of chronic residual symptomatology (withdrawal, etc). In contrast, a rapid onset after good premorbid functioning, possibly following a stressful event, and a good chance of recovery describes the 'reactive' type. The term **acute** replaced reactive because of the implication that the latter was *purely* a 'reaction' to an environmental event.
2. The **paranoid and non-paranoid** division relates to the presence or absence of **paranoid symptoms**. There is an association between the acute (reactive) type course of the disorder and the presence of paranoid symptoms. Thus the presence and absence of paranoid

ideation also corresponds to good and poor prognosis and premorbid function respectively.

3. The **positive–negative symptom (type I and type II schizophrenia)** distinction follows from the above, however the implications were more far-reaching. Crow (1980) presented the first comprehensive hypothesis dividing the disorder in terms of symptom groups, which was also developed by Andreasen in the US. This typology focused on dividing symptoms into positive, i.e. more than normal behaviour, and negative types, i.e. less than normal behaviour. Thus examples of **positive symptoms** would be hallucinations, delusions, 'positive' forms of thought disorder and disorganized behaviour, whereas withdrawal, affective flattening, anhedonia, avolition and poverty of action, speech and its content would be termed **negative symptoms**.

   Crow used the labels **type I** schizophrenia for sufferers with predominantly positive symptoms and **type II** where there is a predominance of negative symptoms. He thus identified two syndromes in the disorder corresponding to a range of important features of schizophrenia as listed in Table 9.1.

   This division has been subject to criticism. There is a large area of overlap between type I and II, labelled 'mixed schizophrenia' by Andreasen and Olsen (1982). Andreasen (1989) points out that Crow's theoretical division has difficulty in accounting for the coexistence of positive and negative symptoms in one individual. The case studies of Sandra and Michael (pp. 157–8) approximate to type I and type II syndromes, respectively.

4. Liddle's (1987) three sub-syndrome typology is based on differences in neurological activity, perhaps indicating more specific **neuropathology**. '**Disorganized schizophrenia**', in this case, corresponds to increased activity in the **right anterior cingulate**, as analyzed using *in vivo* PET scans. The '**reality distortion**' subtype relates to greater **left temporal lobe** activity, and in the '**psychomotor poverty**' type shows a failure of **frontal lobe** activity and reciprocally linked increased activity in the **basal ganglia**.

Table 9.1 *The division of schizophrenia into type I and type II (Crow, 1980)*

Type I	Type II
Positive symptoms	Negative symptoms
Sudden onset	Slow insidious onset
Good prognosis	Poor prognosis
Retain intellectual function	Intellectual impairment
Good premorbid adjustment	Poor premorbid adjustment
Few neurological abnormalities	Cell loss and neurological change
Responsive to medication	Poor response to medication

From the above, it can clearly be seen that the **prognosis** for an individual with schizophrenia can vary greatly and be indicated by features such as poor premorbid function and negative symptoms. The course of the disorder has been broken down into **thirds**: around a third make a reasonably quick recovery with no or limited relapse; a further third will make some recovery, but suffer intermittent relapse, some **residual symptoms** and may need long-term prophylactic medication; the final third will become **chronic sufferers**, dependent on institutional support of one sort or another. Studies have produced variations on these rough figures, but there still tends to be around 20 per cent who recover from their initial episode and never return to hospital, and an unfortunate 10 per cent who never fully recover from their first episode.

Schizophrenic patients are costly in occupying more hospital beds than any other psychiatric disorder. As a result of the rationalization of resources (especially in Britain) there is pressure to *discharge patients into the community* as soon as possible. This, and the difficulty in finding beds for **psychiatric emergencies**, has led to disturbed sufferers wandering the streets fuelling the negative stereotype the public have of schizophrenic individuals. It has also exacerbated the **revolving door** situation where patients are hurriedly discharged, only to return after a short period, often having lost, or failed to take, necessary medication.

CASE STUDY

Schizophrenia

'Sandra'

Sandra's grandfather had been hospitalized for schizophrenia when she was quite young and on one occasion she was present when he relapsed during a home visit. Sandra seemed quite alarmed by this, but forgot about it after a month or so. Her childhood was relatively free of illness but she persisted in having an imaginary friend until she was 10. At 15, she abruptly ended a relationship with a boyfriend and seemed agitated for weeks, having periods when she accused her parents of interfering with her relationship, although this was unwarranted. Near her 23rd birthday a close friend was killed in a car crash and although Sandra was away at the time, she became convinced she was to blame. For days she rambled through explanations, becoming more incoherent in her speech and began referring to her (late) grandfather in the present tense. Her family doctor referred her as a psychiatric emergency when she announced that all her deceased relatives had been visiting her because she had 'killed' her friend, and one now followed in her head telling her how to make amends. Sandra responded well to medication and returned home to her parents after three months. She relapsed twice in the following two years and family therapy was given as part of a research programme. Her last episode began as she was planning her own wedding, which never took place. She has now lived for five years with her widowed mother without relapse. She has a job and has been free of medication for three years.

'Michael'

Michael was a 'sickly' child and was the surviving twin from a difficult birth, during which his brother had died. As an only child his parents encouraged him to socialize with other children but with paradoxical results. Michael seemed less interested in others with each passing year. He had a girlfriend for a while, who left him because she became fearful at some of the things he had said and felt uneasy during the frequent silences in conversation. In his early twenties, Michael visited his family doctor and tried to get her to sign a letter to the police verifying that his ex-girlfriend's family were plotting to kill him. A psychiatrist had Michael admitted to hospital for a week but discharged him, although he still maintained his story. Six months later Michael was rushed to hospital having severed his foot because 'they' now had God helping them, making him kill himself. Michael responded poorly to medication, which made stays with his parents brief and difficult. He made many attempts to move back with his parents over the next 15 years, but is now back in hospital in a very withdrawn often immobile state, with the pronounced side-effects of the many attempts to medicate him with alternative drugs. Some of his delusions persist in milder forms, but his thoughts have never seemed confused or disorganized.

Aetiology and treatment of schizophrenia

As with most psychiatric disorders, effective treatment depends on accurate knowledge of causal mechanisms. In schizophrenia, limited knowledge of the specifics of **neurodevelopment** and **neurochemical interaction** constrains the usefulness of therapies available to the sufferer.

The search for a cause (or causes) for schizophrenia has spanned a number of decades. As a consequence, many texts juxtapose recent technically sophisticated findings alongside relatively crude, often purely speculative, early research, often giving the latter undue credibility. This said, to ignore some early philosophical views may leave an impression of bias. Likewise, early treatments were often crude, desperate measures, almost always discovered by accident and as such, have been somewhat unfairly criticized. This section will deal with the more useful cause and treatment approaches to date, and controversial views will be dealt with in the special issues section.

Aetiological approaches can be grouped under four main headings: genetics, neurological correlates, biochemical correlates, and stress and other environmental factors.

Early **genetic** research suffered from imprecise measurement and poor sampling. However, later studies provided cumulative evidence of a definite genetic component to schizophrenia, in the words of Kety (1974, p. 205) when replying to the critics of the schizophrenia concept, 'If schizophrenia is a myth, then it is a myth with a heavy genetic component.' It is equally clear from genetic research that the disorder is not *purely* genetic, although a recent **meta-analysis** of genetic studies attributes two-thirds of overall influence to genetic factors.

Pedigree studies have shown that the closer the (genetic) relationship to someone with schizophrenia, the greater the chance of developing the disorder (e.g. Slater and Cowie, 1971). For example, if one parent has the disorder the rate in any offspring is around 12 per cent, if both parents are affected the figure doubles to 24 per cent. The concordance rates for **mono-zygotic** twins are substantial, and greater than those for **dizygotic** twins (e.g. Shields, 1978). Such **twin studies** are subject to the criticism that the closer the relationship, the more similar the environments each is exposed to.

In addressing this fundamental criticism, Fisher (1971) points out that the offspring of the non-schizophrenic twins (i.e. where the other twin has the disorder) are still more likely to develop the disorder. Further to this, research on the relatives of adoptees with the disorder more clearly refutes the 'similar environment' criticism (e.g. Kety *et al.*, 1975). This is especially the case when examining adopted half-siblings, i.e. having only a common father (Kety *et al.*, 1976), where even the intra-uterine environment is different. All these studies find significantly higher rates for schizophrenia if the disordered relative is biologically rather than environmentally (adoptive parent) linked.

More recently, attempts have been made to find a **genetic marker** (see Chapter 2) linked to schizophrenia. Sherrington *et al.* (1988) proposed a marker on **chromosome 5**, but this finding has not been replicated (e.g. Kennedy *et al.*, 1988). Such research is limited by family size in trying to differentiate linked subgroups of the disorder. However, a project to map the human genetic constitution, the Human Genome Project, is beginning to aid this type of research. Freedman *et al.* (1997) have shown an inherited defect in inhibiting the **P50 evoked response** (see Chapter 2) found in schizophrenia to be related to a neuronal defect (decreased alpha 7-nicotinic cholinergic receptor activity) and linked this to a site on **chromosome 15**. This may provide a full explanation of **auditory attentional defects** in schizophrenia (see Freedman *et al.*, 1997).

Overall, the case for a genetic cause is overwhelming, albeit only part of the process resulting in schizophrenia. The fact that the disorder is found at about the *same rate* regardless of country, culture or even historical era would seem to support this.

Neurological abnormalities that correspond to the presence of schizophrenia could indicate that the cause may be due to their effect on the sufferer, but it is equally plausible that the abnormalities are a consequence of the **effects** of schizophrenia or the **iatrogenic effects** of drug therapy. The latter argument is stronger when evidence comes from **post-mortem studies,** often following a lifetime of schizophrenic episodes and medication, with inevitable atrophy of brain matter.

The advances in **CAT, PET** and **NMR** technology (see Chapter 2) have enabled the examination of brain structure and function in living patients. Such studies have found **enlarged ventricles** (reduced brain mass), especially in the left hemisphere, in acute and drug-free cases (e.g. Cannon and Marco, 1994). This structural loss, and smaller frontal lobes, craniums and cerebrums, as well as reduced cerebral blood flow, tend to be associated with **negative symptoms** and the other criteria for Crow's type II schizophrenia. With improved measurement in neurophysiology, research has begun to identify the underpinnings of individual symptoms, e.g. the association of auditory hallucinations with Broca's area (speech) of the brain. A number of professionals have attempted to link specific cognitive explanations of schizophrenic symptoms to **neurological abnormalities** (e.g. Frith and Frith, 1991; Strauss, 1993).

If brain abnormalities *led to* schizophrenia (at least the type II), then what caused the abnormalities? Current thinking adopts a **neurodevelopmental** account for this route to schizophrenia (see Roberts, 1990). In this, genetic factors combine with early damage to the developing brain resulting in a form of schizophrenia, which may be less susceptible to later environmental stressors, hence the slow progressive onset that characterizes this form of the disorder. Early damage could be the result of a predisposition to **viral infection** (Kirch, 1993). A more established explanation is that of **perinatal complications** (e.g. forceps delivery), perhaps accounting for more schizophrenic people being born in the late winter months, when the risk of complications is higher, the so-called **season of birth effect**.

Biochemical correlates of schizophrenia have mainly concerned the neurotransmitter **dopamine**. Substances that increase dopamine activity such as **amphetamine** and **L-dopa** (a treatment for **Parkinson's disorder**) can produce schizophrenia-like symptoms (e.g. Angrist *et al.*, 1980). Drugs which reduce the (mainly positive) symptoms of schizophrenia, **neuroleptics**, block dopamine receptors. Thus higher dopamine activity would seem to equate with the occurrence of schizophrenic symptoms such as hallucinations and delusions. However later research showed increased numbers of dopamine type **D2 receptors**, even in acute schizophrenia (Owen and Cross, 1989), indicating that this led to the symptoms rather than being a *product* of the disorder or medication.

However, even a refined form of the **dopamine hypothesis** such as looking at more specific receptors (e.g. **D4**), cannot account for why the effect of medication on symptoms takes several weeks or that levels of dopamine need to be low enough to cause Parkinson's-like symptoms to be effective against schizophrenia. More recent approaches consider the complex interaction of neurotransmitters in the brain, for example, that the transmitter **GABA** may have a central role in schizophrenia via its influence over the level of dopamine turnover (see Carlsson and Carlsson, 1990). Biochemical explanations of schizophrenia seem more relevant to the '**positive symptoms**' of the type I syndrome.

Given a **genetic diathesis**, or predisposition to the disorder, what finally triggers the episode in one predisposed individual rather than the other? Many theories have identified **environmental stress** as a precipitating factor, i.e. the **diathesis–stress** approach. Early approaches identified stressful **family interactions**, but overstated their causal role, often ignoring the stress effect and using psychodynamic theory as a complete explanation for the disorder. Examples of these are Bateson *et al.*'s (1956) idea that **double-**

bind communication (conflicting verbal and nonverbal messages) produces the disorder, and Lidz *et al.* (1957) pointed to distortions in parental relations termed **skew** (one is over-dominant) and **schism** (cold, manipulative relations) creating schizophrenia in the offspring. Most of these explanations ignore the high probability that the schizophrenic offspring could *produce* conflict in the family (e.g. Stirling *et al.*, 1993; Hirsch and Leff, 1975).

Other researchers have been less presumptuous, although **stressful events** may be partly a product of the disorder, e.g. losing a job, the cumulative stress effect may precipitate an episode (e.g. Brown and Harris, 1978). Vaughn and Leff (1976) examined aspects of family interaction such as critical comments, emotional over-involvement and hostility, and measured this **expressed emotion** (EE) in relation to rates of relapse in patients returning home. Higher levels of EE did predict more *rapid relapse*, irrespective of medication. However, it is still difficult to discern what proportion of the measured EE results from a reaction to schizophrenic behaviour. Factors such as to whether the family **attribute** the behaviour to the disorder or the individual and the extent of the family's knowledge of the disorder, have been found to be influential in this equation.

Treatments for schizophrenia are limited by the incomplete understanding of the disorder. Prior to the 1950s, restraint in institutions was the only way of managing sufferers. **Electroconvulsive therapy (ECT)** (previously insulin shock therapy) had been tried, but was inappropriate for psychotic symptoms, and **surgical interventions** altered more than just schizophrenic behaviour. Genetic counselling for schizophrenia is controversial, as there is no definite marker for it and the possibility that the 'schizophrenic genes' may produce **benefits** in some individuals (e.g. creativity and lowered rates of cancer), although some individuals have made their *own decision* not to have children after experiencing schizophrenia in their family.

With the accidental discovery of the neuroleptic effect of the **phenothiazines** in the early 1950s, primarily **chlorpromazine**, many patients were able to leave institutions with their symptoms held in check by these medications. This also prevented the debilitating effects of long-term **institutionalization** for many sufferers. However, the **side-effects** of the neuroleptics are unpleasant, often requiring supplements to control Parkinson's disorder-like iatrogenic symptoms; in addition, neuroleptics are not effective with all patients (especially type II syndrome). Since the 1950s, neuroleptics have been refined and new 'breeds' introduced, such as **clozapine**, which does not directly block dopamine receptors and lacks the associated motor side-effects, but can adversely affect the immune system.

As can be seen from our incomplete knowledge of the role of neurotransmitters in schizophrenia, medications which address only a single biochemical feature are unlikely to counter the exact effects of the disorder and will always produce some side-effects. However, they remain the only help for the individual with profound psychotic symptoms.

Behavioural and occupational therapy approaches are very important in the recovery of patients once their symptoms abate, or are controlled by medication. Behavioural techniques, such as token economies, can be used to rebuild social skills and self-care and may help to reduce the initial stresses of re-entry into the community. Though still under evaluation, **family intervention** has improved interactions in the home to which the patient returns. This has become more focused in the light of EE research and efforts to reduce levels of EE, in an effort to improve relapse rates, have met with some success (e.g. Falloon *et al.*, 1985).

Special issues in schizophrenia

Schizophrenia has been a focus for controversy and debate since it was first defined, perhaps more so than any other disorder. Some of the areas that provide a source of argument and academic interest are

▶ **Whether schizophrenia is a single disease entity.** As outlined above, there have been many attempts to *subdivide* the disorder, e.g. types I and II, but these have never been sufficiently convincing to change the classification of schizophrenia, perhaps due to imprecise underpinnings or large areas of overlap. It has been suggested that the term be reserved for those cases which become chronic with residual defects (a return to Kraepelin?).

▶ **Whether schizophrenia is an organic brain disease.** This is linked to the next issue, but as the above review of aetiological factors indicates, the case for an organic basis to schizophrenia is accelerating with each advance in neurochemistry and neurophysiology.

▶ **Anti-psychiatry views: schizophrenia is an invention of psychiatry.** Laing (1965) described schizophrenia as a sane reaction to an insane situation (the family). He also considered the *interaction* between psychiatrist and patient in detail, proposing that perceptions were not the same as experiences and that the compounding effects of acting on such misperceptions in a clinical setting resulted in a schizophrenic diagnosis. Laing's views provoked some heated (and enjoyable) debate, but were self-indulgent and of little practical value to the average sufferer. However, such views often produce dedicated followers, much like a religious movement, whose members will always fervently believe in any myth with a happy ending, rather than the often depressing reality of schizophrenia. Other critical views of schizophrenia from this era include Szasz (1971), who called it a witch-hunt, and Leifer (1970), who saw it as character assassination.

▶ **The iatrogenic effects of treatment.** Often sufferers have a lifetime battle with the schizophrenia, but they must also battle with the medication that allows them to cope with the symptoms. Side-effects include involuntary movements, weight gain, agitation (**akasthesia**) and other movements which can identify (and therefore stigmatize) a patient. Psychiatric nurses often have the thankless task of administering medication to sufferers, who do not want to take it and often constantly ask to have dosage altered. Arguments arise from this (reinforced by proponents of anti-psychiatry) about the freedom of patient choice (e.g. compared with non-psychiatric patients), treatment alternatives, and the **misuse of medication** to keep patients 'manageable'. Psycho-dynamically-oriented approaches to schizophrenia have not been covered in this chapter as they are largely considered ineffective, but it is worth mentioning here that they have also been found to worsen the condition of patients with this disorder (e.g. by feeding delusions).

▶ **Failures of managing schizophrenia in the community.** Controversy recurs in the media where patients discharged into the community harm themselves or others. Although schizophrenic patients can be more verbally aggressive to others, they do not pose any greater threat to safety than any other group unless they are acutely psychotic, in which case they should be under close supervision. Unfortunately, when **hospitalization** is dependent on factors such as *cost*, or community support is lacking or uncoordinated, such tragic events become unacceptably frequent.

Other psychotic disorders

Some psychotic disorders have been usefully differentiated from schizophrenia. DSM-IV has identified four of these in addition to the routine categories of substance-induced disorder and psychotic disorder due to a general medical condition. The ICD-10 differentiates schizoaffective disorder, persistent delusional disorder, and recognizes acute schizophrenia-like disorder.

Schizophreniform and brief psychotic disorder

In schizophreniform disorder, schizophrenic symptoms last *less than six months* (DSM-IV) but *more than one month*. This usually indicates a better prognosis than schizophrenia and is characterized by a sudden onset and an absence of relatives with schizophrenia, perhaps suggesting substance abuse or stress as precipitating factors. Brief psychotic disorder has a duration of *less than one month*. In each case, the diagnoses are considered provisional until the duration is established.

Schizoaffective disorder

In some cases (especially acute) a mixture of psychotic and affective symptoms prevents a definite diagnosis of either mood disorder or schizophrenia, a diagnosis of schizoaffective disorder is then made. In schizoaffective disorder both types of symptoms occur during the same episode, or separated by only a few days. The disorder was first identified by Kasenin (1933).

Shared psychotic disorder (formerly, induced psychotic disorder)

The individual with shared psychotic disorder (the **primary case**) has a delusion which is very similar in content to that of a second person, usually a close friend, or other people involved. Thus they share the same delusion and this is generally attributed to their living in close proximity and in isolation from others. In the case of only two people being involved, it can be referred to as **folie a deux**.

Substance-induced and psychotic disorder due to a general medical condition

Some psychoactive substances, such as **amphetamine** and some **hallucinogens** among others, can produce schizophrenic-like symptoms. Likewise, some medical conditions, for example, **temporal lobe epilepsy** and **Huntington's chorea,** can also result in these symptoms. These conditions need to be eliminated before a definite diagnosis of schizophrenia can be made. In the case of drug-induced symptoms, these will disappear in time with abstinence (checked by **urine analysis**), which is around 10 days for amphetamine-induced psychosis. Similarly, likely disease states should also be checked for and a thorough neurological analysis should always be carried out where organic damage or disease is suspected alongside schizophrenic symptoms.

Chapter summary

The disorders in this chapter all show evidence of psychotic symptoms, mainly **delusions** and **hallucinations**. These **positive symptoms** characterize schizophrenia and schizophrenia-like disorders. However, recent thinking in schizophrenia research has considered the importance of the **negative symptoms,** which are indicative of a very poor outcome for the sufferer. Negative symptoms, such as withdrawal, are more *difficult to diagnose* reliably and thus have been neglected in producing diagnostic criteria. In dividing the symptoms, the integrity of schizophrenia itself has been questioned, although suggested subdivisions have not been implemented formally. Schizophrenia is a very disturbing and serious disorder, filling many psychiatric beds, and for which there is no **definite aetiology or cure**. Although a minority of patients do recover without relapse, many more suffer a **chronic** version of the syndrome. **Briefer** forms of the disorder are classified separately with other **delusional disorders**.

Self-test questions

▶ Can the unitary concept of schizophrenia be justified?
▶ Evaluate the treatments available for schizophrenia.
▶ Why are the side-effects of neuroleptics especially problematic?
▶ What is the role of stress in relation to schizophrenia?
▶ What is meant by the 'dopamine hypothesis'?
▶ What is the importance of 'negative symptoms' in schizophrenia?
▶ Evaluate anti-psychiatry views of shizophrenia.

Further reading

Abraham, K. and Kulhara, P. (1987) 'The efficacy of electroconvulsive therapy in the treatment of schizophrenia', *British Journal of Psychiatry*, **151**, 152–5.

Andreasen, N. and Carpenter, W. (1993) 'Diagnosis and classification of schizophrenia', *Schizophrenia Bulletin*, **19**, 199–214.

Birchwood, M. and Tarrier, N. (1994) *The Psychological Management of Schizophrenia*. Chichester: John Wiley.

Chua, S. and McKenna, P. (1995) 'Schizophrenia, a brain disease? A critical review of structural and functional cerebral abnormality in the disorder', *British Journal of Psychiatry*, **166**, 563–82.

Crow, T. (1989) 'A current view of the type II syndrome', *British Journal of Psychiatry*, **155** (suppl. 7), 15–20.

Crow, T. (1994) 'Prenatal exposure to influenza as a cause of schizophrenia', *British Journal of Psychiatry*, **164**, 588–92.

David, A. and Cutting, J. (1995) *The Neuropsychology of Schizophrenia*. London: Psychology Press.

Holliday, S., Ancill, R. and Macewan, G. (1996) *Schizophrenia: Breaking down the barriers*. Toronto: John Wiley.

Johnstone, E. (1994) *Searching for the Causes of Schizophrenia*. Oxford: Oxford University Press.

Kavanagh, D. (1992) *Schizophrenia: An overview and practical handbook*. London: Chapman & Hall.

Kirch, D. (1993) 'Infection and autoimmunity as aetiological factors in schizophrenia: a review and reappraisal', *Schizophrenia Bulletin*, **19**, 355–70.

McKenna, P. (1994) *Schizophrenia and Related Syndromes*. Oxford: Oxford University Press.

Pantelis, C. (ed.) (1996) *The Neuropsychology of Schizophrenia*. Chichester: John Wiley.

Reynolds, G. (1989) 'Beyond the dopamine hypothesis: the neurochemical pathology of schizophrenia', *British Journal of Psychiatry*, **155**, 305–16.

Warner, R. (1994) *Recovery from Schizophrenia*, 2nd edition. London: Routledge.

CHAPTER 10

Mood disorders

In this chapter

▶ Phenomenology, diagnosis and prognosis of mood disorders
▶ Aetology and treatment of mood disorders
▶ Special issues in mood disorders

Phenomenology, diagnosis and prognosis of mood disorders

We all experience low moods following difficulties or feel elated with success, but this does not last and we rarely would wish to end it all or be *confident* about plans to rule the world. Mood-disordered individuals experience such extreme feelings daily for long periods after related events have past or even irrespective of life's events. Only 2 per cent of people will experience manic episodes during their lives, whereas ten times that number, mostly females, will experience clinically significant depression, which is thus considered as 'the common cold of psychiatry'. Descriptions of mood disorders use terms (e.g. mania) for **mood states** or diagnosable **episodes,** which may occur in different *combinations* designating *different mood disorders*. The clinical mood states are as follows:

▶ **Depression** is characterized by daily sadness, **anhedonia** (lack of pleasure-seeking), sleep problems (e.g. early wakening), weight change, fatigue with either agitation or lack of activity, lack of concentration, poor sense of self-worth, and morbid, pessimistic or suicidal thoughts. There may also be **anxiety,** with overconcern about relatives or magnified worries.
▶ **Mania** involves persistent elation (or irritability) for at least a week, high self-esteem, engaging in risky and ill thought-out plans or relationships, incessant pressured speech, distractibility and rapid changes of thought, enthusiasm for work and sleeplessness.
▶ **Mixed mood** is when *both* the symptoms of mania and depression occur nearly every day over at least a week. Such rapid and extreme

mood change results in disturbance of social and occupational functioning as moods alternate without compensating for each other.

▶ **Hypomania** means 'below mania' and includes all of the symptoms of mania but not to a disabling degree. The hypomanic individual shows clear differences with their normal functioning but remains in good contact with reality and may find an *improvement* in their social and occupational functioning.

In both ICD and DSM systems, mood disorders are broadly divided into depression without mania (**unipolar depression**) and depression with mania (**bipolar disorder**). Depression used to be thought of as 'endogenous' (coming from within) or 'reactive', i.e. a protracted reaction to an external event. These terms have fallen into disuse as the boundary between them is usually impossible to ascertain. Mood disorders were once described as psychotic disorders along with schizophrenia, but the term **psychotic** is now reserved for hallucinations or delusions occurring in mood disorders, i.e. as a **specifier** of a subtype. The mood disorders listed in DSM-IV are as follows:

▶ **Major depressive disorder** (i.e. unipolar) can be the result of a **single episode** or **recurrent** episodes of depressive states, but in either case there must be *no* episodes of mania, including hypomania or mixed mood.

▶ **Dysthymic disorder** concerns only unipolar depression and although it shares the same symptoms, they are less severe. Rather than being in clear episodes, dysthymic depression tends to be less remitting or chronic over a period of two or more years.

▶ **Bipolar I disorder** can be diagnosed if there is at least **one manic episode** (often with depression, hypomania or mixed mood in their history), but there are six subtypes distinguished by the most recent episode, i.e.
  − single manic episode
  − recent episode hypomanic
  − recent episode manic
  − recent episode mixed
  − recent episode depressed
  − recent episode unspecified

▶ **Bipolar II disorder** involves one or more depressive episodes with at least one hypomanic (but not manic) episode.

▶ **Cyclothymic disorder** is the bipolar equivalent of dysthymic disorder and is diagnosed when hypomania (but no manic or mixed mood episodes) and depressive symptoms (but no major depressive episode) occur for at least two years in a chronic pattern. Although some patients may *look forward* to the hypomanic breaks from depression, social and occupational functioning is poor overall.

Within each of these disorder criteria, there may be some variation in the **severity** of the current episode, information which can be added to any description of the disorder diagnosed. These further descriptions, or **specifiers**, for mood disorders include:

- ▶ **Catatonic features** are severe motor disturbances, immobility or restlessness, that may occur in any of the mood states.
- ▶ **Melancholic features** concern the lack of interest or pleasure in activity (or even good news) sometimes found in depressive episodes.
- ▶ **Postpartum onset** is specified for any episode if it begins up to four weeks after giving birth and may include psychotic features. This is often a confusing time for a new mother, coping with chores and her feelings towards her child. **Hormone** changes at this time may relate to the onset of mood disorder (e.g. see Harris, 1996). Mood disturbance at this time may be hidden as a result of guilt and fear, especially if the mother has negative feelings towards the child. Relatives and even the GP may also be reluctant to acknowledge disorder at this time, thinking it is a matter of the mother adjusting to her new circumstances. It may be referred to as 'postnatal depression'.
- ▶ **Seasonal pattern** is specified in recurrent episodes of mood disorder if depressive episodes regularly start late in the year as winter sets in and daylight shortens, ending in spring. There may also be additional 'hibernation' type symptoms such as oversleeping, carbohydrate food craving, lack of energy and weight gain. It is more common in females, the young and when living in the higher latitudes, although there may be other factors affecting the timing of episodes (see Barbini *et al.*, 1995). This may be referred to as **seasonal affective disorder (SAD)**.

Bipolar I disorder

CASE STUDY

Jean's husband Ken was becoming tired and somewhat irritated with her increasing talkativeness and they had argued more fiercely than ever before, after Jean had switched channels on the TV all night, 'just checking what was happening on the other sides'. Two days later Jean kept him awake till 2 am with her plans for a new career in design, but at 5 am Ken was woken by the sound of Jean 'spring cleaning'. Ken had never seen such enthusiasm or energy in *anyone* before. During the following days Jean slept less, talked more and Ken began to find notepaper all around the house with what seemed to be poetic jottings on it. Jean claimed these were plans for her college work, though some were to be adapted for her 'new book'. Ken was somewhat shocked at this, but was horrified to find out that their bank account had been emptied and all their saving 'invested' in *two* university courses, a computer and various magazine subscriptions for Jean's 'new career'. Ken's initial fears that Jean might be too ambitious for a man like him were beginning to turn to anger. When he confronted her, Jean gibbered wildly, pointing to the lyrics on a music CD, 'Don't you see, it's all in the Don Durham lyrics . . . the world, we're rich . . . it will . . . I'll be worth millions . . . the Prime Minister knows all about me . . .' Ken's anger turned to tears as he realized that behind her wide eyes was illness and he sought emergency help from the GP. Within two months Jean's mood had been stabilized by medication and she returned home from hospital to Ken, who still could not believe he had ignored her symptoms for so long and felt apprehensive for their future should Jean's moods become extreme again.

Around 10–15 percent of mood-disordered individuals become chronic cases and 80 per cent will have more than one episode. Around 15 per cent successfully commit suicide: an ever-present danger in mood disorder.

Aetiology and treatment of mood disorders

Behavioural theorists such as **Ferster** have examined the self-reinforcing nature of depression. Inactivity leads to a lack of reinforcement of actions, leading to less activity, etc. and sympathy merely *reinforces* depressive behaviour. This would suggest a treatment in which depression was *not* reinforced, but activity was. In 1975 Seligman reported on a number of studies showing that **learned helplessness,** or learning that one is unable to control significant events, produces a form of depressed state. He also demonstrated that this learning can result from single experiences, e.g. being assaulted, and rapidly generalized, resulting in failure to tackle tasks, inactivity and **dysphoric** (depression and anxiety) symptoms. This explanation may *also* account for depression and suicide in spoilt or privileged teenagers, who also lack control in that they are **unconditionally rewarded.** Therapy from this perspective would be to encourage **learned effectiveness,** i.e. carrying out achievable rewarding tasks until they become self-perpetuating (see Seligman, 1992). **Cognitive** explanations are similar in that persistent negative expectations and assumptions have self-fulfilling effects and also lead to inactivity.

Genetic studies are confounded by there being *related* but *differing* genetic factors contributing to bipolar and unipolar mood disorders. Linkage studies have implicated a dominant gene on the 11th chromosome for bipolar disorder, but only in a specific population (see Mann, 1989). The genetic component for bipolar disorder is greater than that for unipolar, perhaps indicating that non-genetic factors have a greater part in the origin of unipolar depression and thus accounting for its greater incidence. This is reinforced by the observation that a parent with unipolar disorder does not *tend* to have bipolar offspring, but 'bipolar families' tend to have *both* disorders in their descendants (in fact *more unipolar*). **Hormonal** factors clearly have a causal role in **premenstrual** and **postpartum** type depression, but whether the raised

cortisol levels found in other forms of depression is a cause or consequence of the episode is difficult to resolve. The same difficulty exists in determining if the levels of **dopamine, serotonin** and **noradrenaline**, which are raised in mania and lowered in depression, are *causing* the mood change. However, noradrenaline levels are lowered by learned helplessness and raised by treatments such as **ECT**.

Environmental events can be observed to precipitate depression and elation, but do not account for the persistence of extreme moods in disorders. As in schizophrenia, cumulative **life-events** and **expressed emotion** (see Chapter 9) also increase the *chance* of episodes of mood *disorder*. Geographical latitude and seasonality both determine length of daylight, which seems to influence **seasonal affective disorder**, or mood disorder with a seasonal pattern. Treatments based on artificially extending daylight and influencing **melatonin** levels, altering the sleep cycle **circadian rhythms**, are effective in these cases (see Lewy *et al.*, 1995). Based on this approach, one simple way to reduce depressive symptoms and increase activity is to *miss a night's sleep*. **Cultural** factors can influence the *expression* of mood symptoms. For example, Chinese individuals present more *physical* complaints (somatization) and fewer emotional symptoms (**dysphoria**). The aetiology of mood disorder is often confounded by its comorbidity with alcoholism and personality disorders.

In addition to **circadian rhythm** manipulation and **learned effectiveness**, the other major therapies for mood disorders are **drug, electroconvulsive** (ECT) and **cognitive-behavioural therapies**.

The most widely effective drugs for depression are the **tricyclic antidepressants** (e.g. **amitriptyline**), but numerous side-effects (e.g. strokes) can make them unsuitable for some. **Monoamine oxidase inhibitors** or MAOI (e.g. **tranylcyonize**), can also have serious effects beyond their antidepressive ones. More recent antidepressants such as **fluoxetine** (Prozac), a **selective serotonin reuptake inhibitor**, have become *very* widely used owing to their lack of such side-effects. However, there is controversy over their long-term use following problems with the long-term use of **benzodiazepines**. Where there are difficulties over drug therapy, a course of **ECT** can often prove very effective (see Chapter 2), especially if the patient is older or there is risk of suicide. These treatments are less appropriate for bipolar disorder. Manic episodes are treated with **neuroleptics** in the short term and carefully monitored levels of **lithium** as maintenance medication. Anticonvulsants such as **carbamazepine** may sometimes substitute for lithium and **clozapine** may help if the others are inappropriate (see Calabrese *et al.*, 1996).

Depressive patients stabilized by physical treatments should always be considered for cognitive-behavioural treatment (see Chapter 2). Aaron Beck has helped popularize these methods of reducing the negative thinking patterns which often maintain inactivity and dysphoric symptoms. This is less effective for depression in *bipolar* disorder.

Special issues in mood disorders

There are two issues that need to be considered further, the problem of **suicide** and that of the uneasy relationship between mood disorder and **creativity**.

One of the ever-present dangers when treating mood-disordered patients is that they may kill themselves and this risk needs to be considered when weighing the costs and benefits of some treatments, especially drugs and ECT. Men are four times more likely to commit suicide than women, who are three times more likely to *attempt* suicide. Attempted or **parasuicide** tends to be an appeal for attention or an expression of anger and is often 'advertised' (e.g. phone call) to enable detection. Successful suicide usually involves hopelessness and uses highly lethal methods, with no possibility of detection. Paradoxically, bipolar patients may commit suicide during more manic phases when they are more active and decisive, and perhaps to avoid the onset of depression.

Many gifted creators and performers have been lost to suicide due to mood disorder, in fact, far more than chance would dictate. The reverse side of mood dysfunction is the creative excess that seems to accompany bipolar patients, especially during **hypomanic states**. Herself a sufferer, **Kay Jamison** was amazed to find the incidence of mood disorder to be *many times* that of the general population among successful writers and artists, and seemed to be almost obligatory among poets (see Jamison, 1997). This is perhaps why the genes for these disorders do not die out through the dysfunctional nature of the disorder, they possibly also produce *advantages* in hypomanic individuals (or their relatives) which partly balance the disadvantages in those more mood-disabled. Other observations tend to confirm that we as humans *prefer* optimistic views of ourselves and the future, *even if these are unrealistic*, and that some depressed individuals have *more realistic* views of their future than the normal population. Perhaps very successful comedians such as Tony Hancock and John Cleese have harnessed their (*unwanted*) mood problems to their advantage. A story told in Tony Hancock's honour expresses this dilemma well. A depressed man visits his GP many times, finally pleading, 'Doctor, I am desperate, so depressed I cannot go on.' The doctor, who had tried everything, paused then began speaking excitedly, 'Go see Grock the famous comedian, he is so funny he can make a statue laugh, go see him and he will lift your spirits.' The man lifted his eyes and replied, 'But doctor, I *am* Grock . . .'

Chapter summary

Mood disorders involve states of severe **depression, mania,** a **mixture** of these two and **hypomania.** Various combinations of these states differentiate the types of mood disorder. **Major (unipolar) depression** and its milder chronic form, **dysthymia** do not involve mania. **Bipolar I** disorder always involves mania usually cycling with other states, **bipolar II** disorder alternates hypomania with depression, and **cyclothymia** involves a milder, chronic form of this cycle. There is a **genetic** component to these disorders which is greater for the bipolar form. Cognitive, behavioural and environmental factors such as daylight are also implicated. Treatments can be drugs, ECT and cognitive therapy, with some cases responding to daylight levels and 'learned effectiveness'. **Suicide risk** is an important consideration in mood disorder and the death of very **creative** individuals in this way is sometimes a feature of mood disorder.

Self-test questions

▶ What is meant by a mixed mood episode?
▶ What distinguishes cyclothymic disorder?
▶ How do unipolar and bipolar disorders differ with regard to genetics?
▶ What is meant by 'seasonal affective disorder'?
▶ What is the relationship of 'learned helplessness' to depression?
▶ Discuss the implications suicide has for treatment of mood disorder.
▶ How could hypomanic states account for the survival of 'bipolar genes'?

Further reading

Angst, J. (1995) 'The clinical research of affective disorders: a personal perspective' (English translation), *Pharmacopsychiatry*, **28**, 38–44.

Cassano, G., Tundo, A. and Micheli, C. (1994) 'Bipolar and psychotic depressions', *Current Opinion in Psychiatry*, 7, 528.

Gotlib, I. and Hammen, C. (1992) *Psychological Aspects of Depression*. Chichester: John Wiley.

Schatzberg, A. and Rothschild, A. (1992) 'Serotonin activity in psychotic (delusional) major depression', *Journal of Clinical Psychiatry*, **53**, 52–5.

Seligman, M. (1992) *Helplessness*. New York: Freeman.

Shneidman, E. (1996) *The Suicidal Mind*. Oxford: Oxford University Press.

Tam, E., Lam, R. and Levitt, A. (1995) 'Treatment of seasonal affective disorder: a review', *Canadian Journal of Psychiatry*, **40**, 457–66.

Thase, M. and Kupfer, D. (1996) 'Recent developments in the pharmacotherapy of mood disorders', *Journal of Consulting and Clinical Psychology*, **64**, 646–59.

CHAPTER 11

Anxiety, somatoform (and factitious) and dissociative disorders

In this chapter

▶ Anxiety-related disorder
▶ Anxiety disorders
▶ Somatoform disorders (and factitious disorder)
▶ Dissociative disorders
▶ Aetology and treatment of anxiety, somatoform and dissociative disorders

Anxiety-related disorder

Until recently, the disorders in this chapter were collectively known as the **neuroses,** i.e. anxiety neurosis, and hysterical neuroses conversion (i.e. somatoform) and dissociative types. The ICD-10 has retained the word 'neurotic' in the title for these three disorder groups, but it has been removed (with 'hysterical') from DSM-IV to avoid assumptions of (psychodynamic) aetiology and to focus on symptom *description.* However, some professionals still use these terms and often refer to the **neurotic personality** in describing individuals with **trait anxiety,** who tend to have over-reactive autonomic responses (see Chapter 2) and may be more prone to suggestibility and fantasy (see Brenneis, 1995). Individuals prone to 'neurotic' disorders may *report* more headaches, chest pains, palpitations and will report apprehension up to *20 times* more often than non-neurotic individuals. Around 1 in 4 people will be affected by anxiety-related symptoms at some time in their lives.

A simplified way of distinguishing the following three groups of disorders is to consider the place of anxiety or fear in each of them. In **anxiety disorders** *observable* anxiety is a key symptom. However, in the other two groups anxiety is not overt, but *assumed* to underlie their symptoms. In **somatoform disorders** anxiety is thought to be perceived as physical (bodily) complaints by the patient. In **dissociative disorders,** the patient is thought to be psychologically 'running away' from their anxiety, dissociating themselves from the source of their fear. The traditional descriptions of the *latter* two disorder groups are very **psychodynamically** based, which may be appropriate in cases involving suggestible individuals. **Factitious disorder** has been included in this chapter to show how it is distinguished from the somatoform disorders and **malingering**.

Anxiety disorders

When we are exposed to sudden threat or a fearful situation we experience high levels of arousal or **sympathetic autonomic responses,** which prepare our body to 'fight or escape'. In anxiety disorder this response occurs in the *absence* of real threat and is experienced as anxiety or debilitating fear with their characteristic symptoms of apprehension, tension, increased heart rate and in some cases an inability to move. Most anxiety disorders are characterized by the differing 'triggers' that produce anxiety in sufferers, but not non-neurotic individuals. Sufferers usually have good **insight** into their fears and *realize that they are irrational,* but cannot help their **feelings,** which often override their logical **thoughts.** Some medical conditions such as **hypoglycaemia** and **hyperthyroidism** produce some anxiety-type symptoms and need to be eliminated prior to a psychiatric diagnosis. The individual (DSM-IV) anxiety disorders are as follows:

▶ **Panic disorder** consists of recurrent and unexpected **panic attacks.** Panic attacks can occur in a number of disorders and are characterized by extreme anxiety symptoms such as trembling, breathlessness, choking, numbness, palpitations and a fear of dying or losing control. Clark (1986) proposed the cognitive explanation that panic-prone individuals precipitate their attacks by **catastrophic misinterpretation** of their anxiety symptoms, i.e. their heart rate rises, so they *think* they are going to have an attack (or even die) and the apprehension this causes then intensifies their symptoms in the manner of a *self-fulfilling prophecy.* Panic disorder can be diagnosed as with or without **agoraphobia.**

▶ **Agoraphobia** (literally, fear of the marketplace) is a *complex* phobia, i.e. a number of fears, which involves fear of being outside of secure places or in any situation where escape is difficult, especially if alone. It is made progressively worse by sufferers *avoiding* going out or into inescapable situations altogether. Most agoraphobics have other phobias and are mostly female, which may be a consequence of the traditional 'female role' as homemaker.

▶ **Specific phobias** are fears of particular things or situations such as fire (**pyrophobia**) or heights (**acrophobia**). Phobias are mostly found in females and involve anticipatory fear and avoidance of the phobic situation (see the arachnophobia case study).

▶ **Social phobia** involves a persistent fear of public exposure or social events in which the sufferer could cause embarrassment. More common in females, social phobia can be restricted to, say, social events or **generalized** to most situations and needs to be distinguished from **avoidant personality disorder**.

▶ **Obsessive-compulsive disorder** is characterized by the presence of **obsessions** and **compulsions**. Obsessions are persistent thoughts, images or impulses that are **ego-dystonic** (unwanted) and intrude into the sufferer's life causing distress. Compulsions are repetitive behaviours (checking) or mental acts (e.g. praying), which are carried out to provide *short-term* relief from the anxiety caused by obsessions. For example, an obsessive fear of contamination by germs may be reduced by compulsive hand washing. However, the level of hand washing and time-consuming rituals will steadily increase until the sufferer's life is taken up with these activities, which may begin to involve other members of the family. Hands may be scrubbed until the skin is broken. Thus the compulsive behaviour serves to *increase* the sufferer's anxieties in the long term.

Akhter *et al.* (1975) considered different types of obsessions, e.g. fear of giving way to impulses (to shout obscenities), doubts (did I lock the door?) or images (dead child on the floor). They also considered two types of compulsion, those that *yield* to the obsession, i.e. going to check the door is locked, and those that *control* it, i.e. repeating a verse out loud to blot out the doubting thoughts. To understand something of the obsessional's dilemma of *knowing* they have turned a light off, but continuing to switch it for *hours* until it *feels* off, we need to examine milder items from our own experience. When small, we may have pretended to 'wipe something' onto a friend's arm, who promptly pretends to wipe it off and onto another's arm, and so on. The person at the end of this line still *feels* that there is something on their arm, although they *know* there is nothing there. Thus the obsessive individual *knows* their behaviour to be bizarre, but cannot control the *feelings* that produce it. Normal individuals may also engage in mild obsessive-compulsive behaviour when under great stress and *strong* believers in some religious faiths have been found to have significantly higher levels of obsessive-compulsive behaviours by one of my own researchers.

▶ **Post-traumatic stress disorder (PTSD)** is an extreme response to a severe (usually life-threatening) stressor. The event could be experience of war, homicide, assault, motor accident or the delayed effects of childhood abuse (an important area for new PTSD research). The extreme response is characterized by five groups of symptoms (three in DSM-IV).

1. **Avoidance of reminders of the event,** such as self-distraction to avoid recurring thoughts (perhaps alternating with amnesia) or physically avoiding the location of an attack or accident.
2. **Numbing of responses,** such as anhedonia, difficulty in feeling positive, alienation and lack of emotional or general interest in others.
3. **Reliving the experience** in the form of nightmares, daydreams, and associating everyday sounds (e.g. car backfire) and images with the event.
4. **Increased arousal** results in insomnia, difficulty in concentration, hyper-vigilance (constantly monitoring for danger), an exaggerated startle response, i.e. an over-reaction to change in stimuli, and increased physiological reactions to associated words or images. The latter can be usefully detected using **heart rate** (see Blanchard *et al.*, 1996).
5. **Learned helplessness** can be produced by the single, *uncontrollable* event and generalized to other situations, often leading to depression. This may be coupled with **guilt,** that in some way they are responsible for the outcome of the traumatic event, in that *they survived* and others may have died. These symptoms can be further complicated by **substance abuse** and **suicidal** tendencies.

There may be **psychosomatic** complaints (e.g. abdominal pains) and **dissociative** symptoms, especially when the source of trauma is child sexual or physical abuse. It is becoming increasingly useful to conceptualize the **adult effects of child abuse** as PTSD, especially when considering treatment approaches.

The symptoms must persist for **more than one month,** and can be considered chronic after three months, affecting about 1 per cent of the population. Not everyone who experiences such trauma develops the disorder, so some may be predisposed to PTSD. For example, having an **external locus of control,** i.e. considering one's fate to be outside of personal control, or genetic predisposing factors may contribute to the reaction. Alternatively, it may be that those who do not develop PTSD have greater social support and are more able to accept that the event is in the *past.*

▶ **Acute stress disorder** is a reaction to a similar stressor as found in PTSD, but this lasts only **one month** and includes at least three **dissociative symptoms.**
▶ **Generalized anxiety disorder** or 'free-floating anxiety', is uncontrolled, excessive apprehension, worry and anxiety and occurs in 5 per cent of the population at some point during their lifetime. It is difficult to identify any source for these anxieties which may result in panic attacks, with the sufferer being unable to avoid particular situations or objects, as the fear is *generalized* across most situations.

Specific phobia (arachnophobia)

For most of Mary's life, she and her mother had shared a fear of spiders, even the smallest. As far back as Mary could remember, most situations where spiders would be encountered were avoided and on the rare occasion one was near Mary had vivid recollections of her mother being rigid with fear, hurting Mary's hand with her grip. Now Mary had her own daughter and did not want Amy to have the same fear and tried not to show her anxieties, though with little success. One day, she was giving Amy an 'extended' bath and, as this had lasted half an hour, Mary warmed the water by turning on the hot tap. Mary suddenly fell back to the bathroom door gasping for air: a very large garden spider had been hidden behind the tap. Amy played on oblivious and even approached the spider, but Mary was frozen with fear, she could *not* approach the tap *nor* Amy. After a few minutes Amy's splashing turned to screams and Mary realized her child was being scalded. The situation was saved by Mary's husband hearing the child's screams as he was repairing a neighbour's car. Mary made her mind up to seek therapy, urgently. Six months later, Mary spoke of her exposure therapy with a kind of pride, and kept the promise she made to herself to show spiders to Amy in a relaxed way, so long as they were not too big.

Somatoform disorders (and factitious disorder)

Somatoform disorders are characterized by physical symptoms for which there is no medical basis. Although the symptoms are *not intentionally* created, they are vague, atypical and conform to the patient's *understanding* of such physical complaints. For diagnosis, these disorders must disrupt social and occupational functioning, but the distress is often *less* than would be expected if the patient were to have the genuine medical condition. There are six identifiable somatoform disorders.

1. **Somatization disorder**, known as **Briquet's syndrome** (as well as hysteria), is characterized by a number of clinically significant pseudomedical complaints concerning different parts of the body: at least four different sites for pain; and two gastrointestinal complaints other than pain; and two 'conversion' type (see below) pseudoneurological complaints; and one sexual complaint. Such a level of psychologically based problems could be said to indicate a 'neurotic personality'. The disorder is fairly rare – less than 1 per cent of the population, mostly females.
2. **Undifferentiated somatization disorder** is a milder form of the above with less stringent criteria regarding the number and severity of pseudomedical complaints.
3. **Conversion disorder** involves visceral, motor or sensory complaints, e.g. coughing fits, paralysis or blindness, for which there is no medical basis. Again, these symptoms are not intentionally faked, but they do

correspond to the patient's level of **medical knowledge**, i.e. a patient with poor medical knowledge may present with implausible, even physiologically impossible complaints, e.g. **glove anaesthesia**. There may be *unintentional* 'lapses of convenience' where a paralyzed hand may be temporarily used, then become unusable again. There may be **secondary gain**, i.e. the disability may be advantageous to the patient, e.g. avoiding commitments, but this is *not* the conscious intention of the sufferer (**primary gain** is considered to be the immediate effect of the symptom, i.e. blindness in reaction to a distressing visual experience). The phrase **la belle indifférence** has been used to refer to the conversion patient's tendency to lack the degree of concern normally associated with sudden blindness or paralysis. **Breuer's** classic case study of **Anna O** claimed that her paralyzed arm resulted from the *conversion* of anxiety from a repressed childhood trauma into a physical condition. Other professionals have viewed conversion more sceptically, seeing the process as a continuation of childhood irresponsibility, when flight into sickness became a habitual escape route from responsibility, in which the child convinces *itself* the illness is genuine. The disorder is rare and more common in females, but estimates vary greatly.

4. **Pain disorder** is similar to somatization, except that it involves complaints of significant pain at one or more sites in the body, e.g. back pain. Although the pain may worsen if the patient's psychological stress increases, it is not intentionally 'produced' pain. As with other somatoform disorders, this is diagnosed only when medical causes have been eliminated, which can take time as some pain is difficult to investigate from a medical viewpoint. It is thought to be a common disorder, accounting for a proportion of occupational absenteeism.

5. **Body dysmorphic disorder** involves an obsessive overconcern with some part of their body, usually a facial feature such as the nose. Occasionally there may be more than one area of focus, but it is usually a fairly specific complaint. The patient finds the appearance of this body area unacceptable and even if there *is* a defect, the degree of concern is disproportionate. Plastic surgery (even multiple attempts) often fails to satisfy what is a psychologically based obsession. Patients' embarrassment can be extreme, sometimes resulting in their becoming recluses. They may spend a lot of time examining the body part or may actively avoid mirrors. The disorder has been known under the name **dysmorphophobia**.

6. **Hypochondriasis** is the unintentional misinterpretation of bodily functions so as to be convinced of serious illness or disorder. These individuals continue to be preoccupied with these fears when presented with evidence of normal health. Such individuals may have **poor insight** into their disorder, i.e. do not realize they are exaggerating or misinterpreting functions, which can make treatment approaches difficult. There is a tendency to become obsessed with serious disorders

and be over-sensitive to minor changes in their bodies, which may sometimes *result* from overconcern.

Factitious disorder is a separate heading in DSM-IV. Although the symptoms are *similar* to those of the somatoform disorders, factitious individuals *deliberately* present with physical or psychological symptoms for which there is no medical basis. In another DSM-IV item **malingering** there is some *advantage* to the patient in presenting fake disorders, but in factitious disorder the *only* goal seems to be maintaining the role of a sick person. The term **Munchausen's syndrome** has been used for the disorder when the patient actively seeks *medical treatment* (e.g. surgery) by faking symptoms. These are often young women with extensive knowledge of health services (Folks, 1995). In **Munchhausen's syndrome by proxy**, the fake symptoms are inflicted on *another individual*, often a child, though such individuals may also have a personality disorder (see Bools *et al.*, 1994). These are *not* childish pranks: factitious individuals are serious in their deception, they lie convincingly to cover up evidence and will deny any accusations of their having faked symptoms.

Dissociative disorders

The symptoms of dissociative disorders characteristically involve damage to the integrity (i.e. 'dissociation') of memory, perception, identity and consciousness. The disorders are thought to be a reaction to an unbearable event or source of anxiety, in which the individual escapes *psychologically*. Thus the symptoms are of a psychological nature, e.g. loss of memory or identity. Dissociative symptoms are found in **post-traumatic stress** and **somatization disorders,** but are not primary criteria for the diagnosis of these disorders. In ICD-10 conversion disorder symptoms are considered to be dissociative leading to the heading **dissociative (conversion) disorders,** but in DSM-IV the two symptom types are distinct.

Some individuals seem to be more prone to dissociation and this seems to coincide with higher levels of **suggestibility** and **hypnotizability** (see Butler *et al.*, 1996). This needs to be considered seriously when the source of symptoms is suspected to be sexual or physical **abuse**, in that **false memories** are not inadvertently created in suggestible individuals as a result of assessment or treatment (see Gutheil, 1993). Public perceptions of dissociative disorders tend to be distorted as these relatively *rare* disorders receive a great deal of media interest. Curiously, the **prevalence** of these disorders is *increasing* as media coverage has grown, which could be due to increased public awareness of the disorder, *or* a consequence of the media influencing *suggestible* and dissociation prone individuals. DSM-IV lists four dissociative disorders:

1. **Dissociative amnesia** is the failure to recall important personal information that cannot be accounted for by simple forgetting. The information is usually of a stressful or disturbing nature, or from a period with such connotations. Sometimes the amnesia is generalized over large areas of experience or even *ongoing*, but it is more frequently for a specific period in time or even *selective*, i.e. only certain events from a period cannot be recalled. Where a number of 'blank periods' sequence with remembered ones there is the possibility of undiagnosed **dissociative identity disorder** (see below). Suggestibility can make such individuals prone to **false memory syndrome**, i.e. suggested possible events are adopted by the sufferer to replace dissociated ones and then accepted as a 'real past'.

2. **Dissociative fugue** involves an abrupt departure from one's normal habitat or living area and wandering for hours or even months with partial or total amnesia for their previous life, usually following stress or trauma. It may be some time before the individual is 'discovered', usually due to their lack of identity or key memories, as they may behave quite normally in other respects and may have established a new identity, but *not* in the manner of dissociative identity disorder (see below). After their return there may still be amnesia surrounding the precipitating trauma, or even amnesia for the period of the fugue state. It is probable that some soldiers suffering from dissociative fugue have been shot as deserters during wartime. The prevalence rate of about 2 per 1,000 of the population can rise during times of natural disasters or war.

3. **Depersonalization disorder** involves persistent periods of depersonalization, in which the sufferer experiences a dream-like detachment from their selves. This feeling of detachment has been described as being 'outside' one's body watching one's own actions, almost as a 'detached observer' or **automaton**. This is sometimes accompanied by a lack of emotional involvement or sense of control over one's actions. The sense of passivity may extend to one's thoughts. These are *feelings* not *beliefs* and as good contact with reality is maintained throughout, thus these symptoms are distinguishable from the delusions and hallucinations of **psychotic states**. Many individuals will experience these feelings at some stressful point in their lives, but this is rarely persistent.

4. **Dissociative identity disorder** (DID) is still commonly called by its former title **multiple personality disorder**. It is characterized by the individual having *two or more distinct identities* or personality states that recurrently take control of behaviour. These different personalities may have distinct characteristics, e.g. highly extravert, or insensitive and callous. They usually have their own names, history and way of dressing or speaking. The identities can be unaware of one another or may be in

conflict, and can appear when their particular personality characteristics are the most appropriate to deal with current circumstances. There may be over 100 personalities in some cases, but some identities are more salient than others, although the **primary** identity (with the individual's name) tends to be passive and dependent among these, often carrying the guilt and emotional burden for the rest. More powerful and hostile identities tend to dominate the individual's consciousness and may 'organize' the other identities. There seems to be an inability to integrate these aspects of identity and memory in DID individuals.

Early presenting symptoms of DID involve lapses of memory accompanied by changes in the environment that cannot be accounted for, such as unusual personal items left in the home or finding cigarette ends when one does not smoke. The idea that one's other identity has left these is usually the *last* explanation to be accepted. The concept of DID being an escape from trauma is reinforced by the very high incidence of **incestuous sexual abuse** (70 per cent) and **physical abuse** (80 per cent) in the histories of patients (e.g. Putnam, 1989).

The fact that the symptoms seem implausible and resemble 'possession' have led some professionals to doubt the very existence of the disorder, and others to consider that the 'identities' and memories of abuse arise due to the **suggestibility** and **hypnotizability** of such patients (see Frankel, 1996). This **sociocognitive** model of DID has been challenged (e.g. Gleaves, 1996) and may be seen as unjust in the context of DID arising from genuine incidents of abuse. However, some accounts perhaps illustrate the vulnerability of the dissociative concept to criticism. For example, Ferracuti *et al.* (1996) report on individuals undergoing **exorcism** for 'devil trance possession state', whose symptoms they interpret into a dissociative framework with features of DID. In the course of studying DID, Colin Ross has also reported some controversial accounts of recovered memories involving 'alien abductions' in dissociative patients (see also Ross, 1991). The decision of US **health insurance** companies to recognize DID may have contributed to the acceptability of some of the more controversial accounts of the disorder.

Prevalence rates for the disorder have also been a source of controversy. At the beginning of the twentieth century when the disorder was first described a number of cases were reported, but these declined up until the 1970s. At this point a number of cases had recently received publicity, which was followed by a dramatic increase in the number of new cases reported, more than a 1,000-fold increase in some studies. As mentioned above, increased public awareness and the suggestibility of susceptible individuals are the competing explanations for this change.

Aetiology and treatment of anxiety, somatoform and dissociative disorders

The different paradigms in abnormal psychology have their place in approaching these disorders. However, behavioural (with cognitive) and biogenic approaches appear most effective in explaining and treating anxiety disorders, whereas cognitive and insight therapies (including psychodynamic approaches and hypnosis) have proved useful with somatoform and dissociative disorders.

Anxiety disorders have been known to be partly inherited for some time (e.g. Carey and Gottesman, 1981). Examples of inheritable factors which could influence anxious reactions are **autonomic reactivity, gamma-amino butyric acid** levels (general anxiety levels), **cortisol** production levels (see Abelson and Curtis, 1996), **noradrenaline** levels (PTSD) and **serotonin** levels (obsessive-compulsive disorder). Although the level of genetic influence in anxiety disorders would *not* be sufficient for genetic counselling, related biochemical abnormalities *may* explain the effectiveness of pharmacological treatments (e.g. Lydiard *et al.*, 1996). Many anxious individuals self-medicate with **alcohol**, often confounding their condition as a result. Antidepressants (e.g. **benzodiazepines** and the less addictive **tricyclics** such as **imipramine**) are useful with most anxiety disorders except specific phobias, in which medication is not recommended, and obsessive disorders. Obsessive-compulsive behaviour has a paradoxical relationship to the neurotransmitter **serotonin**. Although *increased* levels have been found in the disorder, treatment with **selective serotonin reuptake blockers**, e.g. **fluoxetine** (Prozac), which are serotonin **agonists** (increase its action), can *reduce* symptoms. However, it must be remembered that serotonin is generally an inhibitory neurotransmitter. The **tricyclic, clomipramine** is also effective in obsessive-compulsive disorder, although **psychosurgery** has been a final resort too in treatment-resistant cases.

The treatment of choice for anxiety disorders is the behavioural approach, usually with the addition of cognitive therapy. Although this implies a behavioural cause for the disorder, this is not necessary for the effectiveness of behavioural treatments. Exposure treatments (*in vivo* for agoraphobia) such as **systematic desensitization** and **flooding** (see Chapter 2) have been found to produce success rates of around 80 per cent across studies. This success is often maintained in the long term, although cognitive aspects of the therapy may be involved in this (Kendall and Southam-Gerow, 1996). **Response prevention** needs to be added to these behavioural techniques when dealing with the compulsions in obsessive-compulsive disorder. Cognitive approaches combine well with behavioural techniques and are often used effectively in this combination by experts in this field such as **Aaron Beck**. Among a number of authors, Foa *et al.* (1996) have shown cognitive bias to threat-related stimuli to be a mechanism in some anxiety disorders. As previously mentioned, disorders such as panic attacks can be greatly exacerbated by faulty cognition (i.e. Clark, 1986). In general, cognitive approaches help to restore a sense of control over the irrational thoughts which often precipitate anxiety, although focus on feared situations can occasionally result in sensitization (e.g. Wells and Dattilio, 1992).

In **somatoform disorders** biological causes for the *complaint* (e.g. paralysis) are specifically *excluded* prior to diagnosis, i.e. the presenting complaint must be in the *absence* of medical causes (and mistakes *can* be made here). This does not eliminate the possibility that there may be biological factors involved in the *cause* of the somatoform disorder itself and **neurological** factors have long been suspected in this respect, although without specific evidence so far. Clearly the pseudophysiological nature of the symptoms implicate psychological factors. These could be viewed in psychodynamic terms, with the symptoms arising from repressed emotional trauma which needs to be relived though **psychoanalysis**. Alternatively, behavioural approaches see the somatoform patient as being rewarded for adopting the **sick role**, by gaining sympathy and attention. Thus behavioural treatments focus on removing the reinforcers of the sick role behaviour, usually supplemented by cognitive restructuring techniques.

In **dissociative disorders** there is no clear evidence of biological factors being involved. However, the dissociation of conscious and unconscious processes may be more likely in some individuals than others, irrespective of their experiences. In most cases of dissociative disorders there is evidence of trauma and severe trauma, in the case of DID. Although some aspects of this are controversial and 'false memories' are possible (see Loftus, 1993), psychodynamic, cognitive and behavioural explanations generally agree on trauma as a causal factor. Some explanations of the resulting dissociative states have returned to the idea of **self-hypnosis** (e.g. Bliss, 1986), first considered for hysteria by Leibeault and Bernheim of the **Nancy school** (see Chapter 1). Antidepressant and antipsychotic medication can help the physical distress in dissociation, but treatment is mainly psychological. Psychodynamic approaches would consider the process of working through the trauma, perhaps under hypnosis, as the immediate goal with **abreaction** or an emotional reliving of the event, as a key to confronting the distress without dissociation. Cognitive-behavioural approaches would follow a similar course, but would emphasize the processes of desensitization and cognitive restructuring as producing positive outcomes. In DID the aim is the **reintegration**, not the elimination of the extra identities (see Putnam, 1989).

Chapter summary

Although anxiety is assumed to relate to **somatoform** and **dissociative disorders**, it is only observable in **anxiety disorders**. The anxiety disorders are: **panic disorder, agoraphobia; specific phobia; social phobia; obsessive-compulsive disorder; post-traumatic and acute stress**

disorders; generalized anxiety disorder. These are all characterized by anxiety that is inappropriate to the situation, that may have come about by a learning experience and facilitated by biological or constitutional predisposing factors, e.g. the **neurotic personality**. They are best treated by behavioural therapies with additional cognitive approaches. **Somatoform disorders** are characterized by physical complaints in the absence of medical conditions and comprise: **somatization disorder; pain disorder; conversion disorder; body dysmorphic disorder; hypochondriasis**. They are of psychological origin and respond to cognitive-behavioural and insight therapies. **Factitious disorder** is similar, but in this case the symptoms are intentionally faked. The **dissociative disorders** are: **dissociative amnesia; dissociative fugue; depersonalization disorder; dissociative identity disorder**. These involve the dissociation of psychological functions, usually as a reaction to trauma. Access to the original experience is difficult, but seen as a treatment aim irrespective of paradigm adopted. There is controversy over the accuracy of events recalled by these suggestible patients.

Self-test questions

▶ What major features distinguish the three groups of disorders in this chapter?
▶ How can a specific phobia best be treated?
▶ How does agoraphobia differ from social phobia?
▶ Discuss the distinction between somatization disorder and factitious disorder.
▶ What explanations are given for conversion disorder?
▶ In what ways are dissociative disorders controversial?
▶ What is meant by dissociative fugue?
▶ What are the possible explanations for dissociative identity disorder?
▶ Why are dissociative symptoms also found in post-traumatic stress disorder?

Further reading

Bass, C. and Benjamin, S. (1993) 'The management of chronic somatisation', *British Journal of Psychiatry*, **162**, 472–80.
Davey, G. (1997) *Phobias*. London: John Wiley.
Fahy, T. (1988) 'The diagnosis of multiple personality disorder: a critical review', *British Journal of Psychiatry*, **153**, 597–606.
Hollander, J., Zohar, J., Marazzitti, D. and Olivier, B. (1994) *Current Insights in Obsessive-Compulsive Disorder*. Chichester: John Wiley.

Jakes, I. (1996) *Theoretical Approaches to Obsessive-compulsive Disorder.* Cambridge: Cambridge University Press.

Joseph, S., Yule, W. and Williams, R. (1997) *Understanding Post-traumatic Stress.* Chichester: John Wiley.

Lader, M. (1994) 'The treatment of anxiety', *British Medical Journal*, **309**, 321–4.

Lydiard, R., Brawman-Minzer, O. and Ballenger, J. (1996) 'Recent developments in the psychopharmacology of anxiety disorders', *Journal of Consulting and Clinical Psychology*, **64**, 660–8.

Mayou, R., Bass, C. and Sharpe, M. (1995) *Treatment of Functional Somatic Symptoms.* Oxford: Oxford University Press.

Merckelbach, H., de-Jong, P., Muris, P. and van den Hout, M. (1996) 'The aetiology of specific phobias: a review', *Clinical Psychology Review*, **16**, 337–61.

Rapee, R. (1996) *Current Controversies in the Anxiety Disorders.* New York: Guilford.

Glossary

Abreaction. A re-experiencing (reliving) of past events, usually with the emotional content. Assumed to be the process bringing about catharsis in psychoanalysis.

Aetiology. The study of causes.

AIDS (acquired immunodeficiency syndrome). A condition resulting from infection by the human immunodeficiency virus (HIV), in which immune defences are reduced to the point of simple infections having fatal results.

Anhedonia. A lack of pleasure-seeking behaviour.

Animus and anima. In Carl Jung's approach, the hidden femininity and masculinity in males and females respectively.

Achetypes. From Carl Jung, these are formless predispositions handed down through evolution awaiting realization.

Automatic thoughts. In Aaron Beck's cognitive therapy, these are habitual negative assumptions made by depressed individuals.

Autonomic nervous system (ANS). Part of the peripheral nervous system. The **sympathetic** division of this system responds to danger by preparing the body to fight or flee (e.g. heart rate increases) with an associated sense of fear. In the absence of threat the **parasympathetic** division stimulates recuperation (e.g. digestion increases).

Autoreceptors. These receptors determine the concentration of a neurotransmitter in the synapse.

Aversion therapy. Associating a 'punisher' with an undesirable stimulus to reduce attraction to it in the client, e.g. alcohol.

Axon. The long 'arms' of neurons through which electrochemical signals are generated and sent out to other neurons.

Behaviour modification. Operant conditioning applied as clinical therapy.

Behaviour therapy. Classical conditioning applied as a clinical therapy.

Biofeedback. Providing clients with information about their body's activity so they can learn to indirectly control it.

CAT scans (computerized axial tomography). Taking X-ray images at different angles enables computerized images of 'slices' through organs (e.g. the brain) to be built up.

Catharsis. The emotionally charged recall and reliving of an anxiety causing early experience, usually as part of psychoanalysis.

Cerebellum. This is the 'flying saucer'-shaped structure at the rear of the brain which integrates information on the body's position and movement.

Chaining. Using the completion of one behaviour to reinforce it and act as a prompt (discriminative stimuli) for the next action in producing a complex behaviour.

Chromosome. Molecules of DNA which are subdivided into 'genes', each of which codes for an individual protein.

Classical conditioning. A form of associative learning in which the association of two stimuli results in the response to one of these also being envoked by the other.

Client-centred therapy. A therapy started by Carl Rogers, in which the object is to have the client realize their own potential and act on it. Now renamed *person*-centred therapy.

Collateral damage. Damage caused to areas adjacent to the 'target', or intended area.

Comorbidity. Having more than one diagnosed disorder at one time.

Confounding effect. Something having an effect on a condition, which has not been anticipated or accounted for.

Cultural relativism. This refers to how the perception and sanctioning of behaviour can vary from culture to culture. Thus the acceptability of a particular behaviour is relative to the culture in which it occurs.

Decompensation. In Freud's theory, where ego defences break down and the personality disintegrates.

Deinstitutionalization. The process of removing people from long-term institutional care and its effects.

Demonology. The earliest explanation of psychological disorder was a belief in possession by demons.

Designer drugs. These are psychoactive substances deliberately designed to mimic the effects of existing psychoactive substances, but differ chemically to evade legislation.

Diagnostic and Statistical Manual (DSM). The US diagnostic classification system (for mental disorders) now in its fourth revision (DSM-IV), produced by the American Psychiatric Association.

Diathesis-stress. An approach to causation which assumes a biological predisposition (diathesis) and an environmental stressor that precipitates the disorder.

Differential reinforcement of incompatible behaviour (DRI). The reinforcement of behaviour which is incompatible with the behaviour one is trying to remove.

Differential reinforcement of other behaviour (DRO). Reinforcing *any* other behaviour in order to reduce the target behaviour.

Discriminative stimuli. A stimulus that acts as a 'signal' as to whether a required behaviour will be reinforced or not.

Dizygotic. Having two zygotes. A pair of fertilized human eggs which will develop into non-identical twins.

DNA (deoxyriboneucleic acid). A double-stranded molecule containing genetic information in its chemical structure.

DSM (Diagnostic and Statistical Manual). The US-based classificatory system for mental disorders.

Dysphoria. Affective depressive symptoms, e.g. sadness.

Eclectic approach. An approach in which different therapies are employed to the extent that they are useful in the individual case.

ECT. See electroconvulsive therapy.

Ego. The reality component of the mind in Freud's personality theory.

Ego-dystonic. 'Against the ego', something unwanted by the individual.

Ego-syntonic. Something agreeable to the individual.

Electra conflict. The female equivalent of Oedipal conflict in which the infant girl comes to identify with the mother.

Electroconvulsive therapy (ECT). The passage of an electric current through the brain to produce a convulsion, which has a marked therapeutic effect in depression and catatonic states.

Electroencephalogram (EEG). Recording brain activity from electrical changes detected on the scalp.

Empiricism. Has come to represent the scientific approach, rejecting subjectivity in favour of objective data based on observation and experimentation.

Endogenous reward system. Connections in the brain, related to pain reduction, which produce a sense of pleasure in response to achievement or successful effort.

Ethology. The study of animal behaviour.

Event-related potentials. These are electrical changes picked up from the scalp (EEG responses) in response to sensory stimuli presented to the individual.

Existential anxiety. Anxiety provoked by the awareness of one's being and inevitable non-being.

Expressed emotion. This refers to a certain kind of interaction within a family characterized by hostility, critical comments and over-involvement, which can be detrimental to individuals with schizophrenia or depression.

Family systems approach. Treats the family as an interactive unit with its own dynamics, requiring therapy as a whole.

Field-dependence/independence. A psychological trait representing the degree to which one depends on, or is distracted by, background cues.

Fixation. In Freud's theory, getting 'stuck' at one of his stages of development.

Flooding. The therapeutic enforced exposure to a feared stimuli without escape until the fear subsides.

Forensic psychology. Work pertaining to the law court, now including psychologists in such roles as expert witnesses, offender profilers and criminological theorists.

Free association. In psychoanalysis, the patient is allowed to speak their thoughts as they come to them, without instruction or preconception.

Freebasing cocaine. Purifying the psychoactive ingredient (freebase) by heating cocaine with ether.

Frequency coding. Communication between neurons is on the basis of the frequency of the pulse (not its intensity).

Functional disorder. A disorder arising from function or non-biological factors.

Gene. A section of a DNA molecule (chromosome) responsible for producing a particular protein.

Gestalt. Concentration on the pattern of the whole rather than its component parts.

Glial cell. A cell which supplies nutrients to neurons.

GP. In Britain the family doctor is termed a GP (general practitioner).

Hallucination. A psychotic symptom in which the individual perceives something which does not exist.

Heterogeneity. Having more than one (usually genetic) cause.

Hormone replacement therapy (HRT). Administering hormones to counter a naturally occurring deficiency.

Hypochondriasis. Overconcern with normal bodily functions to the point of imagining serious illness.

Hysteria. An older term for disorders involving dissociation, pseudomedical symptoms or anxiety.

Iatrogenic symptoms. Symptoms resulting from the effects of therapy, not the disorder.

Id. The most basic of Freud's mental structures formed at birth, the source of all psychic energy and containing inherited needs and instincts.

Ideographic. Literally 'picture of the individual', used to imply the unique nature of one person's illness and its causes.

Implosion. A form of flooding which uses exaggerated imagined versions of the feared stimuli in therapy.

Impulsivity. The tendency to give way to impulses, e.g. eating too much or theft.

In vivo. In life. Conducting therapy in real world situations.

Insight. The patient's ability to realize their own state of disorder.

International Classification of Diseases (ICD). The Geneva-based diagnostic classification system (of mental disorders) compiled by the World Health Organization.

Inuit. Inhabitants of the frozen north of Canada. Part of the group formerly known as 'eskimos'.

Learned helplessness. Learning that one is helpless to control significant events from previous experiences of lack of control.

Libido. Freud's concept of psychic energy, called libido, which had a sexual basis.

Linkage. The tendency for genetic traits to be inherited together if they are on the same chromosome.

MAOI (monoamine-oxidase inhibitor). A drug which inhibits the action of the substance (MAO) that breaks down neurotransmitters in the synapse.

Medical model. An approach to disorders which adopts a medical or biological view of disorder.

Meta-analysis. Usually an analysis of findings across a number of studies, an analysis of a number of analyses.

Modelling. An applied form of social learning theory, in which a behaviour is demonstrated to a client who has difficulty in performing it.

Multiaxial. Referring to the DSM classification system, in which clients are assessed on independent scales or 'axes' representing different aspects of the patient's functioning which contribute to a final formulation.

Negative reinforcement. In operant conditioning, this is the conditional removal of a punisher to increase desired behaviour.

Neuroanatomy. Study of the physical structure of the nervous system, including the substructures of the brain.

Neurochemistry. The study of the chemical transmission of signals within and between nerve cells.

Neuroendocrinology. Study of the effects of hormone activity on the nervous system.

Neuroleptic. A group of antipsychotic (anti-schizophrenic) drugs, which achieve this by blocking dopamine receptors.

Neuron(e). A nerve cell.

Neurophysiology. The study of the responses of the nervous system: how signals are carried.

Neurotic paradox. The apparent resistance of phobic reactions to extinction over time.

Neuroticism. Predisposed to anxiety, having an unstable autonomic nervous system.

Neurotransmitter. Substances that transmit signals between neurons, usually released across the synapses to activate receptors on the other side.

NIMBY ('Not In My Back Yard'). A phrase often used in the context of care in the community to represent the views of those who agree with the principle, but would not like the cared for in their neighbourhood.

NMR (nuclear magnetic resonance imaging). Uses a magnetic field to displace hydrogen in the body's tissue enabling computers to analyze the tiny magnetic emissions as it returns, giving good internal pictures of tissue.

Nomothetic. Literally 'rule giving', used to indicate the way that disorders are classified by looking for general principles and common features that apply to all individuals with the disorder.

Object relations. Derived from Melanie Klein, this is now a therapeutic approach in its own right and examines the effects of early relationships with objects, usually beginning with the breast.

Oedipal conflict. A crucial point in Freud's psychosexual stages in which the superego is formed by the boy identifying with the father, based on the dynamics of the legend of Oedipus.

Omission. In operant conditioning, this is the conditional removal of reward to reduce undesirable behaviour.

Operant conditioning. A form of associative learning in which the consequences following a behaviour serve to reinforce or reduce its re-occurrence, depending on the affective qualities of the consequences.

Ortgeit. Going against the historical culture. Often used to refer to people or events that seem to be in opposition to their historical context.

Outreach work. Describes services sent out into the community to aid people with disorders.

Paradigm. A set of assumptions guiding theory and practice. In abnormal psychology, a way of conceptualizing mental disorder leading to assumptions about its aetiology and treatment.

Paraphilia. Sexual desire of that beyond the normal.

Parasympathetic. See ANS.

Pathologize. To consider a particular set of behaviours to be a disorder, usually controversially.

Perseveration. Persisting in an action or line of thought when it is no longer necessary.

Pervasive developmental disorder. Childhood onset disorders which persist and pervade all aspects of the individual's functioning.

Placebo. A non-active (benign) treatment process used for comparison with an active one.

Positron emission tomography (PET). A means of observing brain activity in living subjects, by mapping the emissions of radioactive metabolites introduced into the brain.

Premorbid. Before the onset of a disorder.

Prodromal. Describes a pattern of behaviour or conditions before the onset of a disorder.

Prophylactic. Preventative, e.g. maintenence medication is prophylactic.

Psychoanalysis. Originating with Freud, an insight therapy in which a client discovers early emotional conflict by the process of free association.

Psychodynamic. The approach derived from Freud of considering mental activity as a mostly unconscious and dynamic activity.

Psychogenesis. Having originated from psychological causes.

Psychotic. Severely disturbed behaviour showing hallucinations, delusions or thought disorder.

Radical behaviourism. An extreme behavioural view that accounts for all behaviour as being learned.

Rational emotive therapy (RET). The cognitive therapy of Ellis in which irrational beliefs about one's behaviour are challenged.

Recessive-dominant genes/traits. Genes have 'opposing partners' on the other chromosome of a pair. As dominant ones are expressed over recessive, it requires matching recessive traits for them to be expressed (but they may still be passed on or 'carried').

Recidivist. An offender who repeatedly offends and seems undeterred by punishment, typically returning to prison on a regular basis.

Reciprocal inhibition. The simple fact that some states of the autonomic nervous system, such as relaxation, are inhibitory of others, such as arousal (anxiety).

Remission. A disorder is 'in remission' when its symptoms reduce and the person seems well again.

Retrospective diagnosis. A diagnosis made long after the onset of a disorder based on descriptions from that time or projecting back from the current state.

Schedules of reinforcement. These are economics of reinforcement in operant conditioning which can produce more durable learning.

Scull's dilemma. After Andrew Scull. Refers to the no-win situation in which you should not institutionalize mental patients, but cannot let them out either.

Self-actualization. In humanistic approaches, it is the aim of the therapist to have the client realize and activate their own potential.

Self-help groups. A form of group therapy in which there is no professional presence, only individuals with experience of the disorder.

Self-injurious behaviour (SIB). Problem behaviour involving physical damage to the client's self, e.g. head-banging.

Self-stimulatory behaviour (SSB). Problem behaviour that involves repeated rubbing or manipulation.

Shaping. Using operant conditioning gradually to create complex behaviours by selectively reinforcing simpler ones.

Social learning. Derived from Rotter and Bandura, it concerns learning by observing the reinforcement of another's behaviour, i.e. vicarious reinforcement.

Somatogenesis. Having originated from 'bodily' or physical causes.

Superego. Freud's concept of a conscience and one of his mental structures formed during Oepidal or Electra conflict.

Symptom substitution. An unsubstantiated claim that new symptoms of anxiety will replace those removed by therapy unless the 'underlying cause' is addressed.

Synapse. The cleft between one neuron's axon terminal button and another's dendritic spine, across which pulses of neurotransmitter substances pass nerve impulses.

Systematic desensitization. Gradually exposing a client to a feared stimulus while they are relaxed.

Terminal button. The end of a neuron's axon, i.e. the output from the neuron sending chemical transmitters across the synapse to the next neuron's dendrites.

Tic. A neurologically based abnormal muscle contraction.

Token economy. A system of using tokens as secondary reinforcers to encourage in-patients to perform desirable behaviours.

Transference. A client projecting onto their psychoanalyst feelings originally aroused by a significant figure from their past experience.

Trephination. Term used to describe the cutting of a hole in the skull as far back as the Paleolithic period, which may have been to relieve pressure on the brain but was more likely intended to release 'evil spirits' from a disturbed person.

Validity. Something being or doing what it claims.

Vasocongestion. The engorging of blood vessels with blood.

Ventricle. The fluid filled spaces in the brain.

Vicarious learning. Learning by watching others behave.

Zeitgeist. Literally, spirit of the times, this is often used to refer to people and events that were in keeping with the prevailing mood of the time. Used in contrast to *Ortgeist.*

References

Abelson, J. and Curtis, G. (1996) 'Hypothalamic-pituitary-adrenal axis activity in panic disorder: prediction of long-term outcome by pretreatment cortisol levels', *American Journal of Psychiatry*, **153**, 69–73.

Akhtar, S. (1996) 'Further exploration of gender differences in personality disorders', *American Journal of Psychiatry*, **153**, 846–7.

Akhter, S., Wig, N., Varma, V., Pershad, D. and Varma, S. (1975) 'A phenomenological analysis of symptoms in obsessive-compulsive neurosis', *British Journal of Psychiatry*, **127**, 342–8.

Andreasen, N.C. (1979) 'Thought, language, and communication disorders 1. Clinical assessment, definition of terms, and evaluation of their reliability', *Archives of General Psychiatry*, **36**, 1315–21.

Andreasen, N.C. (1989) 'Neural mechanisms of negative schizophrenia', *British Journal of Psychiatry*, **155** (suppl. 7), 93–8.

Andreasen, N.C. and Olsen, S.A., (1982) 'Negative and positive schizophrenia', *Archives of General Psychiatry*, **39**, 789–94.

Angrist, B., Retrosen, J. and Gershon, S. (1980) 'Differential effects of amphetamine & neuroleptics on negative vs. positive symptoms in schizophrenia', *Psychopharmacology*, **72**, 17–19.

Asperger, H. (1944) 'Die "Autistschen Psychopathen" in Kindesalter', *Archiv für Psychiatrie und Nervenkrankheiten*, **117**, 76–136.

Asperger, H. (1979) 'Problems of infantile autism', *Communication*, **13**, 45–52.

Ayllon, T. and Azrin, N. (1968) *Token Economy: A motivation system for therapy and rehabilitation*. New York: Appleton-Century-Crofts.

Bailey, A. (1993) 'The biology of autism (editorial)', *Psychological Medicine*, **23**, 7–41.

Barbini, B., Di-Molfetta, D., Gasperini, M., Manfredonia, M. *et al.* (1995) 'Seasonal concordance of recurrence in mood disorder parients', *European Psychiatry*, **10**, 171–4.

Baroff, G. (1986) *Mental Retardation: Nature, cause and management*. Washington DC: Hemisphere Publishing.

Baron, M., Levitt, M., Gruen, R. *et al.* (1984) 'Platelet MAO activity and genetic vulnerability to schizophrenia', *American Journal of Psychiatry*, **141**, 836–42.

Baron-Cohen, S., Leslie, A. and Frith, U. (1985) 'Does the autistic child have "a theory of mind"?', *Cognition*, **21**, 37–41.

Bateson, G., Jackson, D., Haley, J. and Weakland, J. (1956) 'Towards a theory of schizophrenia', *Behavioural Science*, **1**, 251–64.

Bauman, M. and Kemper, T. (1985) 'Histo-anatomic observations of the brain in early infantile autism', *Neurology*, 35, 866–74.

Bernstein, D., Cohen, P., Skodol, A., Bezirganian, S. *et al.* (1996) 'Childhood antecedents of adolescent personality disorders', *American Journal of Psychiatry*, 153, 907–13.

Bettelheim, B. (1967) *The Empty Fortress*. New York: Free Press.

Black, D., Monahan, P., Wesner, R., Gabel, J. *et al.* (1996) 'The effects of fluvoxamine, cognitive therapy and placebo on abnormal personality traits in 44 patients with panic disorder', *Journal of Personality Disorders*, 10, 185–94.

Blanchard, E., Hickling, E., Buckley, T., Taylor, A. *et al.* (1996) 'Psychophysiology of posttraumatic stress disorder related to motor vehicle accidents: replication and extention', *Journal of Consulting and Clinical Psychology*, 64, 742–51.

Bleuler, E. (1911) *Dementia Praecox or the Group of Schizophrenias*. London: Allen & Unwin.

Bliss, E. (1986) *Multiple Personality, Allied Disorders and Hypnosis*. New York: Oxford University Press.

Bools, C., Neale, B. and Meadow, R. (1994) 'Munchausen syndrome by proxy: a study of psychopathology', *Child Abuse and Neglect*, 18, 773–88.

Bowman, E.S. and Nurnberger, J.I. (1993) 'Genetics of psychiatric diagnosis', in D.L. Dunner (ed.), *Current Psychiatric Therapy*. Philadelphia: W.B. Saunders.

Brenneis, C. (1995) 'On Brenner's "The dissociative character" ', *Journal of the American Psychoanalytic Association*, 43, 297–300.

Brigham, J., Herning, R. and Moss, H. (1995) 'Event related potentials and alpha synchronisation in preadolescent boys at risk for psychoactive substance use', *Biological Psychiatry*, 37, 834–46.

Brown, G.W. and Harris, T. (1978) *Social Origins of Depression*. London: Tavistock.

Brussel, J. (1968) *Casebook of a Criminal Psychiatrist*. New York: Bernard Geis.

Burroughs, W. (1959) *The Naked Lunch*. Paris: Olympia Press.

Butler, L., Duran, R., Jasiukiatis, P., Koopman, C. *et al.* (1996) 'Hypnotizability and traumatic experience: a diathesis-stress model of dissociative symptomatology', *American Journal of Psychiatry*, 153, 42–63.

Calabrese, J., Kimmel, S., Woyshville, M., Rapport, D. *et al.* (1996) 'Clozapine for treatment-refactory mania', *American Journal of Psychiatry*, 153, 759–64.

Cannon, T.D. and Marco, E. (1994) 'Structural brain abnormalities as indicators of vulnerability in schizophrenia', *Schizophrenia Bulletin*, 20, 89–102.

Carey, G. and Gottesman, I. (1981) 'Twin and family studies of anxiety, phobic and obsessive disorders', in D. Klein and J. Rabkin (eds.), *Anxiety: New research and changing concepts*. New York: Raven Press.

Carlsson, M. and Carlsson, A. (1990) 'Interactions between glutaminergic and monoaminergic systems within the basal ganglia: implications for schizophrenia and Parkinson's disease', *Trends in Neuroscience*, 13, 272–6.

Catalan, J. and Gath, D. (1985) 'Benzodiazepines in general practice: a time for decision', *British Medical Journal*, 290, 1374–6.

Clare, A. (1980) *Psychiatry in Dissent*, 2nd edition. London: Tavistock.

Clark, D. (1986) 'A cognitive approach to panic', *Behaviour Research and Therapy*, 24, 461–70.

Cleckley, H. (1976) *The Mask of Sanity*, 5th edition. St Louis: C.V. Mosby.

Cloninger, C. and Begleiter, H. (eds.) (1990) *Genetics and the Biology of Alcoholism*. New York: Cold Spring Harbour Laboratory Press.

Cohen, P. (1996) 'Childhood risks for young adult symptoms of personality disorder: method and substance', *Multivariate Behavioural Research*, **31**, 121–48.

Cole, M. (1982) 'Surrogates and sexual dysfunction', *British Journal of Sexual Medicine*, **9**, 13–20.

Cole, M. and Dryden, W. (1988) *Sex Therapy in Britain*. Milton Keynes: Open University Press.

Compton, W. and Guze, S. (1995) 'The neo-Kraepelinian revolution in psychiatric diagnosis. Special issue: Emil Kraepelin and 20th-century psychiatry', *European Archives of Psychiatry and Clinical Neuroscience*, **245**, 196–201.

Crow, T.J. (1980) 'Molecular pathology of schizophrenia: more than one disease process?', *British Medical Journal*, **280**, 66–8.

Cutting, J. (1985) *The Psychology of Schizophrenia*. Edinburgh: Churchill Livingstone.

Deary, I. and Matthews, G. (1993) 'Personality traits are alive and well', *The Psychologist*, July, 299–311.

Dickinson, A. and Dearing, M. (1979) 'Appetitive-aversive interactions and inhibitory processes', in A. Dickinson and R. Boakes (eds.), *Mechanisms of Learning and Motivation*. Hillsdale, NJ: Erlbaum.

Dies, R. (1969) 'Electroconvulsive therapy: a social learning therapy interpretation', *Journal of Nervous and Mental Diseases*, **149**, 334.

Dilks, S. and Shattock, L. (1996) 'Does community residence mean more community contact for people with severe, long-term psychiatric disabilities?', *British Journal of Clinical Psychology*, **35**, 183–92.

Dollard, J. and Miller, N. (1950) *Personality and Psychotherapy*. New York: McGraw-Hill.

Eysenck, H.J. (1964) *Crime and Personality*. London: Routledge.

Falloon, I., Boyd, J., McGill, C., Williamson, M., Razani, J., Moss, H., Gilderman, A. and Simpson, G. (1985) 'Family management in the prevention of morbidity of schizophrenia', *Archives of General Psychiatry*, **42**, 887–96.

Faraone, S. and Biederman, J. (1994) 'Is attention deficit hyperactivity disorder familial?', *Harvard Review of Psychiatry*, **1**, 271–87.

Fedoroff, P. (1991) 'Interview techniques to assess sexual disorders', *Families in Society*, **72**, 140–5.

Feingold, B. (1973) *Introduction to Clinical Allergy*. Springfield, IL: Charles C. Thomas.

Feinstein, A. (1967) *Clinical Judgement*. Baltimore: Williams and Wilkins.

Ferracuti, S., Sacco, R. and Lazzari, R. (1996) 'Dissociative trance disorder: clinical and Rorschach findings in ten persons reporting demon possession and treated by exorcism', *Journal of Personality Assessment*, **66**, 525–39.

Ferster, C. (1961) 'Positive reinforcement and behavioural deficits of autistic children', *Child Development*, **32**, 437–56.

Fisher, M. (1971) 'Psychoses in the offspring of schizophrenic monozygotic twins and their normal co-twins', *British Journal of Psychiatry*, **118**, 43–52.

Foa, E., Franklin, M., Perry, K. and Herbert, J. (1996) 'Cognitive biases in generalised social phobia', *Journal of Abnormal Psychology*, **105**, 433–9.

Folks, D. (1995) 'Munchausen's syndrome and other factitious disorders. Special issue: malingering and conversion reactions', *Neurologic Clinics*, **13**, 267–81.

Frankel, F. (1996) 'Dissociation: the clinical realities', *American Journal of Psychiatry*, **153**, 64–70.

Freedman, D., Coon, H., Myles-Worsley, M., Orr-Utreger, A., Olincy, A. *et al.* (1997) 'Linkage of a neurophysiological deficit in schizophrenia to a chromosome 15 locus', *Proceedings of the National Academy of Science*, **94**, 587–92.

Freeman, B. and Ritvo, E. (1984) 'The syndrome of autism: establishing the diagnosis and principles of management', *Pediatric Annals*, **13**, 284–305.

Friedman, M. and Rosenman, R. (1974) *Type A Behavior and Your Heart*. New York: Alfred Knopf.

Frith, C. and Frith, U. (1991) 'Elective affinities in schizophrenia & childhood autism', in P. Bebbington (ed.), *Social Psychiatry: Theory, methodology & practice*. New Brunswick: Transaction Publishers.

Frith, U. (1989) *Autism: Explaining the enigma*. Oxford: Basil Blackwell.

Frith, U., Morton, J. and Leslie, A. (1991) 'The cognitive basis of a biological disorder: autism', *Trends in Neuroscience*, **14**, 433–8.

Gillberg, C. and Gillberg, J. (1983) 'Infantile autism: a total population study of reduced optimality in the pre-, peri-, and neonatal period', *Journal of Autism and Developmental Disorders*, **13**, 153–66.

Gleaves, D. (1996) 'The sociocognitive model of dissociative identity disorder: A re-examination of the evidence', *Psychological Bulletin*, **120**, 42–59.

Goffman, E. (1968) *Asylums*. Harmondsworth: Penguin.

Goldberg, D.P. and Huxley, P. (1980) *Mental Illness in the Community. The pathway to psychiatric care*. London: Tavistock.

Grilo, C., Levy, K., Becker, D., Edell, W. *et al.* (1995) 'Eating disorders in female inpatients with versus without substance use disorders', *Addictive Behaviours*, **20**, 255–60.

Gutheil, T. (1993) 'True or false memories of sexual abuse? A forensic psychiatric view', *Psychiatric Annals*, **23**, 527–31.

Hare, R. (1986) 'Twenty years' experience with the Cleckley psychopath', in W. Reid, D. Dore, J. Walker and J. Bonner (eds.), *Unmasking the Psychopath: Antisocial personality and related syndromes*. New York: W.W. Norton.

Harris, B. (1996) 'Hormonal aspects of postnatal depression', *International Review of Psychiatry*, **8**, 27–36.

Hirsch, S. and Leff, J. (1975) *Abnormalities in Parents of Schizophrenics*. Maudsley Monograph No. 22. London: Oxford University Press.

Hobson, R. (1986) 'The autistic child's concept of people', *Communication*, **20**, 12–17.

Hobson R. (1990) 'On aquiring knowledge about people and the capacity to pretend: response to Leslie (1987)', *Psychological Review*, **97**, 114–21.

Hollin, C. (1989) *Psychology and Crime: An introduction to criminological psychology*. London: Routledge.

Holmes, D. (1994) *Nonverbal Behaviour in Autism and Schizophrenia*. Unpublished PhD thesis (British Library copy held).

Holmes, R. (1989) *Profiling Violent Crimes: An investigative tool*. Newbury Park, CA: Sage.

Hugdahl, K. (1981) 'The three systems model of fear: a critical examination', *Behaviour Research & Therapy*, **19**, 75–85.

Hunter, R. (1973) 'Psychiatry and neurology: psychosyndrome or brain disease', *Proceedings of the Royal Society of Medicine*, **66**, 17–22.

Isometsa, E., Henriksson, M., Heikkinen, M., Aro, H. *et al.* (1996) 'Suicide among subjects with personality disorders', *American Journal of Psychiatry*, **153**, 667–73.

Jacobsen, C., Wolfe, J. and Jackson, T. (1935) 'An experimental analysis of the functions of the frontal association areas in primates', *Journal of Nervous and Mental Disorders*, **82**, 1–14.

Jacobson, R., Le Couteur, A., Howlin, P. and Rutter, M. (1988) 'Selective subcortical abnormalities in autism', *Psychological Medicine*, **18**, 39–48.

Jamison, K. (1997) 'Manic depressive illness and creativity', *Scientific American, Special issue: Mysteries of the mind*, **7(1)**, 44–9.

Jones, K. (1982) 'Scull's dilemma', *British Journal of Psychiatry*, **141**, 221–6.

Jones, K. and Poletti, A. (1985) 'Understanding the Italian experience', *British Journal of Psychiatry*, **146**, 341–7.

Jones, M.C. (1924) 'The elimination of chidren's fears', *Journal of Experimental Psychology*, **7**, 383–90.

Kanner, L. (1943) 'Autistic disturbances of affective contact', *Nervous Child*, **2**, 217.

Kanner, L. (1948) 'Problems of nosology and psychodynamics in early infantile autism', *American Journal of Ortho-psychiatry*, **19**, 416–26.

Kaplan, H. (1983) *The Evaluation of Sexual Disorders: Psychological and medical aspects.* New York: Brunner/Mazel.

Kasenin, J. (1933) 'The acute schizoaffective psychoses', *American Journal of Psychiatry*, **90**, 97–126.

Kay, P. and Kolvin, I. (1987) 'Childhood psychoses and their borderlands', *British Medical Bulletin*, **43**, 570–86.

Kendall, P. and Southam-Gerow, M. (1996) 'Long-term follow-up of a cognitive-behavioural therapy for anxiety-disordered youth', *Journal of Consulting and Clinical Psychology*, **64**, 724–30.

Kennedy, J., Giuffra, L., Moisis, H., Cavalli-Sforza, L., Pakstis, A., Kidd, J., Castigleone, C., Sjorsen, B., Wetterberg, L. and Kidd, K. (1988) 'Evidence against linkage to markers on chromosome 5 in a northern Swedish pedigree', *Nature*, **336**, 167–70.

Kessel, W.J.N. (1960) 'Psychiatric morbidity in a London general practice,' *British Journal of Preventive and Social Medicine*, **14**, 16.

Kety, S. (1974) 'Problems in biological research in psychiatry', in J. Mendels (ed.), *Biological Psychiatry*. New York: John Wiley.

Kety, S., Rosenthal, D., Wender, P., Schulsinger, F. and Jacobson, B. (1975) 'Mental illness in the biological and adoptive families of adopted individuals who have become schizophrenic: a preliminary report based on psychiatric interviews', in R. Fieve, D. Rosenthal and H. Brill (eds.), *Genetic Research in Psychiatry*. Baltimore: Johns Hopkins University Press.

Kety, S., Rosenthal, D., Wender, P., Schulsinger, F. and Jacobson, B. (1976) 'Mental illness in the biological and adoptive families of adopted individuals who have become schizophrenic', *Behavioural Genetics*, **6**, 219–25.

King, M. (1990) 'Sneezing as a fetishistic stimulus', *Sexual & Marital Therapy*, **5**, 69–72.

Kinsey, A., Pomeroy, W., Martin, C. and Gebhard, P. (1948) *Sexual Behaviour in the Human Male*. London: W.B. Saunders.

Kinsey, A., Pomeroy, W., Martin, C. and Gebhard, P. (1953) *Sexual Behaviour in the Human Female*. London: W.B. Saunders.

Kinzl, J., Traweger, C. and Biebl, W. (1995) 'Sexual dysfunctions: relationships to childhood sexual abuse and early family experiences in a nonclinical sample', *Child Abuse and Neglect*, **19**, 785–92.

Kirch, D. (1993) 'Infection and autoimmunity as aetiologic factors in schizophrenia: a review and reappraisal', *Schizophrenia Bulletin*, 19, 355–70.

Klein, D. (1995) 'What's new in DSM-IV?', *Psychiatric Annals*, 25(8), 465–6, 469–74.

Klin, A., Volkmar, F., Sparrow, S., Cicchetti, D. *et al.* (1995) 'Validity and neuropsychological characterisation of Asperger syndrome: convergence with nonverbal learning disabilities syndrome', *Journal of Child Psychology and Psychiatry and Allied Disciplines*, 36, 1127–40.

Kraepelin, E. (1899). *Kompendium der Psychiatre*, 6th edition. Leipzig: Abel.

Kraepelin, E. (1919) *Dementia Praecox and Paraphrenia*. Edinburgh: E. & S. Livingstone.

Kwapil, T. (1996) 'A longitudinal study of drug and alcohol use by psychosis-prone and impulsive nonconforming individuals', *Journal of Abnormal Psychology*, 105, 114–23.

Laing, R.D. (1965) *The Divided Self*. UK: Pelican Books.

Lang, P. (1968) 'Fear reduction and fear behaviour: problems in treating a construct', in M. Shilen (ed.), *Research in Psychotherapy*, Vol. III. Washington: American Psychological Association.

Last, C., Barlow, D. and O'Brien, G. (1984) 'Cognitive changes during *in vivo* exposure in an agoraphobic', *Behaviour Modification*, 8, 93–113.

Lazarus, A. (1984) 'Multimodal therapy', in R. Corsini (ed.), *Current Psychotherapies*. Ithaca: Peacock.

Leifer, R. (1970) 'The medical model as ideology', *International Journal of Psychiatry*, 9, 13–19.

Leslie, A. (1990) 'Pretence, autism and the basis of "theory of mind"', *The Psychologist: Bulletin of the British Psychological Society*, 3, 120–3.

Lewis, S. (1994) 'ICD-10: a neuropsychiatrist's nightmare?', *British Journal of Psychiatry*, 164, 157–8.

Lewy, A., Ahmed, S. and Sack, R. (1995) 'Phase shifting the human circadian clock using melatonin', *Behavioural Brain Research*, 73, 131–4.

Liddle, P. (1987) 'The symptoms of chronic schizophrenia: a re-examination of the positive negative dichotomy', *British Journal of Psychiatry*, 151, 145–51.

Lidz, T., Cornelison, A., Fleck, S. and Terry, D. (1957) 'The intrafamilial environment of schizophrenic patients II. Marital schism and marital skew', *American Journal of Psychiatry*, 114, 241–8.

Lieberman, M., Yalom, J. and Miles, M. (1973) *Encounter Groups: First facts*. New York: Basic Books.

Loftus, E. (1993) 'The reality of repressed memories', *American Psychologist*, 48, 518–37.

Lovaas, O. (1987) 'Behavioural treatment and normal educatonal and intellectual functioning in young autistic children', *Journal of Consulting and Clinical Psychology*, 55, 3–9.

Lydiard, R., Brawman-Minzer, O. and Ballenger, J. (1996) 'Recent developments in the psychopharmacology of anxiety disorders', *Journal of Consulting and Clinical Psychology*, 64, 660–8.

Mann, J. (ed.) (1989) *Models of Depressive Disorders: Psychological, biological and genetic perspectives*. New York: Plenum.

Masters, W. and Johnson, V. (1966) *Human Sexual Response*. London: J.A. Churchill.

Masters, W. and Johnson, V. (1970) *Human Sexual Inadequacy*. London: J.A. Churchill.

Mawson, D., Grounds, A. and Tantam, D. (1985) 'Violence and Asperger's syndrome: a case study', *British Journal of Psychiatry*, 147, 566–9.

Mayer-Gross, W., Slater, E. and Roth, M. (1969) *Clinical Psychiatry*. London: Baillière, Tindall & Cox.

Meehl, P. (1962) 'Schizotaxia, schizotypia, schizophrenia', *American Psychologist*, 17, 827–38.

Meichenbaum, D. (1986) *Stress Inoculation Straining*. New York: Pergamon.

Merckelbach, H., de-Jong, P., Muris, P. and van den Hout, M. (1996) 'The aetiology of specific phobias: a review', *Clinical Psychology Review*, 16, 337–61.

Millon, T. (1981) *Disorders of Personality: DSM-III, Axis II*. New York: John Wiley.

Morel, B.A. (1852) *Traité des maladies mentales*. Paris: Masson.

Morey, L. (1988) 'Personality disorders in DSM-III and DSM-IIIR: convergence, coverage and internal consistency', *American Journal of Psychiatry*, 145, 573–7.

Morgan, H. and Murray, H. (1935) 'A method of investigating fantasies: The Thematic Apperception Test', *Arch Neurol Psychiat*, 34, 289–306.

Offer, D. and Sabshin, M. (1991) *The Diversity of Normal Behaviour*. New York: HarperCollins.

Ogata, S., Silk, K., Goodrich, S. *et al.* (1990) 'Childhood sexual and physical abuse in adult patients with borderline personality disorder', *American Journal of Psychiatry*, 147, 1008–13.

O'Kane, A., Fawcett, D. and Blackburn, R. (1996) 'Psychopathy and moral reasoning: comparison of two classifications', *Personality and Individual Differences*, 20, 505–14.

Owen, F. and Cross, A.J. (1989) 'Schizophrenia', in R.A. Webster and C.C. Jordan (eds.), *Neurotransmitter, Drugs and Disease*. Oxford: Basil Blackwell.

Pace, G., Ivancic, M., Edwards, G., Iwata, B. and Page, T. (1985) 'Assessment of stimulus preference and reinforcer value with profoundly retarded individuals', *Journal of Applied Behaviour Analysis*, 18, 249–55.

Passamanick, B., Dinitz, S. and Lefton, M. (1959) 'Psychiatric orientation and its relation to diagnosis and treatment in mental hospital', *American Journal of Psychiatry*, 116, 127–32.

Pinizzotto, A. and Finkel, N. (1990) 'Criminal personality profiling: an outcome and process study', *Law and Human Behaviour*, 14, 215–33.

Potts, S. and Bhugra, D. (1995) 'Classification of sexual disorders', *International Review of Psychiatry*, 7, 167–74.

Preskorn, S. (1995) 'Beyond DSM-IV: what is the cart and what is the horse?', *Psychiatric Annals*, 25, 53–62.

Prior, M.R. (1987) 'Biological and neuropsychological approaches to childhood autism', *British Journal of Psychiatry*, 150, 8–17.

Putnam, F. (1989) *Diagnosis and Treatment of Multiple Personality Disorder*. New York: Guilford Press.

Quill, K., Gurry, S. and Larkin, A. (1989) 'Daily Life Therapy: a Japanese model for educating children with autism', *Journal of Autism & Developmental Disorders*, 19, 625–35.

Roberts, G.W. (1990) 'Schizophrenia: the cellular biology of a functional psychosis', *Trends in Neuroscience*, 6, 207–11.

Robertson, G. (1992) 'Objections to the present system', *Criminal Behaviour and Mental Health*, 2, 114–23.

Rogers, C.R. (1951) *Client-centered Therapy*. Boston: Houghton Mifflin.

Rosen, R. and Leiblum, S. (1995) 'Treatment of sexual disorders in the 1990s: an integrated approach', *Journal of Consulting and Clinical Psychology*, **63**, 877–90.

Rosenhan, D. (1973) 'On being sane in insane places', *Science*, **179**, 250–8.

Ross, C. (1991) 'Epidemiology of multiple personality disorder and dissociation', *Psychiatric Clinics of North America*, **14**, 503–17.

Rutter, M. (1974) 'The development of infantile autism', *Psychological Bulletin*, **4**, 147–63.

Rutter, M. (1979) 'Maternal deprivation, 1972–1978: new findings, new concepts, new approaches', *Child Development*, **50**, 283–305.

Rutter, M. (1983) 'Cognitive deficits in the pathogenesis of autism', *Journal of Child Psychology & Psychiatry*, **24**, 513–31.

Salan, S., Zinberg, N. and Frei, E. (1975) 'Antiemetic effects of delta-9-THC in patients receiving cancer chemotherapy', *New England Journal of Medicine*, **293**, 795–7.

Sartorius, N., Ustin, T., Korten, A., Cooper, J. *et al.* (1995) 'Progress toward achieving a common language in psychiatry: II Results from the international field trials of the ICD-10 Diagnostic Criteria for Research for mental and behavioural disorders', *Americal Journal of Psychiatry*, **152**, 1427–37.

Satterfield, J, Swanson, J., Schell, A. and Lee, F. (1994) 'Prediction of antisocial behaviour in attention-deficit hyperactivity disorder boys from aggression/defiant scores', *Journal of the American Academy of Child and Adolescent Psychiatry*, **33**, 185–90.

Schneider, K. (1959) *Clinical Psychopathology*, trans. M.W. Hamilton. New York: Grune & Stratton.

Seligman, M. (1992) *Helplessness*, revd. edition. New York: Freeman.

Shah, A. and Frith, U. (1983) 'An islet of ability in autism: a research note', *Journal of Child Psychology and Psychiatry*, **24**, 613–20.

Shapiro, D. and Firth, J. (1987) 'Prescriptive v. exploratory psychotherapy. Outcomes of the Sheffield Psychotherapy Project', *British Journal of Psychiatry*, **151**, 790–9.

Sherrington, R., Brynjolfsson, J., Peutrsson, H., Potter, M., Duddleston, K., Barraclough, B., Wasmuth, J., Dobbs, M. and Gurling, H. (1988) 'The localisation of a susceptibility locus for schizophrenia on chromosome 5', *Nature*, **336**, 164–7.

Shields, J. (1978) 'Genetics', in J.K. Wing (ed.), *Schizophrenia: Towards a new synthesis*. London: Academic Press.

Siever, L., Silverman, J., Horvath, T. *et al.* (1990) 'Increased morbid risk for schizophrenia-related disorders in relatives of schizotypal personality disordered patients', *Archives of General Psychiatry*, **47**, 634–40.

Slater, E. and Cowie, V. (1971) *The Genetics of Mental Disorders*. London: Oxford University Press.

Slater, E. and Roth, M. (1969) *Clinical Psychiatry*. London: Baillière, Tindall & Cassell.

Smalley, S. (1991) 'Genetic influences in autism', *Psychiatric Clinics of North America*, **14**, 125–39.

Snowden, D. (1996) *Spiritual and Sexual Attitudes: Special issue, masochism as a product of a strict religious upbringing*. Unpublished thesis, the Manchester Metropolitan University.

Spitzer, R., Endicott, J. and Robins, E. (1978) 'Research diagnostic criteria: rationale & reliability', *Archives of General Psychiatry*, **38**, 773–82.

Steffenberg, S., Gillberg, C., Hellgren, L., Andersson, L. *et al.* (1989) 'A twin study of autism in Denmark, Finland, Iceland, Norway and Sweden', *Journal of Child Psychology and Psychiatry and Allied Disciplines*, **30**, 405–16.

Stern, M. and Stern, A. (1981) *Sex in the Soviet Union*. London: W.H. Allen.

Stirling, J., Tantam, D., Thomas, P., Newby, D., Montague, L., Ring, N. and Rowe, S. (1993) 'Expressed emotion and schizophrenia: the ontogeny of EE during and 18 month follow up', *Psychological Medicine*, **23**, 771–8.

Stone, M. (1993) 'Cluster C personality disorders', in D. Dunner (ed.), *Current Psychiatric Therapy*. Philadelphia: W.B. Saunders.

Strauss, M. (1993) 'Relations of symptoms to cognitive deficits in schizophrenia', *Schizophrenia Bulletin*, **19**, 215–33.

Szasz, T. (1960) 'The myth of mental illness', *American Psychologist*, **15**, 113–18.

Szasz, T. (1971) *The Manufacture of Madness*. London: Routledge & Kegan Paul.

Szasz, T. (1980) *Sex: Facts, frauds and follies*. Oxford: Basil Blackwell.

Szatmari, P. (1992) 'The validity of autistic spectrum disorders: a literature review', *Journal of Autism and Developmental Disorders*, **22**, 583–600.

Tantam, D. (1988). *A Mind of One's Own: A guide to the special difficulties and needs of the more able autistic person, for parents, professional and autistic people*. The National Autistic Society.

Tantam, D. (1992) 'Characterising the fundamental social handicap in autism', *Acta Paedopsychiatrica*, **55**, 83–91.

Tantam, D. and McGrath, G. (1989) 'Psychiatric day hospitals – another route to institutionalisation?', *Social Psychiatry and Psychiatric Epidemiology*, **24**, 96–101.

Tantam, D., Holmes, D. and Cordess, C. (1993) 'Nonverbal expression in autism of Asperger's type', *Journal of Autism and Developmental Disorders*, **23**, 111–33.

Tantam, D., Stirling, J., Monaghan, L. and Nicholson, H. (1989) 'Autistic children's ability to interpret faces: a research note', *Journal of Child Psychology & Psychiatry*, **39**, 623–30.

Vaughn, C. and Leff, J. (1976) 'The measurement of expressed emotion in the families of psychiatric patients', *British Journal of Social and Clinical Psychology*, **15**, 157–65.

Watson, J.B. and Rayner, R. (1920) 'Conditioned emotional reactions', *Journal of Experimental Psychology*, **3**, 1–14.

Weissman, M. (1993) 'The epidemiology of personality disorders: a 1990 update', *Journal of Personality Disorders*, Spring Supplement, 44–62.

Welch, M. (1989) 'Towards prevention of developmental disorders', *Pre- and Peri-Natal Psychology Journal*, **3**, 319–28.

Wells, A. and Dattilio, F. (1992) 'Negative outcomes in cognitive behavioural therapy: a case study', *Behavioural Psychotherapy*, **20**, 291–4.

Widiger, T. (1991) 'Personality dimensional models proposed for the DSM-IV', *Journal of Personality Disorders*, **5**, 386–98.

Wing, L. (1981) 'Asperger's syndrome: a clinical account', *Psychological Medicine*, **11**, 115–29.

Wing, L. and Gould, J. (1979) 'Severe impairments of social interaction and associated abnormalities in children: epidemiology and classification', *Journal of Autism and Developmental Disorders*, **9**, 11–29.

Wise, R. (1987) 'The neurobiology of craving: implications for the understanding and treatment of addictions', *Journal of Abnormal Psychology*, **97**, 118–32.

Wolf-Schein, E. (1996) 'The autistic spectrum disorder: a current review', *Developmental Disabilities Bulletin*, **24**, 33–55.

Wolpe, J. (1958) *Psychotherapy by Reciprocal Inhibition.* Stanford, CA: Stanford University Press.

Wood, J. (1993) 'Reform of the Mental Health Act 1983: an effective tribunal system', *British Journal of Psychiatry,* **162**, 14–22.

World Health Organization (1973) *The International Pilot Study of Schizophrenia.* Geneva: WHO.

Zilboorg, G. and Henry, G. (1941) *A History of Medical Psychology.* New York: W.W. Norton.

Index